THE CANINE SOURCE BOOK

FOURTH EDITION

ALMOST EVERYTHING YOU ALWAYS WANTED TO KNOW ABOUT DOGS

by Susan Bulanda

D O R A L
Publishing, Inc
Portland, Oregon
1994

Published by Doral Publishing, 2619 Industrial St NW, Portland OR 97210.
Printed in the United States of America.

Copyedited by Luana Luther
Cover design by Fred Christensen
Cartoons by Joe Murray

Library of Congress Card Number: 93-74008
ISBN: 0-944875-35-1

Bulanda, Susan
    The canine source book: almost everything
you wanted to know about dogs / Susan Bulanda.
-- 4th ed. -- Portland, Or. : Doral Pub., 1994, c1993.
    p. ; cm.
    ISBN:0-944875-35-1

    1. Dogs--North America--Handbooks, manuals, etc.
2. Dogs--North America--Bibliography. 3. Dogs-- North
America--Societies, etc.-- Directories. I. Title.

SF426.B   636.7 dc20

The purpose of this publication is to provide lists of organizations, companies, and agencies that are involved in every level of canine activity and interest.

I have been involved with dogs as a breeder, professional trainer, canine behaviorist, and, since 1961, have participated in many sports involving dogs. During that time, I saw a need for a publication such as this. While the sources listed are not exhaustive, they do represent my experience in the canine world. The reader will be able to use the listings in this book to locate nearly every canine organization and find information on many subjects of interest.

The first chapter, *General Suggestions*, provides hints for making maximum use of this publication. Each chapter has a brief explanation and specific suggestions for the type of information listed.

The chapter, *Selecting a Dog Trainer*, offers some hints on how to find the right trainer for you and lists a state-by-state directory of trainers.

To help you find a breeder for the dog you want, the chapter on *How to Choose a Dog Breeder* provides some guidelines.

The chapter on *Breed Clubs* includes a list of breeds recognized (and not recognized) by most of the major kennel clubs in the United States and Canada. In some cases, a club may not have been formed, and in those cases the name of a person to contact is listed. Local breed clubs are not listed because information about them can be obtained from the parent club or registry for that breed.

The *Rare-Breed Clubs* chapter lists organizations involved with more than one breed of dog, but which are limited to those breeds that are considered rare. In most cases, this will mean dogs with limited numbers in the United States and/or are not recognized by a major registry, such as the American Kennel Club (AKC) or the United Kennel Club (UKC).

The chapter that lists *Miscellaneous Clubs* includes clubs that did not fall into the first two chapters. Generally speaking, they are involved with a type of dog, such as mixed breeds.

Activity Clubs contains a list of organizations involved in a dog sport or activity, such as ring sport, obedience, hunting, etc. This type of club is growing in popularity, with many local clubs forming all the time. If you cannot find one listed for your area, contact your local breed club or parent breed club.

The chapters on *Herding* and *Dog Sledding* list organizations that deal specifically with those activities.

The *Rescue Clubs* chapter contains a list of groups concerned about the welfare of dogs in general, or they deal with specific breeds and are generally associated with a breed club. The rescue organizations are always a good place to start to find a dog, but many are filled to capacity and unable to take in a dog.

For those of you who want to keep up on the latest events for your favorite breed, the chapter on *Breed Publications* offers a list of publications by breed. These publications may be independent of the parent club or published by the parent club. They range from simple newsletters to glossy magazines.

The publications that do not deal with a specific breed, but do cover general interests are listed in the *General Publications* chapter. Subjects might include dog training, canine psychology, dog hobbies, health concerns, sports and special-interest groups.

The chapter listing *Registry Organizations* includes most of the major canine registry organizations in the United States, as well as those in other countries. This chapter also includes some special-interest organizations, which only register certain types of dogs.

The chapter on *Health and Safety Organizations* lists organizations that are concerned about the health—both mental and physical—and safety of dogs.

Dog Show Services lists dog-show-related topics, such as entry services, photographers and show superintendents. If you want to find out which shows are offered in your area, you can contact the dog show superintendents and request to be put on their mailing lists. You will then receive the entry forms for the dog shows in the area covered by that superintendent.

The *Supply Catalogs* section provides a sampling of catalogs available to order by mail almost anything related to dogs. Some of the suppliers listed specialize in specific equipment and are not as widely known as the general suppliers.

The chapter on *Associations* lists all the professional associations that attempt to regulate the professionals in their fields. Some of the listings are associations that are groups fighting for specific causes and are not actually clubs.

The *Awards and Contests* chapter lists the contests and awards that are related to the canine world.

The chapter on *Places to Visit* lists places that are dog-related that might be of interest to visit.

The chapter on *Veterinary Medicine Colleges* lists all of the colleges in the United States and Canada. This is a useful chapter for those who would like a career as a veterinarian, as well as those who have need of the facilities offered by veterinarian colleges.

The *Search and Rescue Units* chapter lists units in the United States and Canada that are involved in using dogs to locate lost people.

Hotlines lists telephone numbers to call for information about dogs. Be aware that some organizations charge for their services and you should inquire before requesting information.

The chapter on *Wolf/Wildlife and Humane Treatment of Animals* contains a list of organizations devoted to wolves, animal rights or general humane treatment of animals.

Support Dogs for the Handicapped lists organizations that are dedicated to providing support dogs for people who are handicapped, including guide dogs for the blind, hearing ear dogs and assistance dogs.

The chapter on *Videos and Computers* offers a list of videos available for sale or rent. Because this service is rapidly growing, the reader should ask the organizations offering videos for their latest listings. A number of organizations are offering computer bulletin board services and these are included in this chapter.

The *Just Because* chapter is my fun chapter and it lists all of those rather unusual organizations, publications, etc. that I thought you might find of interest.

Every two years, this book will be updated to provide the reader with the latest information available.

When requesting information from an organization, try to be very specific as to what you want. Some of the larger breed clubs offer a wide range of information and may not mail everything available to you unless you request it. You can ask the club what information is available in addition to the general information typically sent. It is a good idea when requesting information to include a stamped, self-addressed, legal-sized envelope with your request. Club officials also like to know how you heard of their organizations, so be sure to include that information. As a general rule, allow eight weeks for a response. Remember, most organizations have elected members who volunteer time to fulfill duties of corresponding—response may be slow.

I have also discovered that it is not a good idea to mail a check for a subscription or reproduction fee because may clubs are very slow to deposit checks. A money order is a better choice. It is also a good idea to record the date you mailed your request. This way you will know how long ago you requested the information and how soon you should try again. Sometimes, it seems as though you mailed your request for information ages ago when in reality just a few weeks have passed.

If you do not find the information you need in this book, write to a related organization and try there. For example, if you do not find a publication for your breed of dog, write to a club devoted to that breed. It's best to start with the national or parent club because they usually produce a club newsletter you can subscribe to without joining the club. The same is true for activity clubs. If the club listed in this book is too far away, write for information to include a list of the clubs nearest you. Many times, a publication can direct you to a club in your area. For example, if you are interested in canine search and rescue, and there is no unit listed close enough to you, the *SAR Dog Alert* or the National Association for Search and Rescue may be able to provide names of units or personnel in your area.

If you cannot find a club near you, a list of all clubs (all-breed, specialty, or breed clubs, obedience clubs and sanctioned specialty clubs) for your state can be obtained free from most of the major registries. They are listed in the chapter on *Registry Organizations*.

If you are interested in buying a dog, the best way to find a reputable breeder is to write the parent club. Many clubs publish literature about their breeds and are eager to help interested persons. I cannot stress enough how important it is to research a breed of dog to be sure it is the right one for you. If you are looking for a dog as a pet, give serious consideration to adopting one from the rescue groups. You can get a wonderful pet that way. See the chapter on rescue clubs.

Occasionally, the telephone company will add a new area code to a state. Recently, this happened in New Jersey and the 201 area code was divided into 201 and 908. If you try to use a number in this book and receive a message that the number is no longer in service, call information and check the area code.

Addresses for the countries of the United States and Canada are not designated as such.

Selecting the correct person to help you train your dog can be just as critical as selecting the correct dog for your lifestyle and needs. The field of dog training is an ever changing field, but the criteria for selecting a dog trainer have been fairly consistent over the years. Before you can select the correct trainer, it is important to understand a little about dog training. To begin with you need to decide exactly what you want to train your dog to do. Is your ultimate goal to have your dog trained well enough to compete in field trials, obedience trials (to what level) or are your interests in some of the other dog-related sports such as sled racing, hunting, lure coursing, etc., or do you just want a well-behaved companion dog?

Once you have decided what you want to train your dog to do, you can look for the trainer who specializes in that type of training. For specialized types of training, it is usually a good idea to contact the clubs that are involved with that type of activity. If you cannot find a club in your area, contact your local breed club, which you can locate through the parent clubs listed in this book or by writing directly to a canine registry organization, such as the United Kennel Club or the American Kennel Club.

Usually, your local breed club will know of a trainer who specializes in the sport associated with your pedigreed breed of dog and any dog training club will know where to send you for your mixed-breed dog. If you have a mixed breed, you can still train the dog to do things designated for pedigree dogs, but you may not be able to earn a title.

You can also check the listings in this book in the *Activity Clubs* chapter. If you are interested in obedience training, there are classes offered in almost every town, either through adult school programs, obedience clubs, recreation departments, or the local YW/MCAs. There are also local trainers who operate on a limited basis from their homes, as well as those who have regular businesses and run obedience schools. These people are usually listed in the yellow pages of your phone book or can be located through your veterinarian or nearest animal shelter.

Keep in mind that just because a trainer buys an ad in the yellow pages doesn't mean he/she is competent. Be sure to investigate further. The best method is word-of-mouth. A competent trainer will have a good reputation in his community, and, conversely, the bad trainer will also be well known, but not favorably.

Many people are not aware there are a number of techniques used to train dogs. These techniques vary in degrees from very harsh to very passive. Most trainers develop their own techniques based on all they have learned, therefore it is important to know the techniques a trainer uses to decide which trainer to select. Do not hesitate to ask questions and discuss the techniques and methods a trainer uses to train dogs. Some key questions would be: 1) How do you correct an adult dog, a puppy? 2) What methods do you use to motivate a dog? 3) Do you use leadership or dominance?

A dog trainer's primary job is to motivate a dog to respond in a prescribed manner to specific commands or to do a specific job in a specific way, such as obedience, field work, K-9 work, etc.

It is my opinion that a good trainer is one who uses the technique best suited for that type of dog. It takes an experienced trainer to make the correct decision as to which technique is best for which dog. How many dogs has the trainer worked with in his career? How long has this person been a trainer? Are names of former clients available? Bear in mind that the trainer is only going to give you the names of his successes, but it does not hurt to ask anyway.

It is very difficult to establish what makes a good trainer when there are no standards in the field to determine quality. Therefore, the only measure of quality seems to be success. To determine success, ask to watch the trainer work with some of his clients. Do the dogs respond in a positive manner to the trainer? What about people? Can the trainer take a dog who is giving an owner difficulty and get the dog to perform better than the owner was able to? Does the trainer explain carefully what is going on, what to expect, and how to do it? Does the trainer give each client the attention needed to solve any problems? Are the trainer's methods humane? Be sure to ask the clients how they feel about the classes and trainer.

If the trainer specializes in any specific form of training such as field trials, be sure to ask how many champions he has trained. Ask to see demonstrations of dogs he has trained. With a little investigation and the right questions, even someone who knows nothing about dog training can determine what types of trainers are available to them.

As you research your dog trainer, you will have to decide whether you want to train your dog yourself in a class with other people, if you want to be tutored, or if you want to board your dog with a trainer to be trained for you. If your dog has no special problems, a class will work for you. The advantage of a class is that you get to see other dogs work, and your dog learns in an environment full of distractions. The negative side is that the distractions may be too much for you and your dog to learn properly, and the trainer cannot tailor the lessons for your needs.

If your dog has problems, you may want to consider a tutor. You will still train your dog yourself, but the trainer will work with you and your dog in a private setting. This allows the trainer to use the techniques that work best for you and your dog.

If you decide to get private instructions, it is sometimes a good idea to enroll in a class after the dog has learned his lessons so he can practice in a group setting.

The last option is to send your dog to a trainer to be trained for you. If you decide that this is the best method for you, it is important that you spend a few weeks with the trainer and study his techniques. Be sure to ask questions such as: How do you deal with aggressive dogs or with passive dogs? What equipment do you use—prong collars, shock collars, slip (choke) collars, head harnesses or buckle collars? How do you handle my breed or type of dog? The answers to these questions, as well as similar questions, should give you an idea what type of trainer a person is. Do learn the proper way to handle your dog after he is trained.

Another aspect of the canine world is the growing field of canine behavior or psychology. Before attempting to define the credentials associated with an animal behaviorist, it would be helpful to understand the difference between an animal behaviorist and a dog trainer.

The animal behaviorist is primarily involved with assessing and treating behavioral problems in dogs and sometimes other animals. As a rule, dog trainers do not deal with the same types of behavioral problems that a behaviorist would. Many animal behaviorists have received formal academic training from universities in the field of animal behavior. The departments that offer these courses are psychology, zoology, or biology. Ideally, the behaviorist must have the knowledge necessary to make a competent evaluation of his client. This would include the animal's owner since most behavioral problems involve the interaction between owner and dog.

The behaviorist must be able to communicate effectively to bring about a change in the behavior. The behaviorist must be able to view the behavior of the dog without using anthropomorphic reasoning—attributing human reasoning to animal behavior. An example would be the belief that the dog chewed the couch for spite. The behaviorist should keep up on the latest research in his field through additional courses and professional journals.

Keep in mind that there are no regulations controlling the field of animal behavior. Anyone can call himself an animal behaviorist. Again it is up to you to question qualifications. Question the person's educational background and experience, and require references. Discuss hypothetical situations, how they would handle it and why. Keep in mind that a Ph.D. or a MA/MS degree does not guarantee that the person is competent. Hands on experience counts a great deal. Pure behavior modification techniques are not sufficient if the person does not have a strong working knowledge of dogs. Dog training and rehabilitating behavior problems in dogs is not as simple as was once thought. Consider also whether the behaviorist uses the same technique for all dogs or varies it with different types of dogs.

Keep in mind that not all behaviorists without college degrees are bad or incompetent. However, it takes a great deal of dedication to learn what is necessary study to be a true behaviorist. A final note about the difference between dog trainers and behaviorists—there are some very good dog trainers who know intuitively how to handle behavioral problems and are very successful. Just as there are some college-educated behaviorists who know very little about dogs. The truly professional dog trainer and behaviorist will work together for the benefit of the client.

We'd like to thank *Dog Fancy* magazine for many of the following listings.

CANADA

Grey-Bruce Kennel & Obedience Club
Mary Morris
PO Box 481
Owen Sound ONT N4K 5P7
519/ 376-0401

Hamilton Dog Obedience Club, Inc
Robert D Smith
93 Lake Avenue Dr
Stoney Creek ONT L8G 1X7
416/ 662-6104

Hub City Kennel & Obedience Club
Brenda Hagel
PO Box 561
Saskatoon SK S7K 3N9
306/ 665-8289

Lakeshore Dog Training Assoc
Janis Carruthers
54 - 11th St
Roxboro PQ H8Y 1K9
514/ 684-2515

Mountain City Obedience Club
Kay Wells
42 Brentwood Rd
Beaconsfield PQ H9W 4L6
514/ 630-3760

North York Obedience Inc
Mrs Pat Longman
40 Blewsky Cres
Richmond Hill ONT L4C 8H9
416/ 884-7089

Peterborough and District Obedience Club
Elaine Hopkins
680 Otonabee Dr
Peterborough ONT K9J 7P9
705/ 743-7894

Simcoe County Obedience Club, Inc
29 - 80 Bradford
St. Barrie ONT L4N 6S7
705/ 726-0190

St Catharines and District Kennel & Obedience
Mrs Beverley Harvey
20 Berkwood Pl
Fonthill ONT L0S 1E2
416/ 892-6474

St Francis Kennel & Obedience Club
Maria Duschkanits
440 Pierre Laporte
Bromont PQ J0E 1L0
514/ 534-1242

Swansea Dog Obedience Club
Nancy Minaker
2383 Dundas St W
Oakville ONT L6J 4Z3
416/ 827-4844

Sydenham Valley DTC, Inc
Mavis J Colyer
RR 3
Wallaceburg Ont N8A 4K9
519/ 627-6374

York Regional Dog Obedience Club
Jennifer Morgan
22 Colony Trail Blvd
Holland Landing ONT L0G 1H0
416/ 830-0138

ALABAMA

Birmingham Obedience Training Club, Inc
Sale Calhoun
5590 Rex Ridge Ln
Leeds AL 35094

Dog Obedience Club Inc.
PO Box 231091
Montgomery AL 36104
205/ 277-6489

Huntsville OTC
Karen R Paulukaitis
134 Portal Ln
Madison AL 35758

Mobile Bay DTC
Dee Hyland
1117 Greenway Dr West
Mobile AL 36608

Montgomery Alabama DOC
Laura Ward
336 Dublin Place
Montgomery AL 36108

ALASKA

Angie Grossaro OTC
5146 E 26th
Anchorage AK 99508

Dog OTC, Anchorage Inc
Beverly Holaday-English
11900 Northern Raven
Anchorage AK 99516

OTC of Chugiak
Shelia Martin
2737 Needels Lp
Chugiak AK 99567

ARIZONA

Old Pueblo DTC, Inc
Ms Anne Sharp
1318 W Wabash St
Tucson AZ 85704

Phoenix Field and Obedience Club
Becki Johnson
7308 W Griffin
Glendale AZ 85303

ARKANSAS

Little Rock DTC, Inc
A Hurd c/o Greg Davis
7 Heatherbrae Cr
Little Rock AR 72212

CALIFORNIA

Bakersfield OTC
Sharon Schmidt
1842 Main St
Delano CA 93215

County-Wide DTC, Inc
Ms Charleen McGrath
1309 Tuliptree Rd
Santa Rosa CA 95403

Davis DTC
Cherrie Brown
PO Box 4879
Davis CA 95617

Deep Peninsula DTC
Debee Cox
1945 Serge Ave
San Jose CA 95130

DTC of Salinas Valley, Inc
Sheri Harrell
564 Inca Way
Salinas CA 93906

Fremont DTC, Inc
Martha Stuart
41956 Paseo Padre Pkwy
Fremont CA 94539

Fresno DTC, Inc
Dee Morrison
3385 W Roberts
Fresno CA 93711

High Desert Obedience Club
8641 W Ave E4
Lancaster CA 93535
805/ 943-5037

Hollywood DOC, Inc
Ms Karen Maillous
1143 Viking Ave
Northridge CA 91326

Los Angeles Poodle Obedience Club
Doris Schlicht
101 East Las Flores Ave
Arcadia CA 91006

Marin County DTC
Elinore Green
27 Madrone Ave
Kentfield CA 94904

Monterey Bay DTC, Inc
Betty Garcia
640 Bronte Ave
Watsonville CA 95076

Mt Diablo DTC, Inc
Bonnie Heitz
4435 Crestwood Circle
Concord CA 94521

Napa Valley DTC
Karen Povey
1131 Second Ave
Napa CA 94558

Oakland DTC, Inc
Ms Ellen Michael
3524 Harbor View Ave
Oakland CA 94619

Obedience Club of San Diego County, Inc
Dennis Van Sickle
4550 Panorama Dr
La Mesa CA 91941

Orange Coast Obedience Club
A Robbie Robbison
4510 Cervato
Long Beach CA 90815

Palo Alto Foothills Tracking Assoc
Syndi Sweeney
679 W Garland Terr
Sunnyvale CA 94086

Pasanita Obedience Club, Inc
Ms Betty Shively
3805 Greenhill Rd
Pasadena CA 91107

Sacramento DTC
Betty Barker
4413 Dolly Cot
Sacramento CA 95842

San Francisco DTC, Inc
Ms Karen Schoettler
142 Los Banos
Daly City CA 94014

San Joaquin DTC
Sandy Schneider
13296 Alabama Rd
Galt CA 95632

San Lorenzo DTC, Inc
Barbara A Portoni
534-C Lewelling Blvd
San Leandro CA 94579

San Mateo DTC, Inc
Miriam K Hillier
3 Emerald Ct
San Mateo CA 94403

Santa Clara DTC, Inc
Mrs Beverly Z Cobb
12366 Priscilla Lane
Los Altos Hills CA 94024

Southwest Obedience Club of Los Angeles, Inc
Delalah Fragnola
PO Box 1113
Lomita CA 90717

Vallejo DTC, Inc
Christy Rose
700 Sutter St
Vallejo CA 94590

Valley Hills Obedience Club, Inc
Moira Cornell
18960 Keswick St
Reseda CA 91335

West Los Angeles Training Club
11157 1/2 Luceren Ave
Culver City CA 90230
213/ 559-1234

COLORADO

Blue Springs N Katydid DTC
2980 W Oxford Ave
Englewood CO 80110
303/ 781-9027

Denver Foothills Tracking Assoc
Carole-Joy Evert
861 E Dogwood Ave
Littleton CO 80121

Longs Peak DTC
Susan Reece
609 Cook Dr
Ft Collins CO 80521

Mountain States DTC, Inc
Ms Carol Hoekstra
2512 S Xavier St
Denver CO 80219

Pikes Peak Obedience Club, Inc
Dunning Idle
4540 Whispering Ct
Colorado Springs CO 80917

CONNECTICUT

Hartford OTC
Mrs L A Dalburg
50 Dorset Lane
Farmington CT 06032
203/ 956-1589

Nathan Hale Obedience Club, Inc
Sheila Foran
206 Cedar Ridge Terr
Glastonbury CT 06033

Obedience DTC, Waterbury, Inc
406 Benson Rd
Middlebury CT 06762
203/ 758-9684

Port Chester OTC
25 Beverly Pl
Norwalk CT 06850
914/ 946-0308

Waterbury Obedience DTC
Ellen T Horlbut
406 Benson Rd
Middlebury CT 06762

FLORIDA

Brevard County DTC
Patricia Umerski
1330 Arlington Circle
Merritt Island FL 32952

Central Florida Obedience Dog Club
Marie F Zaman
1208 North Ave
Tavares FL 32778

Daytona Obedience Club
310 Bucknell Dr
Daytona Beach FL 32118

DOC of Hollywood, Inc
Rose Doan
9021 NW 7th Court
Pembroke Pines FL 33024

DOC of Lee County Florida
Shirl Silverthron
2909 23rd St SW
Lehigh Acres FL 33971

DTC of St Petersburg, Inc
Joanne Killeen
7811-47th St N
Pinellas Park FL 34665
813/ 393-4629

DTC of Tampa, Inc
Carol Lukes
PO Box 452
Durant FL 33530

Five Flags DTC of Pensacola
Beth Hudson
9500 N Loop Rd
Pensacola FL 32507

Heartland Dog Club Inc
c/o Affordable Pet Supplies
3911 Skipper Rd
Sebring FL 33870

Imperial Polk Obedience Club of Lakeland
Laura Lindemann
541 Young Pl
Lakeland FL 33803

K-9 Obedience Club of Jacksonville, Inc
Patricia Stanton
2467 Ridgewood Ave
Orange Park FL 32065
904/ 733-1907

Marion Alachua Dog Training Assoc
Laureen Ford
12009 NE 8th Ct
Ocala FL 34479

Miami Obedience Club Inc
Miriam Glaser
10544 SW 112 Ave
Miami FL 33176

Obedience Club of Daytona, Inc
Shirley Shalansky
55105 4th St
Astor FL 32102

Obedience Dog Club of Central Florida
Ms Ethel Dwyer
34916 CR 437
Eustis FL 32726
904/ 357-1144

OTC of Palm Beach County
Marjorie E Butcher
4601 121st Terr N
Royal Palm Beach FL 33411

Orlando DTC
Lenn Stone
1012 Manchester Circle
Winter Park FL 32792

Sarasota OTC, Inc
Valerie Clows
5701 Old Ranch Rd
Sarasota FL 34241

St Petersburg DTC, Inc
10097 Duncan St
Seminole FL 34632

Tracking Club of Central Florida
Fran Smith
4096 Happiness Ln
West Palm Beach FL 33406

Upper Suncoast DOC
730 Broadway St
Dunedin FL 34698
813/ 799-0353

GEORGIA

Albany DOC
316 Brown St
Albany GA 31705

Atlanta Obedience Club Inc
Ms Heather McLendon
6153 Traveler Court
Stone Mountain GA 30087

DOC of Albany
Van Presley
316 Brown St
Albany GA 31705

Savannah DTC
Sylvia H Clark
609 Windsor Rd
Savannah GA 31419

HAWAII

Hawaii OTC, Inc
618 Paopua Loop
Kailua HI 96734

Hawaii OTC, Inc
94-306 Kahualena St
Waipahu HI 96797

Hilo OTC
Tammy Brihante
Hilo HI 96720

Leeward Training Club of Hawaii, Inc
Charlene Shelton
95-344 Kalopau
Mililani HI 96789

Maui OTC
PO Box 246
Pukalani HI 96788

OTC of Hawaii, Inc
Ms Pam Haley
304 Iliwahi Lp
Kailua HI 96734

IDAHO

Upper Snake River Valley DTC, Inc
Ms LaDawn Moad
PO Box 132
Iona ID 83427

ILLINOIS

Amundsen Park All-Breed Obedience
6N400 Lloyd Ave
Itasca IL 60143

Capitol Canine Training Club of Springfield
Vera Herst
1538 W Governor St
Springfield IL 62704

Car-Dun-Al OTC, Inc
Judith E Lantinen
35 W 837 Crispin Dr
Elgin IL 60123

Champaign-Urbana DTC
1614 W Clark St
Champaign IL 61821
217/ 333-0625

De Kalb Dog Obedience Group
209 N Bridge
De Kalb IL 60115

Decatur OTC, Inc
Barbara Sheay
4839 Beacon Dr
Decatur IL 62521

DTC of Champaign-Urbana
Genevieve L Handke
1614 W Clark St
Champaign IL 61821

Dunes DTC, Inc
RR 2 Box 53F
Beecher IL 60410

Edwardsville Kennel Club
3603 Horn
Alton IL 62002
618/ 465-1334

Fox Valley DTC, Inc
Carolyn A Pearson
3N161 Timberline Dr
West Chicago IL 60185

Gage Park All-Breed Dog Training
2415 W 55th St
Chicago IL 60632

German Shepherd DTC of Chicago, Inc
Arleve Moody
1845 Prairie Ave
Downers Grove IL 60515

Glenbard All-Breed Obedience
Karen L Zorn
28W034 Country View Dr
Naperville IL 60564

Highland Parks & Recreation
7304 W 174th St
Tinley Park IL60477
708/ 532-8922

Kewanee Kennel Club
317 Lyle St
Kewanee IL 61443
309/ 852-3734

Lincolnwood Training Club Inc for GSD
Barbara Robin
4229 Bobolink Terrace
Skokie IL 60076

Lyons Township DTC, Inc
Sue Pedersen
611 Burlington Ave
Western Springs IL 60558

Middletown DTC
Julie Long
3845 N Bell Ave
Chicago IL 60618

NW Obedience Club of Suburban Chicago Inc
Amber Perri
26 Ascot Cr
Schaumberg IL 60194

North Shore DTC, Inc
Ms Sue Jackson
23815 W Milton Ave
Wauconda IL 60084

North St Louis City OTC
51 Red Bud Lane
Edwardsville IL 62025

Pecatonica Tracking Club
Missi Roland
PO Box 15306
Rockford IL 61132

Peoria OTC
Chris Ericson
7709 W Redwing Dr
Peoria IL 61604

Quad Cities DOC, Inc
Deanna Fuller
804 W 2nd Ave
Milan IL 61264

Rand Park DTC
Jan Meyers
7720 N Keeler
Lincolnwood IL 60646

River Forest Training Group
2525 N Rutherford
Chicago IL 60635

Ruff n Stuff Dog Obedience
1771 W Winnemac
Chicago IL 60640

South Side All-Breed DTC Inc
Tanya Maloney
14452 Trumbull
Midlothian IL 60445

Starved Rock Kennel Club
RR 1
Grand Ridge IL 61325
815/ 249-6409

Westside DTC
Ms Nancy Babizrz
1832 W School
Chicago IL 60657

INDIANA

Anderson OTC, Inc
1947 Romine Rd
Anderson IN 46011

Dunes DTC, Inc
110 Jonathon Lane
Box 49
Hebron IN 46341

Evansville Obedience Club, Inc
Michele Brown
112 North Marine Ave
Evansville IN 47712

Fort Wayne OTC
Debbie Connelly
218 W Washington Ctr Rd
Fort Wayne IN 46825

Indianapolis OTC
4101 E Michigan St
Indianapolis IN 46201
317/ 359-2030

Indianapolis OTC, Inc
Ms Susan Girvin-Quirk
801 Coolee Lane
Indianapolis IN 46229

Kentuckiana German Shepherd Club
3343 Corydon Pike
New Albany IN 47150
812/ 944-3355

Mississinewa Valley OTC
2115 W 8th St
Marion IN 46953

South Central Indiana Obedience
6131 W 450 S
Columbus IN 47201

Trail Creed DTC, Inc
Francile Willson
217 Overhill Trail
Michigan City IN 46360

Whitewater Valley DTC, Inc
Gloria Jacob
2329 Glen Court
Richmond IN 47374

IOWA

Cedar Valley DTC
Sandra Kipp
5244 Rottinghaus Rd
Waterloo IA 50701

Illiamo DTC of Keokuk
RR 2 Box 187
Keokuk IA 52632

Iowa City Dog Obedience
RR 1 Box 50W
North Liberty IA 52317

KANSAS

Wichita DTC, Inc
Brenda Brill
950 S Royal Rd
Wichita KS 67207

KENTUCKY

Bi-State Kennel Assoc
204 Monottan Dr
Louisville KY 40207

Greater Louisville Training Club, Inc
Jeanette Jackson
5446 Bruce Ave
Louisville KY 40214

LOUISIANA

Deep South All-Breed OTC, Inc
Sue Nolan Melancon
4208 Troy St
Metairie LA 70001

Louisiana Capital City Obedience Club
Holly Reed
5025 Tulane
Baton Rouge LA 70808

Red River OTC
Myra Grosbach
PO Box 3936
Shreveport LA 71133

Triple C Obedience Training
918 Nashville Ave
New Orleans LA 70115

MAINE

Casco Bay DTC
Wilma G Sarna
RFD 2 Box 2068A
Brunswick ME 04011

Saccarappa Obedience Club, Inc
Ms Kathie Barry
28 Morse St
Portland ME 04102

MARYLAND

Capital DTC of Washington DC
RT 1 Box 54L
Golts MD 21637

Dog Owner's TC of Maryland
4869 Avoca Ave
Ellicott City MD 21043

Hyattsville DTC
Ann H Nagler
3516 Old Largo Rd
Upper Marlboro MD 20772
301/ 422-8548

Oriole DTC
Helen Blakey
2800 Pelham Ave
Baltimore MD 21213

Southern Maryland DTC of Forestville
2116 Glendors Dr
Forestville MD 20747
301/ 336-6047

MASSACHUSETTS

Bristol County DTC
31 Parker St
New Bedford MA 02740

Concord DTC, Inc
Ms Betty Anketell
10 Crum Hill
Amesbury MA 01913

East Long Meadow Dog OTC
Cindy Olson
127 Gillette Ave
Springfield MA 01118

Great Barrington Kennel Club
74 Briggs Ave
Pittsvield MA 01210

Holyoke Dog OTC
Debra Wilkinson
PO Box 666
Chicopee MA 01021

New England DTC, Inc
Ms Annette H Champion
22 Barnard Rd
Belmont MA 02178
617/ 944-6088

Shrewsbury DTC, Inc
M Orene Smart
Box 567
S Lancaster MA 01561

South Shore DTC, Inc
Elaine Campbell
1040 Central St E
Bridgewater MA 02333

Tracking Club of Massachusetts
Marianne F Wood
PO Box 56
Ayer MA 01432

MICHIGAN

Ann Arbor DTC
Margaret Haselden
4041 Flynn Dr
Highland MI 48356

Companion DTC of Flint, Inc
Ms Shirley J Buroughs
10343 Coolidge Rd
Goodrich MI 48438

Detroit GSD OTC, Inc
Diane Sachs
18597 Golfview Dr
Livonia MI 48152

Detroit-Windsor Dog Obedience Assoc
2789 Pembroke Rd
Birmingham MI 48009
313/ 643-7282; 313/ 368-3123

Flint Companion DTC
1471 Lasalle St
Burton MI 48509

Kalamazoo DTC
Grace Stevens
1223 Bretton Dr
Kalamazoo MI 49006

Kalamazoo Kennel Club & The Third Leg Club
1963 36th St
Allegan MI 49010
616/ 673-4218

OTC of Greater Lansing
Robin Barfoot
13260 Eaton Hwy
Grand Lodge MI 48837

Rochester DOC
Cinda Strehlow
1527 19th Ave SE
Rochester MI 55904

Southern Michigan OTC
Christine Kloski
33841 Vista Way
Fraser MI 48026

Sportsmen's DTC of Detroit, Inc
Mira Jilbert
2789 Pembroke Ave
Birmingham MI 48009

Trainers Obedience Center
3845 Lincoln Dr
Birmingham MI 48010

Tri Cities DTC of Saginaw Bay
Barb Tahash
358 W Prevo Rd
Linwood MI 48634

Wolverine DTC of Livonia
35582 Elmira
Livonia MI 48150
313/ 476-8650

MINNESOTA

Croix Valley Tracking Club
Joann Oja
14042 63rd Ave N
Maple Grove MN 55311

Iron Range DTC
Angela Swanson
605 12th St S
Virginia MN 55792

St Paul DTC
Eileen Erickson
649-23rd Ave NW
New Brighton MN 55112

Twin Cities OTC, Inc
W Dale Weyhrich
PO Box 17225
4910 39th Ave S
Minneapolis MN 55417

Twin Ports DTC
Kathy Bakke
4250 Kingston Rd
Duluth MN 55803

MISSISSIPPI

Jackson OTC
Angie Gillespie
5747 Horton Ave 9
Jackson MS 39206

MISSOURI

Gateway Tracking Club
Elaine Dodson
300 Meadow Dr
Washington MO 63090

Greater Kansas City DTC
Mollie Stroff
25613 NE 136th St
Excelsior Springs MO 64024

Greater Ozarks OTC
RT 2 Box 275A6
Marshfield MO 65706
417/ 468-4903

Greater St Louis Training Club, Inc
Ms Mary Jane Thibault
10157 Meadowfield Ln
St Louis MO 63128

Mound City OTC
Laura Carr
5300 Brooktop Ct
St Louis MO 63128

North St Louis OTC
Sue Bierman
12384 Woodline Dr
St Louis MO 63141

Springfield Missouri DTC, Inc
Tommie Sue Bailey
607 East Kerr
Springfield MO 65803

MONTANA

Great Falls DTC
Lex Van Tighem
2907 3rd Ave N
Great Falls MT 59405

NEBRASKA

Bellevue DOC of Nebraska, Inc
Marge Danielson
RT 1 Box 120
Greenwood NE 68366

Greater Lincoln Obedience Club
Andrew Pitcher
1846 Euclid Ave
Lincoln NE 68502

NEVADA

Truckee Meadows DTC
Beatrice M Schmidt
810 W 12th St
Reno NV 89503

NEW JERSEY

Bayshore Companion Dog Club, Inc
Audrey Wright
450 Kings Hwy E
Middletown NJ 07748

Cape May County DOT Club
Lori Girard
502 Hughes Ave
N Cape May NJ 08204

First DTC of Northern NJ, Inc
Ms Betsi Hartman
678 Woodside Ave
River Vale NJ 07675

K-9 OTC of Essex County, NJ
Ms Marianna West
52 Dodd St
Montclair NJ 07042

Lower Camden County DTC
119 Berlin Rd
Voorhees NJ 08043
609/ 429-9239

Lower Camden County DTC
Mary H Kimball
237 Salem Ave
Bellmawr NJ 08031

Mid Jersey Companion DTC
Mrs Winifred C Sogan
134 Ethel Rd
Edison NJ 08817

Morris Hills DTC, Inc
Debbie Barner
16 Mountain Way
Morris Plains NJ 07950

Northwest New Jersey DTC
RD 1 Box 310
Lafayette NJ 07848
201/ 579-5969

Poodle OTC of Greater NY
Sheila Seligman
14 Hickory Ave
Oradell NJ 07649

Princeton DTC
Nancy Washabaugh
97 Linvale Rd
Ringoes NJ 08551

Somerset County DOC
Cynthia M Clarke
60 Daugherly Ave
Gillette NJ 07933
201/ 537-4009

Town & Country DTC, Inc
A J Sauerborn
989 Ingersoll Terr
Union NJ 07083

NEW MEXICO

DOC of Las Cruces, Inc
Terri Mayfield
1100 Calle Del Encanto
Las Cruces NM 88005

Enchantment Training Club
Vicki McCabe
1165 Los Pueblos
Los Alamos NM 87544
505/ 662-2463

Los Alamos DOC
Olga Rauenzahn-Grovic
44 La Paloma Dr
Los Alamos NM 87544

Sandia DOC, Inc
Ms Susan Boswell
6708 Mayhill Ct NW
Albuquerque NM 87120

Santa Fe DOC
Janet Moffett
1073 Encantado Dr
Santa Fe NM 87501

NEW YORK

Adirondack High Peaks DTC
PO Box 822
Saranac Lake NY 12983
518/ 891-0051

Albany Obedience Club, Inc
Lois J Plitnick
RD 1 Box 25
Hannacroix NY 12087

Canine Companions Dog Training School
Robin Kovary
98 Charlton St 19A
New York NY 10014
212/ 243-5460

DOC of South Nassau Inc
566 Lincoln Blvd.
Long Beach NY 11561
516/ 431-2944

DOTC of Rochester
Ginger Cobb
71 Hinchey Rd
Rochester NY 14624

Hamburg All Breed Obedience Club
Patty Andolina
4193 Glenwillow Dr
Hamburg NY 14075

Hudson Valley Tracking Club
Gail Fowler
RD 5 Box 51
Wynantskill NY 12198

Independent Trainers Organization Inc
Barbara Axel
7 Red Oak Rd
St James NY 17780
516/ 862-6780

K-9 Obedience Club of Elmire
Matthews Rd
Brudett NY 14818
607/ 546-4033

Nassau DTC, Inc
Mrs Clement F Plessner
217 Dix Hills Rd
Huntington Station NY 11746

OTC of Horseheads
4893 Pine Crest Rd
Millport NY 14864
607/ 739-8168

Patroon DTC
7 Petticoat Lane
Troy NY 12180

Port Chester OTC, Inc
Ms Cindy Rubin
78 East St
South Salem NY 10590

Queens OTC, Inc
Mary Bloom
53-07 Douglaston Pkwy
Douglastown NY 11362

Schenectady DTC, Inc
Ann Kaczkowski
458 Cleveland Ave
Schenectady NY 12309

South Towns Working Dog Club
E Main St
Brocton NY 14716
716/ 792-9929

Staten Island Companion DTC, Inc
Jane Raymond
263 South Ave
Staten Island NY 10303

Suffolk OTC, Inc
Kathi Galotti
42 South Lane
Huntington NY 11743

Syracuse OTC
Margaret Wheeler
231 Willington Rd
Dewih NY 13214

Ulster DTC
Colleen Grossbohlin
26 Mulvin Dr
Lake Katrine NY 12449

Western Lakes Training Club of Buffalo
Rebecca Iannone
2750 Dodge Rd
East Amherst NY 14051

NORTH CAROLINA

Animal Protection Society of Orange County
1081 Airport Rd
Chapel Hill NC 27514
919/ 967-7383

Azalea DTC
2123 Wisteria Dr
Wilmington NC 28401

Cape Fear DTC
Evette Squires
108 Willborough Ave
Fayetteville NC 28303

Carolina DTC, Inc
Mrs Harriet Ward
808 Larkwood Dr
Greensboro NC 27410

Charlotte DTC
Martha Cromartie
31243C Heathstead Pl
Charlotte NC 28210

Greater New Bern Kennel Club, The
270 Nine Mile Rd
Newport NC 28570

Greater Raleigh DTC
Susan Lambiris
5701 Crutchfield Rd
Raleigh NC 27606
919/ 859-1689

Obedience Club of Ashville
Laura DeWald
Box 5025 701
Warren Wilson Rd
Swannanoa NC 28778

Western Carolina Tracking Club of Tyron
Elizabeth Patterson
28 Troy Terr
Marion NC 28752

Winston-Salem Dog Training
3618 Vandalis Dr
Winston-Salem NC 27104

OHIO

All Breed Training Club of Akron
Winona Schelat
3864 Tallmadge Rd
Rootstown OH 44272

Animal Behavior Clinic
D B Cameron, DVM
18250 Main St
Middleburg Hts OH 44130
216/ 826-0013

Buckeye Tracking Club
Marianne Reder
3630 Haas Rd
Cuyahoga Falls OH 44223

Canton All-Breed Training Club
Tina Reynolds
503 32nd St NW
Canton OH 44709

Champion School of Dog Obedience
1201 Manning Rd
Hartville OH 44632

Cleveland All-Breed Training Club, Inc
Ms Sandra Nannfeldt
210 Hayes Dr Ste H
Brooklyn Heights OH 44131

Columbus All-Breed Training Club
Bette Rodman
179 W Dunedin Rd
Columbus OH 43214

Crawford County Kennel Club
3987 Lincoln Hwy
Bucyrus OH 44820

Dayton DTC, Inc
Linda M Miller
4504 Kingview Ave
Dayton OH 45420

Greater Toledo OTC
2360 Whitehouse-Spencer Rd
Swanton OH 43558

Hamilton DTC, Inc
Carrol Armacost
65 Wisconsin St
Hamilton OH 45011

Kuliga DTC
PO Box 399001
Cincinnati OH 45251
513/ 351-4649; 513/ 471-1032

Parkersburg OTC
Betsy A Augenstein
412 1/2 Front Street
Marietta OH 45750

Queen City DTC, Inc
Ms Donna Woodyard
2432 Lysle Ln
Cincinnati OH 45255

Tarbe All-Breed Training Club
Mary Krebs
303 W Main St
PO Box 272
New Washington OH 44854

Youngstown All-Breed Training Club, Inc
Judith Ann Drotar
2470 Spruce St
Girard OH 44420

OKLAHOMA

Indian Nations Tracking Club
Jo Ellen Corley
218 E Chestnut
Coweta OK 74429

OTC of Bartlesville, Inc
PO Box 454
Bartlesville OK 74005
918/ 333-5781

Oklahoma City OTC
Marilyn Smith
12409 Teakwood
Edmond OK 73013

Tulsa DTC, Inc
Ursula Ling
2351 S 100 E Ave
Tulsa OK 74129

OREGON

Emerald DOC, Inc
Connie Alber
39125 Deerhorn Rd
Springfield OR 97478

Luckiamute DTC
Margie Douma
340 Gentle Ave E
Monmouth OR 97361

Portland DOC, Inc
James Primmer
12601 SE Market
Portland OR 97233

Pudding River DOC
934 NW 22nd Ave
Canby OR 97013
503/ 266-3089

PENNSYLVANIA

Admiral Perry Obedience Club
6951 Rohl Rd
North East PA 16428
814/ 864-3175

Allentown DTC, Inc
Karen Hooks
721 Willow Dr N
Catasauqua PA 18032

Beaver Valley Training Club, Inc
JoAnn Thielman
360 Wolfe Run Rd
Freedom PA 15042

Berks County DTC
Nancy Withers
1 Clayton Cir
Wernersville PA 19565

Bulanda's Canine Behaviorial Services
Pottstown PA 19464
215/ 323-6725

Butler Dog Training Assoc
Judith Charlton
7224 Franklin Rd
Evans City PA16033

DTC of Chester County
Kristie Deyerle-Brooks
431 W Boot Rd
Chester PA 19380

Dauphin DTC, Inc
Mimi Weakland
1229 Blue Ridge Rd
Harrisburg PA 17110

Golden Triangle OTC
Terry Deluliis
926 Norfolk St
Pittsburg PA 15217

Mt Nittany DTC
Janet Lewis
RR 2 Box 361
Huntingdon PA 16652

OTC of Harrisburg
RD 1 Box 160
Pine Grove PA 17963

Owner Handler Assoc
PO Box 133
Ottsville PA 18942
215/ 847-2229

Philadelphia DTC, Inc
Ms Margery R Braunstein
4019 Crescent Ave
Lafayette Hill PA 19444

Suburban DTC of East Montgomery
1235 Easton Rd
Warrington PA 18976
215/ 825-1362

PUERTO RICO

Puerto Rico DOC
Ruben Villalba
Pajaros 33 Hato Tejas
Bayamon PR 00619

RHODE ISLAND

Key DTC of Rhode Island
547 Child St
Warren RI 02885

OTC of Rhode Island
240 Tarkiln Rd
Chepachet RI 02814

SOUTH CAROLINA

Aiken DTC
Nanette Schlegel
18 Oakleaf Drive N
Augusta SC 29841

Charleston DTC
Betty Wenner
027 Leadenwah Drive
Wadmalaw Island SC 29487

DOC of Greenville, Inc
Tracy Gardner
2072 Howlong Ave
Greenville SC 29609

Greater Columbia Obedience Club, Inc
Barbara Teusink
217 Rushing Wind Drive
Irmo SC 29063

Palmette OTC, Inc
Margaret Taylor
103 Bain Dr
Spartanburg SC 29302

TENNESSEE

Knoxville DTC
Jeanne Ringe
1824 Vickes Ln
Sevierville TN 37862

Memphis OTC, Inc
Gene Weakley
3802 Waynoka St
Memphis TN 38111

Murfreesboro OTC
Denniese Burns
9798 Hwy. 99
Rochvale TN 37153
615/ 793-9686

Nashville DTC
Pat Sinnott
1033 Miller Creek Rd
Goodlettsville TN 37072

Obedience Club of Chattanooga Inc
Dale Hughes
3207 Berkeley Dr
Chattanooga TN 37415

TEXAS

Alamo DOC
Dorothy Kohlman
434 Pike Rd
San Antonio TX 78209

Amarillo OTC
Annette R Brooks
408 Holman Ln
Canyon TX 79015

Capitol DTC of Austin Inc
Janet L Smith
1514 Alameda Dr
Austin TX 78704

DOTC of Dallas County
Janet Frick
6924 Middle Cove
Dallas TX 75248
214/291-1547; 214/749-6969

Den-Tex Golden Triangle
Dog Obedience Group
PO Box 2779
Denton TX 76202
214/ 539-9309

Fort Worth DTC
4350 Twilight Trl Rt 5
Fort Worth TX 76126

Houston OTDC
Glenda Boykin
RT 2 Box 481P
Waller TX 77484

OTC of Wichita Falls
Lori Fenoglio
RT 1 Box 214E
Henrietta TX 76365

Obedience Club of Corpus Christi Inc
PO Box 270723
Corpus Christi TX 78427

Permian Basin OTC of Texas
Gwen Anderson
2207 Sinclair
Midland TX 79705

Plano OTC
1908 Armstrong Dr
Plano TX 75074

Rio Grande ODC
Judy M West
13257 Montana Ave
El Paso TX 79936

San Antonio DTC
Kellie Jones
9322 Lands Point
San Antonio TX 78250

South Plains OTC of Lubbock Inc
Carrie Berry
308 N Englewood
Lubbock TX 79416

South Texas Obedience Club, Inc
Ms Elizabeth McMillen
13201 Cottingham St
Houston TX 77048

Sugarland Obedience School
14123 Panhandle Dr
Sugar Land TX 77478

Texas Tri-Cities OC
Jeanne Hurt
2408 Shady Meadow Dr
Bedford TX 76021

Tyler OTC
Carole L Massey
12237 CR 1113
Tyler TX 75709

Victoria DOC
Judy Dorman
210 Briarmeadow
Victoria TX 77904

West Houston ODC
Scotty Griffey
14435 Chadbourne
Houston TX 77079

UTAH

Golden Spike DOC
Laurie Spease
2005 E 2200 N
Layton UT 84040

Good Manners DOC
7820 E Emigration Canyon
Salt Lake City UT 84108

Great Salt Lake DTC
1840 E 7020 S
Salt Lake City UT 84121

VERMONT

Burlington OTC
Pat McMahon
RR 1 Box 67
Richmond VT 05477

VIRGINIA

Blue Ridge DTC
Carol Machovec
PO Box 2672
Winchester VA 22601

Capitol DTC of Washington DC Inc
Ms Betty Alexander
1312 Knox Place
Alexandria VA 22304

DOTC of Lynchburg, Inc
Annabel Irene Maley
1824 Maiden Lane SW
Roanoke VA 24015
804/ 239-9605

Dogwood OTC
7402 Oak Ridge St
Richmond VA 23294
804/ 672-8898

Hampton Roads OTC
Christina Roeske
7421 Glenrole Ave
Norfolk VA 23505

Merrimac DTC
Kay Routten
PO Box 1685
Newport News VA 23601

Mount Vernon DTC
Miss Neville Worthington
1009 Saber Lane
Herndon VA 22070

Portsmouth-Chesapeake OTC
Paula Dayton
2712 Victory Blvd
Portsmouth VA 23702

Richmond DOC, Inc
Joy James
8950 Country View Ln
Hopewell VA 23860

Virginia Beach DTC
201 Windsor Woods Ct
Virginia Beach VA 23452

WASHINGTON

Chuckanut Dog Training Assoc
Roberta Anderson
4953 N Puget Sound Lane
Oak Harbor WA 98277

Lilac City DTC
E 1612 Houston
Spokane WA 99207
509/ 487-9542

Olalla DTC
Colleen Edwards
14231 Anatevka Lane SE
Olalla WA 98359

Spokane DTC, Inc
Kathleen S Walshon
N5506 Estep
Newman Lake WA 99025

Washington State OTC, Inc
Ms Marilyn Monk
3733 SW 99th St
Seattle WA 98126

WEST VIRGINIA

Blue Ridge DTC
Vicky Mattingly
29 Timberview Farm
Inwood WV 25428

Kanawha OTC
Roberta McDaniel
1605 West Virginia Ave
Dunbar WV 25064

Parkersburg OTC
Erin Bird
81 Tarrytown
Washington WV 26181

Upper Ohio Valley OTC
74 Elm Crest Dr
Wheeling WV 26003
304/ 242-5178

WISCONSIN

K-9 OTC of Menomonee Fall
Cindy Melk
11002 W Wells St
Wauwatosa WI 53226

Lakeland DTC, Inc
Inge Suchanek
2366 Bowers Lake Rd
Milton WI 53563

Milwaukee DTC
Gail A Wegner
2982 S 52nd St
Milwaukee WI 53219

Where to get a dog is probably the aspect of dog ownership that gives more people problems than anything else. Even those people who decide they want to buy from a breeder have difficulty determining which breeder to buy from. To make this decision with the best possible results, you must become aware of a few facts concerning purebred dogs.

As soon as you start to shop for a dog, the term quality comes up. Generally speaking, the quality of a dog refers to the inherited aspects, such as physical appearance, mental health, temperament and trainability. Trainability and temperament are determined by the job the dog was bred to do, as well as his desire and ability to do that job. Conformation, the dog's physical appearance, is defined by the breed standard as accepted by the organization that registers the dog. There are some breeds that do not have a set standard of conformation, but rather the quality resides in the dog's ability to perform a certain job.

Another confusing factor of dog ownership is the papers issued with a dog. Registration papers originate in the organization that registers the dog. Examples of a registering organization are the American Kennel Club (AKC) and the United Kennel Club (UKC).

There is a wide-spread misconception held by the general public concerning registration papers. Unfortunately, people believe that because their dog has papers, he is a quality dog. This is not necessarily true. A registry organization only guarantees that, as reported to it, the lineage of a dog represented by the papers is accurate. This means that the papers issued with a dog are only as accurate as the information provided to the registry organization. The accuracy of the papers depends on the honesty of the breeder reporting the information. No registry organization can guarantee the quality of a dog.

Papers issued with a dog do not guarantee that the dog is purebred, healthy, trainable, of showable quality or worth what the breeder is asking you to pay. Although breed clubs try to set standards and ethical practices and some registries require certain tests before issuing titles on a dog, there is no agency that controls the ethics of breeders.

Technically, anyone who breeds dogs can be considered a breeder. With this in mind, consider the types of breeders outlined below.

Lowest on the list is the puppy mill operation run by breeders in the business for profit only. They do not care about the dogs themselves, the quality of what they breed, the health of their animals, or the feelings of the customers. In fact, they seldom ever meet the customers. They sell to dog dealers who in turn sell to outlets, such as pet shops. Puppy mill operators may have a number of bitches, one or two studs (which may be purchased champions of record), and will breed the bitches every season until they die. Sometimes the bitch will never leave her small, confined area. Her puppies are usually taken from her as soon as they start to eat solid food. In some cases they are issued false health certificates even though they may be in poor mental and physical condition. Yet the pet shops that sell these dogs charge as much or more than you would pay for a dog from an ethical breeder. Although these dog dealers may offer a health guarantee, be aware that major problems may not be covered, the time limit may be too short for some diseases to appear, and the dealer is counting on your affection for the dog to keep you from giving him up.

Next on the list is the accidental breeder. This is someone whose bitch got caught by the neighbor's dog who happened to be the same breed. Sometimes these offspring will be sold as purebred without papers. (Papers may be obtainable if the neighbors come to an agreement and if both dogs are registered.) It is almost impossible to determine the quality of puppies from this type of breeding because no planning took place and the bitch probably didn't receive proper care. This is usually a quick money-making scheme for the owner of the bitch.

Another type of breeder is the person who planned the litter for sentimental reasons. These people will probably breed only one time, but when you consider how many owners do this, you begin to see how many puppies result. The only difference between this type of breeder and the accidental breeder is that the litter was planned.

There is another kind of breeder for financial gain. This is the breeder who believes in making the family pet earn its keep or help support the family. This breeder is commonly known as the backyard breeder. Backyard breeders must cut corners to make the venture pay off. They may use the closest and cheapest mates, not provide a proper diet, not give shots, and sell the puppies as soon as they are weaned. This type will usually deal with the 20 most popular breeds so the puppies will be sure to sell.

The above breeders do not care who buys their dogs and will sell to anyone without question.

Next, is the breeder who does care about his dogs and is concerned about who buys them. But, if you question this breeder carefully, you'll find that he has no motive to breed except to sell puppies. His puppies will be happy, healthy and have had some socialization, but are probably not show or working quality. These pups are not what you want for a good pet or working prospect, but will still cost you the same as the good-quality puppy.

The best type of breeder to buy from is the one who breeds his dogs to improve the breed. This breeder is serious about his dogs. He knows the good and bad points of his lines for the last four generations. He usually keeps one or two pups from each litter and knows each pup in a litter because he has studied them and kept complete records. A good breeder will not sell a pup that has a major mental or physical defect. He will question prospective buyers carefully to insure a good match. He will be honest about the genetic problems associated with his breed. (For those of you who want to research on your own, see *Medical & Genetic Aspects of Purebred Dogs*, by Ross D. Clark, DVM and Joan Stainer, published by Veterinary Medicine Publishing Co., Edwardsville KS.)

Remember that other types of breeders will not turn down a sale and will sell to anyone, even if it's not a good match. The good breeder will not sell you a dog if he thinks you're not suited for the breed, or if he feels you cannot do justice to his dogs. He is very concerned that the dog might end up in a shelter, be abandoned or abused. He will usually offer to take the dog back if you find you cannot keep him or are dissatisfied. He will offer a health guarantee and will take the dog back or refund your money if genetic defects show up.

The bottom line in selecting a dog is for you to do your homework. Don't buy a dog on an impulse, from a pet shop, dog dealer or puppy mill operator. Check the prospective breeder's claims and reputation. Avoid breeder's terms when buying a dog, or if you must, have your contract checked by a knowledgeable dog person as well as a lawyer.

The bottom line, then, is: buyer beware.

The breed clubs listed in this chapter are alphabetical and are not broken down by group. If your breed has an alternate name, check under that name. If there are variations of a breed that are considered two separate breeds and only one is listed, contact the one listed. In many cases, they will know who to contact in the other varieties. Examples are the American and English Cocker Spaniels and the Cardigan and Pembroke Welsh Corgis.

Unless "American" is part of the breed name, such as American Spaniel, the club will be listed under the actual breed name, for example the American Brussels Griffon Association is listed in the Bs for Brussells Griffon.

If the size of the dog is considered part of the name of the breed, such as Miniature Schnauzer, it will be listed under the size—Miniature.

If a club is not for a specific size, it will be listed by breed, such as the Poodle Club of America, found under "P."

In some cases, there is no formal club established for some of the rare breeds. When possible, a person has been listed who can be contacted for more information about that breed.

In the event one major parent club does not exist for a breed, as in the case of the Border Collie, a number of local or regional clubs have been listed.

If you want to find out how to locate a local club for your breed, see the chapter, *General Suggestions*, for information about how to find your breed's local club.

Most national breed clubs offer breed columnists and education coordinators who are available for lectures about their special breeds, as well as dogs in general. You may find out who they are by contacting the national breed clubs listed in this chapter. Judges are also available for lectures and they may be contacted through the Senior Conformation Judges Association listed in the *Associations* chapter.

Affenpinscher Club of America
Ms Terry Graham
2006 Scenic Rd
Tallahassee FL 32303

Afghan Hound Club of America Inc
Norma Cozzoni
2408-A Rt 31
Oswego IL 60543

Afghan Hound Club of Canada
Sandra Gahan
156 Ch Scott RR #2 Box 76
Rigaud, PQ J0P 1 P0
514/ 451-4724

Airedale Terrier Club of America
Dr Suzanne H Hampton
47 Tulip Ave
Ringwood NJ 07456

Airedale Terrier Club of Canada
Valerie Adkinson
4044 Aberdeen Rd
Beamsville ONT L0R 1B6
416/ 563-0539

Akbash Dogs International
Ms Orysia Dawydiak
R.R. 3 Union Rd
Charlottetown PEI C1A 7J7
902/ 672-3036

Akita Club of America
Nancy Henry
761 Lonesome Dove Ln
Copper Canyon TX 75067-8599

Akita Club of Canada
Lorraine Burch
3281 Aubrey Rd
Mississauga ONT L5L 5C9
416/ 828-8059

Alaskan Malamute Club of America Inc
Sharon Weston
187 Grouse Creek Rd
Grants Pass OR 97526

Alaskan Malamute Club of Canada
Jeff Loucks
PO Box 417
Millbrook ONT L0A 1G0
705/ 932-3099

American Cocker Spaniel Club of Canada
Kathy Fullerton
17 Manitoba St
Stouffville ONT L4A 4T2
416/ 640-7823

American Dog Breeders Assoc
 [Pit Bull Terrier]
180 S Hwy 89 N
Salt Lake City UT 84054

American Eskimo Dog Assoc, National
DeAnn Lee
468 Moreland Wy
Hopeville GA 30354
404/766-0604

American Eskimo Dogs of America
Carolyn Jester
RT 3 Box 211B
Stroud OK 74079
918/ 968-3358

American Foxhound Club
Mrs Jack H Heck
1221 Oakwood Ave
Dayton OH 45419

American Indian Dog Assoc
R Kim LaFlamme
PO Box 558
Selma OR 97538

American Spaniel Club Inc
Mrs Margaret M Ciezkowski
846 Old Stevens Creek Rd
Martinez GA 30907-9227

American Staffordshire Terrier Club of
Canada
Lisa Wysminity
525 Pasqua St
Regina SASK S4R 4M9
306/ 545-2598

American Water Spaniel Club
Linda Hattrem
E 2870 Cedar Rd
Elvea WI 54738

Anatolian Shepherd Dog Club of America
Quinn S Harned
PO Box 1271
Alpine CA 91903
619/ 445-3334

Anatolian Shepherd Dogs International Inc
117E 14th St
Grand Island NE 68801
308/ 382-2849

Appenzeller Mountain Dog Club of America
Bill Coleman
Box 279A1 RD 1
Pedricktown NJ 08067
609/ 299-7197

Argentine Dogo Club of America Inc
2014 Albany St
Lafayette IN 47904

Australian Cattle Dog Club of America
Billie Johnson
24605 Lewiston Blvd
Hampton MN 55031

Australian Cattle Dog Club of Canada
Meaghan Thacker
Box 307
Savona BC V0K 2J0
604/ 373-2389

Australian Shepherd Assoc, United States
Sherry Ball
PO Box 4317
Irving TX 75015

Australian Shepherd Club, Arkansas
Mrs Dovie Gagen
2336 Highway 5
Mt Vernon AR 72111
501/ 849-2219

Australian Shepherd Club of America
6091 E State Hwy 21
Bryan TX 77803-9652
409/ 823-3591

Australian Shepherd Club of Greater St
Louis
Kris Toft
RT 10 8797 Nature Ln
Columbia MO 65202

Australian Terrier Club of America Inc
Ms Marilyn Harbana
1515 Davon Ln
Nassau Bay TX 77058

Azawakh Assoc, American
Debra Rookard
PO Box 312
Thornburg VA 22656-0312

Basenji Club of America Inc
Ms Susan Patterson-Wilson
PO Box 1076
South Bend IN 46624

Basenji Club of Canada
Christine Kempster
3452 Dunrobin Rd RR #3
Woodlawn, ON K0A 3M0
613/ 832-3480

Basque Shepherd Club of America
RD 1 Box 101E Long
Eddy NY 12760-9637
914/ 887-5122

Basset Hound Club of America Inc
Ms Andrea Field
2343 Peters Rd
Ann Arbor MI 48103

Basset Hound Club of Canada
Patricia Nurse
588 Pinewood St
Oshawa, ONT L1G 2S4
416/ 723-7668

Beagle Club, National
Joseph B. Wiley Jr
River Rd
Bedminister NJ 07921

Bearded Collie Club of America Inc
Ms Diana Siebert
1116 Carpenters Trace
Villa Hills KY 41017

Bearded Collie Club of Canada
Bea Sawka
RR #1
Queensville ONT L0G 1R0
416/ 478-2175

Beauceron Club, North American
Susan Bulanda
106 Halteman Rd
Pottstown PA 19464
215/ 323-6725

Bedlington Terrier Club of America
Ms Carole Anne Diehl
604 Lafayette Ln
Altoone PA 16602

Belgian Malinois Club, American
Ms Barbara Peach
1717 Deer Creek Rd
Central Valley CA 96019

Belgian Sheepdog Club of America Inc
Mrs Geraldine B Kimball
211 W Elm St
Pembroke MA 02359

Belgian Sheepdog Club of Canada
Agnes Jeske
1523 Kilmer Place
North Vancouver BC V7K 2M8
604/ 980-5860

Belgian Shepherd Dog Assoc, United
Alleyne Dickens
6812 Woodcock Ln
Spotsylvania VA 22553
703/582-2879

Belgian Tervuren Club Inc, American
Nancy Carman
4970 Chinook Trail
Casper WY 82604

Bernese Mountain Dog Club of America Inc
Mary Jane Mielke
156 Hillview Dr
Sullivan WI 53178-9793

Bernese Mountain Dog Club of Canada
Terry Ricard
Box 12 Site 9 RR #2
Tofield AB T0B 4J0
403/ 662-2242

Bichon Frise Club of America Inc
Bernice Richardson
RT 2 Gulch Ln
Twin Falls ID 83301

Bichon Frise Club of Canada
Norma Dirszowsky
12 Mill Pond Ln
Udora ONT L0C 1L0
705/ 228-1148

Black and Tan Coonhound Club Inc,
American
Victoria Blackburn
700 Grand Ave
Elgin IL 60120

Bleu de Gascogne Club of America, The
Margaret Dietrich
5590 Wing Ave SE
Kentwood MI 49512

Bleu de Gascogne Club of America
ES Traverse
RT 1 Box 28
Castleton VT 05735
802/ 468-5484

Bleu de Gascogne Hound Assoc, American
Mary Ann Powell
RT 3 Box 5458
Crawfordville FL 32327
904/ 926-5401

Bloodhound Club, American
Ed Kilby
1914 Berry Ln
Daytona Beach FL 32124

Bloodhound Club, Canadian
Bev Kezar
5 St Laurente
Maple Grove QUE J6N 1J2
514/ 429-2402

Bluetick Breeders & Coon Hunters Assoc
D John Vanderbeck, PhD
RR 1 Box 114
Wheatland IN 47597
812/ 321-3201

Bolognese Club of America
Box 1461
Montrose CO 81402

Border Collie Assoc, American
Mrs Patty Rogers
82 Rogers Rd
Perkinston MS39573
601/ 928-7551

Border Collie Assoc, Eastern Ontario
Evelyn Neuendorff
Box 468
Munster ONT K0A 3P0

Border Collie Assoc, Heartland
Claudia J Frank
5373 St Rt 138 NE
Greenfield OH 45123

Border Collie Assoc, Indiana
Dick Bruner
3583 N 900 W
Andrews IN 48702

Border Collie Assoc, Iowa
Doug Petersen
RR1 Box 53
Spragueville IA 52074
319/ 689-6647

Border Collie Assoc, Michigan
Dick McClure
142 2nd St
Belleville MI 48111-2710

Border Collie Assoc, Mid-Atlantic
Nancy Cox Starkey
12895 Colonial Dr
Mt Airy MD 21771
301/ 253-4732

Border Collie Assoc, North Carolina
Kent Kuykendall
RT 2 Box 335A
Franklinville NC 27248
919/ 824-4278

Border Collie Assoc, Northeast
Doug McDonough
RFD 1 Box 2280 Dickey Hill Rd
Brooks MA 04921
207/ 525-3223

Border Collie Assoc, San Juaquin Valley
Jim Oxford
24577 Ave 188
Porterville CA 93257

Border Collie Assoc, Virginia
Stu Ligon
RT 1 Box 147
Shipman VA 22971
804/ 263-5912

Border Collie Club, Inland Empire
Dale Dietich
RT 1 Box 64
Reardan WA 99029

Border Collie Club, North-West
Mrs J Richardson
Padiham Farm Engine Ln
Shackley, Tilsley
Greater Manchester England UK

Border Collie Club, Ontario
Amanda Milliken
RR 2
Kingston ONT K7L 5H6

Border Collie Club, Southern
Mr J Gascoine
85 Faversham Rd
Seasalter Cross, Whitstable
Kent, England UK

Border Collie Club, United States
Candace Terry
RT 1 Box 148
Stoneleigh VA 22132

Border Collie Club of America
Lois J Larson
Pinecrest Ln
Durham NH 03824

Border Collie Club of Great Britain
Miss K E Lister
Fieldbank
55 Waverley Rd
Rugby, Warwickshire
England 0788 72003

Border Collie Club of Ireland
Miss J A Holmes
46 Landsdowne Park
Templeogue Dublin 16

Border Collie Club/N Island BC Club,
Ontario
Karen Greenlees
RR1
Joyceville ONT K0H 1Y0

Border Collie Handlers Assoc, US
Francis Raley
RT 1 Box 14A
Crawford TX 76638
817/486-2500

Border Collie Stockdog Assoc, The Arizona
Jeanne Bosson
5638 E Enrose St
Mesa AZ 85205
602/ 396-8938

Border Terrier Club of America Inc
Mrs Laurale Stern
832 Lincoln Blvd
Manitowoc WI 54220

Borzoi Club of America Inc
Mrs Karen Mays
29 Crown Dr
Warren NJ 07059

Borzoi Club of Canada
Judy Carleton
Box 248
Blackfalds AB T0M 0J0
403/ 885-4314

Boston Terrier Assoc, National
Charles Rodriguez
2925 South 10th St
Milwaukee WI 53215
414/482-1633

Boston Terrier Club of America Inc
Ms Marian Sheehan
8537 E San Burno Dr
Scottsdale AZ 85258

Boston Terrier Club of Canada
Doreen B Jones
7127-5th St SW
Calgary AB T2V 1B2
403/ 259-3295

Bouvier Assoc, North American Working
PO Box 114
Gorham ME 04038
207/ 839-6593; 207/ 839-6595

Bouvier des Flandres Club Inc, American
Ms Dianne Ring
RT 1 Box 201
Delaplane VA 22025

Bouvier des Flandres Club of Canada Inc
Bonnie L Bailey
PO Box 1131
Belleville ONT K8N 5E8
613/ 966-1782

Boxer Club of Canada
Bernice Langley
65 Glendora Ave
Willowdale ONT M5N 2V8
416/ 226-1880

Boxer Club Inc, American
Mrs Barbara E Wagner
6310 Edward Dr
Clinton MD 20735-4135

Braque du Bourbonnais, Club du
M Francoise Sarrett
13 Place Delille 63000m
Clermont-Ferrand France

Briard Club of America
Ms Janet G Wall
547 Sussex Ct
Elk Grove Village IL 60007

Brittany Club Inc, American
Ms Joy Watkins
RT 1 Box 114B
Aledo TX 76008

Brittany Spaniel Club of Canada
Sue Deyell
Box 45, Site 20, RR 2
Calgary AB T2P 2G5
403/ 288-3204

Brussels Griffon Assoc, American
Mr Terry J Smith
221 East Scott Box 56
Grand Ledge MI 48837

Brussels Griffon Club, National
5921 159th Ln NW
Anoka MN 55303
713/ 783-8887

Bull Terrier Club of America
Betty Desmond
RD 2 Box 315
Claysville PA 15323
412/ 663-5345

Bull Terrier Club of Canada
Ken Lock
195 Virginia Ave
Toronto, ONT M4C 2T5
416/ 425-8808

Bull Terrier Confederacy of the Southeast
Ron Ultz
RT 15 Box 395
Athens AL 35611
205/ 233-1183

Bulldog Club of America
Ms Linda Sims
8810 M St
Omaha NE 68127

Bulldog Club of Central Canada
Mrs N Daniels
536 Clement Ave
Dorval, PEI H9P 2H4
514/ 631-8920

Bullmastiff Assoc Inc, American
Ms Zoe Murphy
13850 Forsythe Rd
Sykesville MD 21784-5811

Bullmastiff Fanciers of Canada
Nancy Bullock
2306 Homelands Dr
Mississauga ONT L5K 1G6
416/ 855-2814

Cairn Terrier Club of America
Susan Vertz-Millward
3149 Arkona Rd
Saline MI 48176

Cairn Terrier Club of Canada
Joanne Potter
Decew Rd RR 1
Fonthill ONT L0S 1E0
416/ 684-6869

Canaan Dog Club of America
Lorraine Stephens
Box 555
Newcastle OK 73065-0555

Cane Corse Club & Registry, United States
Sandra Freeman
5107 Darkmoor
Imperial MO 63052
314/ 464-3275

Cane Corso Club of America
PO Box 250307
Montgomery AL 36125
205/ 284-4211; FAX 609/ 358-8254

Cardigan Corgi Club, Canadian
Shelly Camm
603 Lydia St
Newmarket ONT L3Y 1M4
416/ 836-1712

Cardigan Welsh Corgi Club of America Inc
Dr Kathleen Harper
544 Bridletrace Dr
Leeds AL 35094

Caucasian Ovtcharka Club of America
PO Box 745
Painesville OH 44077

Cavalier King Charles Spaniel Club,
National
Suzanne Brown
434 Country Ln
Louisville KY 40201
502/ 897-9148

Cavalier King Charles Spaniel Club of
Canada
Frances Bowness
860 Anderson Ave
Milton ONT L9T 4X9
416/ 875-2626

Cesky Club, The National
PO Box 217
Miximo OH 44650

Cesky Terrier Club of America
Lori Moody
PO Box 1318
Goldsboro NC 27534

Chesapeake Bay Retriever Club, American
Janet E Hopp
1705 RD 76
Pasco WA 99301

Chesapeake Bay Retriever Club of Canada
Nancy Ind
18 Dartwell Ave
Toronto ONT M5R 3A4
416/ 961-8666

Chihuahua Club of America Inc
Lynnie Bonten
5019 Village Trail
San Antonio TX 78218-3830

Chihuahua Club of Canada
Angela Bartnik
2114 Dublin St
New Westminster BC V3M 3A9
604/ 525-0123

Chinese Crested Club Inc, American
Ms Lynda McMillian
3101 East Blount St
Pensacola FL 32503

Chinese Shar-Pei Club of America Inc
Ms Jocelyn Barker
6101 Alpine Woods Dr
Anchorage AK 99516

Chinese Shar-Pei Club of Canada
Norm Fargo
2989-4th Concession RR#1
Goodwood, ON L0C 1A0
416/ 649-1875

Chinook Owners Assoc
Grace Anderson
PO Box 3282
Jackson WY 83001
307/733-3182

Chow Chow Club Inc
Irene Cartabio
3580 Plover Place
Seaford NY 11783

Chow Chow Fanciers of Canada
Suzanne Staines
32829 Bakerview Ave
Mission BC V2V 2P8
604/ 826-3284

Clumber Spaniel Club of America
Barbara Stebbins
9 Cedar St
Selden NY 11784

Collie Club of America Inc
Carmen Leonard
1119 S Fleming Rd
Woodstock IL 60098
815/ 337-0323

Collie Club of Canada
Diane Lodon
349 Jefferson Ave
Winnipeg MB R2V 0M9
204/ 582-1225

Collie/Shetland Sheepdog Assoc, Dominion
Mrs Wendy Jackson
RR 2
Harley ONT N0E 1E0
519/ 424-2373

Collie/Shetland Sheepdog Assoc
Inc,Canadian
Ann C Mitchell
160 Campeau Ave
Les Cedres, PQ J0P 1L0
514/ 452-4008

Coton de Tulear Club of America, The
PO Box 7152
Van'Nuys CA 91409-7152
818/ 988-8978; 818/ 989-7567

Cur and Feist Breeders Assoc, National
Claude Thomas
713 E Sycamore
Jasonville IN 47438
812/ 665-3263

Curly-Coated Retriever Club of America
Gina Columbo
24 Holmes Blvd
Walton Beach FL 32548

Dachshund Club of America Inc
Mr Walter M Jones
390 Eminence Pike
Shelbyville KY 40065

Dalmatian Club of America Inc
Mrs Anne T Fleming
4390 Chickasaw Rd
Memphis TN 38117

Dalmatian Club of Canada
Kathleen Charlton
11005-159 St
Edmonton ALTA T5P 3C2
403/ 484-1794

Dandie Dinmont Terrier Club of America
Mrs Mixon M Darracott
25 Ridgeview Rd
Staunton VA 24401

Dandie Dinmont Terrier Club of Canada
Mrs Anne Clune
36 Plateau Crescent
Don Mills ONT M3C 1M8
416/ 444-2861

Doberman Club, United
PO Box 659
Spring Valley NY 10977-0659
914/ 352-0244; 617/ 522-0253

Doberman Pinscher Club of America
Ms Judy Reams
10316 NE 136th Pl
Kirkland WA 98034

Doberman Pinscher Club of Canada
Michelle Limoges
9111-84 Ave
Edmonton ALTA T6C 1E5
403/ 468-6245

Dogo Argentino Club of America
Jose Ricardo Vidal
RT 2 Box 11
Goodland IN 47948

English Cocker Spaniel Club of
America Inc
Kate D Romanski
PO Box 252
Hales Corners WI 53130

English Cocker Spaniel Club of Canada
Linda Beason
RR#2 Site G, C-30
Nanaimo BC V9R 5K2
604/ 722-2912

English Setter Assoc of America
Mrs Dawn Ronyak
114 S Burlington Oval Dr
Chardon OH 44024

English Setter Club of Canada
Hilary Tunstil
5223 Rundlehorn Dr NE
Calgary AB T1Y 3A4
403/ 285-1646

English Shepherd Club
Marianne Dwight
Old Greenfield Rd
Shelburne MA 01370
413/774-5888

English Springer Spaniel Field Trial Assoc
Marie Andersen
29512 47th Ave S
Auburn WA 98001

English Toy Spaniel Club of America
Susan Jackson
18451 Sheffield Ln
Bristol IN 46507-9454

Entlebucher Club of America
RD 2 Box 899 RT 206
Chester NJ 07930
201/ 584-1229

Feist, *see Cur*

Fell Terrier, *see Patterdale Terrier*

Field Spaniel Society of America
Sally Herweyer
11197 Keystone
Lowell MI 49331

Fila Brasileiro Club of America
244 Flat Rock Church Rd
Zebulon GA 30295
706/ 567-8085

Finnish Spitz Club, Canadian
Kay Bunker
11016 - 149th St
Edmonton AB T5P 1M8
403/ 484-4959

Finnish Spitz Club of America
Connie Britt
7870 Lakewood Dr
Austin TX 78750

Flat-Coated Retriever Soc of America Inc
Ann Mortenson
6608 Lynnwood Blvd
Richfield MN 55423

Flat-Coated Retriever Society of Canada
Heather Stewart
RR #4 Queenston Rd
Niagara-on-the-Lake ONT L05 1J0
416/ 684-6187

Fox Paulistinha Brazilian Terrier, Clube do
Rua Dr Lopes de Almeida
87 Sao Paulo-SP-044120

Fox Terrier Club, American
Mr Martin Goldstein
PO Box 604
South Plainfield NJ 07098

French Bulldog Club of America
Mr David F Kruger
6336 Berkley Dr
New Orleans LA 70131-4106

German Pinscher Breeders Assoc, Amer
Rhonda Parks
701 Calvin Ave
Portage PA 15946
814/736-9699

German Pinscher Club of America
RT 1 Box 290
Champion MI 49814
906/ 339-2953

German Shepherd Dog Club of America
Inc
Blanche Beisswenger
17 W Ivy Ln
Englewood NJ 07631

German Shepherd Dog Club of Canada
Christine Gibbons
RR 2
Rockwood ONT N0B 2K0
519/ 856-4363

German Shorthaired Pointer Club of
America
Geraldine A Irwin
1101 W Quincy
Englewood CO 80110

German Wirehaired Pointer Club America
Inc
Ms Barbara Hein
3838 Davison Lake Rd
Ortonville MI 48462

Giant Schnauzer Club of America Inc
Ms Dorothy Wright
4220 S Wallace
Chicago IL 60609

Giant Schnauzer Club of Canada
Dan Hennaert
RR 1
Wyoming ONT N0N 1T0
519/ 845-3653

Golden Retriever Club of America
Ms Ginny Kell
4387 W Highway 94
Marthasville MO 63357

Golden Retriever Club of Canada
Brenda Wilson
6266 Island Hwy West
Qualicum Bay BC V9K 2E4
604/ 757-9276

Gordon Setter Club of America Inc
Ms L Alison Rosskamp
945 Font Rd
Glenmore PA 19343

Gordon Setter Club of Canada
Bev Holoboff
217-52150 Range Rd
Sherwood Park AB T8E 1C8
403/ 922-4113

Great Dane Club of America Inc
Marie A Fint
442 Country View Ln
Garland TX 75043

Great Dane Club of Canada
Ruth A Dalton
RR #1
Red Deer AB T4N 5E1
403/ 341-3875

Great Dane Fanciers Assoc of Canada
John Kuntze
RR 1
Milverton ONT N0K 1M0
519/ 595-4749

Great Pyrenees Club of America Inc
Charlotte Perry
RT 1 Box 119
Midland VA 22728

Great Pyrenees Club of Canada
Winston Cheatley
2442 Hwy 2 West
Alberton ONT L0R 1A0
416/ 648-3515

Greater Swiss Mountain Dog Club of
America
Julianne Wilson
Hwy 1861 Box 286A
Smithfield KY 40068

Greyhound Club of America
Ms Patricia A Clark
227 Hattertown Rd
Newton CT 06470

Greyhound Club of Canada
Christina DePierre
263 1st Ave
Ste Anne des Plaines, PQ J0N 1H0
514/ 478-0833

Havanese Club, Original
Joseph Sleziak
40667 Newport Dr
Plymouth MI 48170-4742

Ibizan Hound Club of Canada
Andrea Walters
RR 2
Alton ONT L0N 1A0
519/ 927-3473

Ibizan Hound Club of the United States
Lisa Puskas
4312 E Nisbet Rd
Phoenix AZ 85032

Irish Red & White Setter
Curtis Humphrey
PO Box 216
Townville SC 29689

Irish Setter Club of America Inc
Ms Marion J Pahy
16717 Ledge Falls
San Antonio TX 78232

Irish Setter Club of Canada
Joan Lock RR #1
Hillsburgh ON N0B 1Z0
519/ 855-4388

Irish Terrier Assoc of Canada
Glenda M Carscadden
82 Alamosa Dr North
York ONT M2J 2N9
416/ 229-6156

Irish Terrier Club of America
Mr Bruce Petersen
RR 3 Box 449
Bloomington IL 61704

Irish Water Spaniel Club of America
Ms Renae Peterson
24712 SE 380th
Enumclaw WA 98022

Irish Wolfhound Club of America
Mrs Williams Pfarrer
8855 US Route 40
New Carlisle OH 45344

Irish Wolfhound Club of Canada
Helga Lavigne
2336 Ogilive
Gloucester ONT K1J 7N6
613/ 749-7082

Italian Greyhound Club of America Inc
Ms Jamie Daily
13403 Lacewood
San Antonio TX 78233

Italian Greyhound Club of Canada
Mrs Karen Chant
1831 Holmstrom Rd
Campbell River BC V9W 3T3
604/ 286-0530

Italian Spinone Club
Mr Jim Channon
PO Box 307
Warsaw VA 22572
804/ 333-0309

Jack Russell Terrier Breeders Assoc
Holly Lestinsky
PO Box 23
Winchester Center CT 06094
203/ 379-3282

Jack Russell Terrier Club of America
Ailsa Crawford
PO Box 365
Far Hills NJ 07931
201/ 234-0126

Jack Russell Terrier Club of Canada
Yvonne Downey
242 Henrietta St
Fort Erie ONT L2A 2K7
416/ 871-8691

Jack Russell Terrier United World
Federation
Jack Batzer
2644 Beckleysville Rd
Millers MD 21107

Japanese Chin Club of America
Ms Faith G Milton
2113 Tract Rd
Fairfield PA 17320-9235

JinDo
Barbara R Abrams
16815 Germantown Rd
Germantown MD 20874
301/ 972-1423

Kai Ken Club, National
PO Box 217
Maximo OH 44650

Karelian Bear Dog
Arlene Sherrod
1550 Bitterroot Dr
Marion MT 59925
406/ 854-2240

Keeshond Club of America
Ms Jan Wilhite
8535 N 10th Ave
Phoenix AZ 85021-4414

Keeshond Club of Canada
Paula Lewis-Taylor
24 Niles Way
Thornhill ONT L3T 5B8
416/ 886-2689

Kelpies Inc, Working
Cindy Vondette
RT 3 Box 243
Willard MO 65781

Kerry Blue Terrier Club Inc, US
Ms Barbara Beuter
2458 Eastridge Dr
Hamilton OH 45011

Kerry Blue Terrier Club of Canada
Ms Barb Thompson
875 Concession St
Hamilton ON L8V 1E4
416/ 574-7999

Komondor Club Inc
The Middle Atlantic States
102 Russell Rd
Princeton NJ 08540

Komondor Club of America
Sandy Hanson
W359 S10708 Nature Rd
Eagle WI 53119

Kuvasz Assoc, American
Ann Cogburn
PO Box 485
Welton AZ 85356
602/ 782-4647

Kuvasz Club of America
John R. Fulkerson
16603 SW 5th Place
Newberry FL 32669

Kuvasz Club of Canada
Christine Thomas
PO Box 3786
Airdrie AB T4B 2B9
403/ 948-5260

Kuvasz Fanciers of America
Gail S Dash
PO Box 7115
Mission Hills CA 91346

Kyi-Leo Club
Harriet Linn
1757 Landana Dr
Concord CA 94520

Labrador Owners Club
Nadia Townshend
25 Treegrove Circle
Aurora ONT L4G 6S5
416/ 713-0448

Labrador Retriever Club of America
Christopher G Wincek
9690 Wilson Mills Rd
Chardon OH 44024

Labrador Retriever Club of Canada
Diane Smith
7078 Mark Ln
PO Box 69 RR#5
Victoria BC V8X 4M6
604/ 652-0180

Lakeland Terrier Club, US
Carol Griffin
PO Box 214
Bayport NY 11705

Lapphund Club of America
Linda Marden
1870 Locke-Cuba Rd
Millington TN 38053
901/ 876-3205

Leonberger Club of America
Marlene Stuteville
PO Box 97
Georgetown CT 06829-0097

Leonberger's Canada
Hans & Marion Horst
General Delivery
Clyde AL T0G 0P0
403/ 348-5790

Lhasa Apso Canada
Arlene Miller
2685 Trillium Place North
Vancouver BC V7H 1J2
604/ 929-3570

Lhasa Apso Club Inc, American
Amy J Andrews
18105 Kirkshire
Birmingham MI 48025

Little Lion Dog Club of America
Sandra Lunka
2771 Graylock Dr
Willoughby Hills OH 44094
216/ 951-5288

Louisiana Catahoulas, National Assoc of
PO Box 1041
Denham Springs LA 70727

Lowchen, *see Little Lion Dog*

Magyar Agar Club of America
Lance House
2280 Grass Valley Hwy # 230
Auburn CA 95603

Majestic Tree Hound Assoc, National
Lee Newhart
155 West Haven Rd
Ithaca NY 14850
607/ 273-6391

Maltese Assoc Inc, American
Ms Pamela G Rightmyer
6145 Coley Ave
Las Vegas NV 89102

Manchester Terrier Club, American
Ms Diana Haywood
RD 2 Box 208A Hampton Rd
Pittstown NJ 08867-9802

Maremma-Abruzzese Club
Sue Drummond
1451 Sisson
Freeport MI 49325
616/ 765-3056

Mastiff Club, Canadian
Lori Isnor-Dobrucki
57 Pine St
Welland ONT L3C 4G2
416/ 732-2222

Mastiff Club of America Inc
Ms Carla Sanchez
45935 Via Esparanza
Temecula CA 92590

McNab Dog
Donna L Seigmund
21526 Hwy 299 East
Redding CA 96003
916/ 547-3324

Miniature Bull Terrier Club of America
Marilyn Drewes
16 Fremont Rd
Sandown NH 03873

Miniature Dachshund Club of Canada
Jean Fletcher
14875-59th Ave
Surrey BC V3S 4S6
604/ 594-6809

Miniature Pinscher Club, Canadian
Beverly Creed
8532 Addison Dr SE
Calgary AB T2H 1P1
403/ 252-6018

Miniature Pinscher Club of America Inc
Kay Phillips
RT 1 Box 173
Temple TX 76501

Miniature Schnauzer Club, American
Susan R Atherton
RR 2 Box 3570
Bartlesville OK 74003

Miniature Schnauzer Club of Canada
Gary Cohen
13410 - 56th Ave
Surrey BC V3X 2Z6
604/ 594-6644

Miniature Shar-Pei Club, The National
14121 Rancho Vista
Riverside CA 92508

Mudi Assoc, North American
Cheryl A Kelly
3039 Hance Rd
Macedon NY 14502
315/ 986-2695

Neapolitan Mastiff Assoc
23000 Santa Susana Pass
Chatsworth CA 91311

Neapolitan Mastiff Club, United States
RD 5 Box 11 Damascus Rd
Franklinville NJ 08322
609/ 728-8937

Neapolitan Mastiff Club of America
PO Box 250307
Montgomery AL 36125
205/ 284-4401; 205/ 284-4838

Newfoundland Club of America Inc
Mr Clyde E Dunphy
RR 3 Box 155
Carlinville IL 62626

Newfoundland Dog Club of Canada
Carol Bodnieks
3 Toulon Rd
Scarborough ON M1G 1V6
416/ 439-3143

Norwegian Buhund Club of America
Mrs Jan Christoferson Barringer
RR 1 Box 8A
Bethalto IL 62010-9801
618/ 466-3777

Norwegian Elkhound Assoc of America Inc
Mrs Diane Coleman
4772 Mentzer Church Rd
Convoy OH 45832

Norwegian Elkhound Club of Canada
Linda Reed
54 Pontiac Ct
Brampton ON L6Z 1C1
416/ 846-5288

Norwegian Lundehund Club of America Inc
Harvey Sanderson
33 Amsterdam Rd
Milford NJ 08848
908/ 995-7422

Norwich & Norfolk Terrier Club
Mrs Maurice J Matteson
407 Grenoble Dr
Sellersville PA 18960

Nova Scotia Duck Tolling Retriever Club
Gretchen Botner
951 Moon Ct
Marco Island FL 33937

Nova Scotia Duck Tolling Retriever Club
Club,Canada
Lynn E Vail
9388 123 A St
Surrey, BC V3V 6S8
604/ 588-9189

Old English Sheepdog & Owners Club of
Canada
Susanne Kitchen
RR #3 North Gower ON K0A 2T0
613/ 489-2480

Old English Sheepdog Club of America
Ms Kathryn L Bunnell
14219 E 79th St S
Derby KS 67037

Otterhound Club of America
Dian Quist-Sulek
RT 1 Box 247 Ave
Palmyra NE 68418

Papillion Canada
Mrs Cindy Hook
RR #12 Site 22 Comp 5
Thunder Bay ON P7B 5E3
807/ 767-5783

Papillon Club of America Inc
Mrs Janice Dougherty
551 Birch Hill Rd
Shoemakersville PA 19555

Patterdale Terrier
Venita Henson
RT 5 Box 195
Neosho MO 64850

Pekingese Club of America Inc
Mrs Leonie Marie Schultz
RT 1 Box 321
Bergton VA 22811

Pembroke Welsh Corgi Assoc
of Canada QUE/ONT
Anne Cunnington, secretary
82 Morningside Village
265E Bleams Rd
New Hamburg ONT N0B 2G0
519/ 662-3490

Pembroke Welsh Corgi Assoc of Canada
Miss Susan O'Heir
25 Nottingham Dr
Etobicoke ONT M9A 2W4
416/ 234-5431

Pembroke Welsh Corgi Club of America
Inc
John Vahaly
1608 Clearview Dr
Louisville KY 40222

Peruvian Inca Orchid Club of America
1160 Cattell Rd
Wenonah NJ 08090

Petit Basset Griffon Vendeen
 Club of America
Ms Shirley Knipe
426 Laguna Way
Simi Valley CA 93065

Petit Basset Griffon Vendeen
  Fanciers—Canada
Mary Legault
1150 Des Sittelles St
Lazare QUE J0P 1V0
519/ 424-9203

Pharaoh Hound Club, Canadian
Mrs Kathie Lanyon
9952 Ridge Rd RR 4
Welland ONT L3B 5N7
416/ 384-9613

Pharaoh Hound Club of America
Rita Sacks
RT 209 Box 285
Stone Ridge NY 12484

Pit Bull Terrier Assoc, National American
Patti Murley
Rt 2 Box 1157
Denton TX 76201
817/ 387-2107

Pointer Club Inc, American
Ms Lee Ann Stagg
RT 1 Box 10
Branch LA 70516

Pointer Club of Canada
Cathy McNeil
537 Woodland Ave
Burlington ON L7R 2S4
416/ 632-4595

Polish Owczarek Nizinny Club
Kaz and Betty Augustowski
1115 Delmont Rd
Severn MD 21144
410/ 551-6750

Polish Owczarek Nizinny Society Inc
Thomas E Ferraro, International
9N580 Nokomis Ln
Elgin IL 60123
708/ 697-0559

Polish Tatra Sheepdog Club of America
Carol Wood
N 11724 Forker Rd
Spokane WA 99207

Pomeranian Club Inc, American
Ms Frances J Stoll
RR 3 Box 429
Washington IN 47501

Pomeranian Club of Canada
Gerrie Bucsko
Box 385
Irricana ALTA T0M 1B0
403/ 935-4730

Poodle Advancement Assoc of Canada
Anne Bell
10546 Guelph Line
Campbellville, ON L0P 1B0
416/ 854-0616

Poodle Club of America Inc
Mrs Harold C Kinne
2514 Custer Parkway
Richardson TX 75080

Portuguese Water Dog Club of America
L Ann Moore
16 Auspice Circle
Newark DE 19711

Portuguese Water Dog Club of Canada
Brian & Monica Burke
RR 1
Barrie ONT L4M 1N0

Pug Club of Canada
Noreen Talbot
RR #16 Ste 5
Thunder Bay ONT P7B 6B3
807/ 767-8991

Pug Dog Club of America Inc
James P Cavallaro
1820 Shadowlawn St
Jacksonville FL 32205-9430

Puli Canada
Stephanie Horan
General Delivery
Crossfield AB T0M 0S0
403/ 946-5762

Puli Club of America Inc
Dodie Atkins
6036 Peachmont Terrace
Norcross GA 30092

Pyrenean Shepherd Club of America
Mrs Jean Cave-Pero
4501 Old Pond Dr
Plano TX 75024-4708

Retriever Club of Canada, National
Jane Schmidt
1348 Mills Rd, RR 2
Sydney BC V8L 3S1
604/ 656-5987

Rhodesian Ridgeback Club
 of Western Canada
Terri Tracy
RR 9 1439 - 242nd St
Langley BC V3A 6H5
604/ 530-9888

Rhodesian Ridgeback Club of US Inc
Ms Betty Epperson
PO Box 121817
Ft Worth TX 76121-1817

Rottweiler Club, American
Ms Doreen LePage
960 South Main St
Pascoag RI 02859

Rottweiler Club of Canada
Deb Bombenon
31 Hawkside Close NW
Calgary AB T3G 3K4
403/ 290-4502

Saint Bernard Club of America Inc
Ms Carole A Wilson
719 East Main St
Bellerville IL 62220

Saint Bernard Club of Ontario
Stephanie Paterson
PO Box 441
Bolton ONT L7E 5T3

Saluki Assoc, American
Judy Lauer
RT 1 Box 344
Fairmont WV 26554

Saluki Club of America
Marilyn LaBrache Brown
PO Box 753
Mercer Island WA 98040

Saluki Club of Canada
Lin Jenkins
5315 Pearl Rd RR 1
L'Orignal ONT K0B 1K0
613/ 678-3626

Samoyed Assoc of Canada
Judi Elford
PO Box 8516
Manuels NFLD A1X 1B5
709/ 834-9346

Samoyed Club of America Inc
Ms Kathie Lensen
W6434 Francis Rd
Cascade WI 53011

Schipperke Club of America Inc
Ms Diana Dick
5205 Chaparral
Laramie WY 82070

Schipperke Club of Canada
Jean Hodgins
#33, 219 Grant St
Saskatoon SK S7N 2A5
306/ 931-8975

Scottish Deerhound Club of America Inc
Joan Shagan
545 Cummings Ln
Cottontown TN 37048

Scottish Terrier Club, Canadian
Anne Newlands
RR 1
Peterborough ONT K9J 6X2
705/ 657-1154

Scottish Terrier Club of America
Mrs Diane Zollinger
PO Box 1893
Woodinville WA 98072

Sealyham Terrier Club, American
Mrs Barbara Carmany
PO 76 - 6160 State Rd
Sharon Center OH 44274
216/ 239-1498

Sealyham Terrier Club of Canada
Dr William R Greenwood
RR 7
Dresden ONT N0P 1M0
519/ 352-6418

Shetland Sheepdog Assoc, American
Ms Susan Beachum
2125 E 16th Ave
Post Falls ID 83854

Shetland Sheepdog Assoc, Canadian
Joanne Pavey
26 Gorsey Square
Scarborough ONT M1B 1A7
416/ 292-6808

Shiba Club of America, National
Miss Frances M Thorton
100 Peaceful Dr
Converse TX 78109

Shiba Inu Club of Canada
Heather Logan
12 Dervock Crescent
Willowdale ON M2K 1A7
416/ 229-4263

Shiba Ken Club
172 Jewett St
Akron OH 44305
216/ 434-2921

Shih Tzu Club, Canadian
Cora Lee Romano
1874 West Arthur St
Thunder Bay ONT P7C 4V1
807/ 577-7753

Shih Tzu Club Inc, American
JoAnn Regelman
837 Auburn Ave
Ridgewood NJ 07450

Shiloh Shepherd Dog Club of America
Dusty Sue Hellmann
PO Box 309
Silver Springs NY 14550
716/493-5747

Siberian Husky Club of America Inc
Ms Carol Nash
54 Newton Rd
Plaistow NH 03865

Siberian Husky Club of Canada
Mrs Shayne Moon
421 Stoney Creek Rd
York ONT N0A 1R0
416/ 765-1892

Silky Terrier Club, National Maple Leaf
Valerie Vankoesveld
35782 Hartley Rd RR 3
Mission BC V2V 4S1
604/ 820-3040

Silky Terrier Club of America Inc
Louise Rosewell
27835 S Saulsbury St
Denver CO 80227

Skye Terrier Club of America
Mrs Karen Sanders
11567 Sutter's Mill Cir
Gold River CA 95670

Sloughi Assoc, American
Vicki Barter
PO Box 308
North Liberty IA 52317-0308

Slovak Tchouvatch Dog Club of America
Joseph and Maya Schon
49 Old Middletown Rd
Nanuet NY 10954
914/ 623-8185

Smooth Fox Terrier Club of Canada
Kathrine Grant
983 Ormsby St
London ONT N5Z 1K5
519/ 453-1750

Soft-Coated Wheaten Terrier Assoc of
Canada
Shelia Teichreb
Box 634
Broadview SASK S0G 0K0
306/ 696-2709

Soft-Coated Wheaten Terrier Club of
America
Mary Anne Dallas
4607 Willow Ln
Nazareth PA 18064

Spanish Mastiff Club of America
1045 RT 18
New Brunswick NJ 08816

Spinone Italiano
PO Box 284
Carmel IN 48032

Staffordshire Bull Terrier Club Inc
Linda Barker
PO Box 7021
Knoxville TN 37918-7000

Staffordshire Bull Terrier Club of Canada
Patrica Beard
972 Connaught Ave
Ottawa ONT K2B 5M9
613/ 828-3850

Staffordshire Terrier Club of America
H Richard Pascoe
785 Valley View Rd
Forney TX 75126

Standard Schnauzer Club of America
Kathy A Donovan
4 Deerfield Rd
Brookfield CT 06804

Standard Schnauzer Club of Canada
Clive Davies
Silver Spoon Manor, RR#2
Tottenham ONT L0G 1W0
416/ 936-2879

Sussex Spaniel Club of America
Joan Dunn
N3W31535 Twin Oaks Dr
Delafield WI 53018

Swedish Vallhund Enthusiasts of America
Mr & Mrs John B. Thell
RR 1 Box 102 Waterman Hill Rd
Greene RI 02827
401/ 397-5003

Telomian Dog Club of America
Audrey Palumbo
28765 White Rd
Perrysburg OH 43551

Tibetan KyiApso Club
Daniel Taylor-Ide
PO Box 10
Franklin WV 26807
304/ 358-2749

Tibetan Mastiff Assoc, American
920 Bonnie Ln
Auburn CA 95603

Tibetan Spaniel Club of America
Shirley Howard
29 W 028 River Glen Rd W
Chicago IL 60185

Tibetan Terrier Club of America Inc
Brenda Brown
127 Springlea Dr
Winfield WV 25213

Tibetan Terrier Club of Canada
Jo Hannam
Site 2, Comp 14, RR #1
Tappen BC V0E 2X0
604/ 835-8258

Tosa of America
10330 Sepulveda Bl Suite 101
Mission Hills CA 91345
818/ 892-4944

Tosa-Ken Assoc, International
8949 Herrick Ave
Sun Valley CA 91352
818/ 768-0691

Toy Fox Terrier Assoc, National
Ann Mauermann
211 Exchange Ave
Louisville KY 40207
502/ 895-2303

Transylvanian Black Hound Club of
America
Charleve Benson
PO Box 3425
Morgantown WV 26505

Treeing Walker Assoc, Southeastern
Richard A Guill, PhD
Stony Point NC 28678
704/ 585-2727

Treeing Walker Breeders and Fanciers
Assoc
Connie Wade
PO Box 399
Guy TX 77444
409/ 793-4133

Vizsla Club of America Inc
Ms Jan Bouman
15744 Hampshire Ave S
Prior Lake MN 55372

Walker Assoc, NK.C. Region VII
Sean M Wonder
341 South Jefferson St
Bloomfield IN 47424

Weimaraner Assoc of Canada
Wendy McKay
Follyhill RR 2
Woodlawn ONT K0A 3M0
613/ 832-3223

Weimaraner Club of America
Dorothy Derr
PO Box 110708
Nashville TN 37222-0708

Welsh Springer Spaniel Club, North East
Linda S Brennan
60 Leo Ave RD 1
Stanhope NJ 07874
201/ 398-7143

Welsh Springer Spaniel Club of America
Inc
Karen Lyle
4425 N 147th St
Brookfield WI 53005

Welsh Springer Spaniel Club of Canada
Gerry Curry
RR 1
Millgrove ONT L0R 1V0
416/ 659-7376

Welsh Terrier Assoc of Canada
Mrs Brenda Olmstead
6606 Mark Ln, RR5
Victoria BC V8X 4M6
604/ 652-6630

Welsh Terrier Club of America Inc
Helen Chamides
698 Ridge Rd
Highland Park IL 60035
708/ 831-0313

West Highland Terrier Club of America
Ms Anne Sanders
33101 44th Ave NW
Stanwood WA 98292

West Highland White Terrier Club,
Canadian
Lynda Scott
Box 81A RR #5
Winnipeg MB R2C 2Z2
204/ 224-0778

Whippet Club Inc, American
Ms Harriett N Lee
14 Oak Circle
Charlottesville VA 22901

White Shepherd Club of Canada
Lynda Rroulx
RR 7
Alvinston ONT N0N 1A0
519/ 847-5206

Wire Haired Fox Terrier Club of Canada
Mrs Ann Gold
RR 1
Erin ONT N0B 1T0
519/ 855-4629

Wirehaired Pointing Griffon Assoc,
American
Denny Smith
90566 Coburg Rd
Eugene OR 97401

Wirehaired Pointing Griffon Club of
America
Mrs Joan Bailey
11739 SW Beaverton Hwy #201
Beaverton OR 97005
503/ 629-5707

Xoloitzquintli, *See Mexican Hairless*

Yorkshire Terrier Assoc Inc, Canadian
Deborah Tatham
34 Byron St
Georgetown ON L7G 3W7
416/ 877-9249

Yorkshire Terrier Club of America Inc
Mrs Betty R Dullinger
PO Box 100
Porter ME 04068

The popularity of rare breeds is increasing rapidly and there are many reasons for this. Some people enjoy owning a unique dog. Others may prefer the look of one of the rare breeds. Still others may have ethnic ties to the breed's country of origin.

There are more than four hundred different breeds of dog throughout the world. Some of the rarest breeds are not easily found in the United States (often they are not easily located in their native countries) and many people have no idea where to turn to find a rare breed. One of the ways to find the breed you may be interested in is to contact the rare-breed club nearest you. Since so many are being formed all of the time, you can usually find out about them through the clubs that already exist. If that does not prove to be fruitful, then you can always request information from a dog magazine.

Because rare breeds are rapidly gaining in popularity, the two major registries in the Unites States (the American Kennel Club and the United Kennel Club) are becoming more involved with the rare breeds. Organizations, such as the American Rare Breed Association, are growing rapidly and now offer dog shows that cater to the rare breeds; therefore, if you are patient and keep looking, you will find the breed you want. However, before you consider buying a rare breed of dog you should research the characteristics of that dog first. Often the rare breed is still used for the purpose for which it was bred and its instincts are very strong. Some of the rare breeds are not kept as pets in their native countries and may not adapt to becoming a pet in a populated area.

It is also extremely important that you research and investigate the breeder of rare breeds as well, because often there are no peers or club ethics to insure that the breeder is honest. When considering the rare breed you should also keep in mind that there may be problems due to a limited gene pool from which to breed. Because some countries do not allow certain breeds to be exported, some dogs have been smuggled out of their countries and few if any new lines are available for breeding.

Be aware of the con-artist who mixes common breeds of dogs and passes them off as exotic breeds. While this practice is not too common, it does occur.

American Rare Breed Association
Anita Bryant
PO Box 76424
Washington DC 20013
202/ 722-1232

Federation of International Canines
Kathy W Sottile
PO Box 250307
Montgomery AL 36125
205/ 284-4401

Federation of Rare Breed Dog Clubs
Madeline Eaton
PO Box 220
Hillside NJ 07205

Garden City Kansas Kennel Club
PO Box 725
Garden City KS 67846

Hudson Valley Rare Breed Club
Stacey Kubyn
PO Box 745
Painesville OH 44077
216/ 639-0567

International All Breed Kennel Club
 of America (IABKCA)
21115 Devonshire #385
Chatsworth CA 91311
818/ 882-5636

International Rare Breed Dog Club
PO Box 757
Blooming Prairie MN 55917-0757

Mid-West Rare Breed Club
Carol Neumann
PO Box 365
Miles MI 49120
616/ 684-1320

Natiional Rare Breed Assoc
PO Box 253
Moorestown NJ 08057
609/779-7404

Oriental Breeds International, The
open to rare breeds
Herb Rosen
11404 Lhasa Lane RD 1
Lutherville MD 21093
301/ 252-7555

Rare Breed Connection
PO Box 3804
Fontana CA 92334
714/ 823-5450

Rocky Mountain Rare Breed Club
Karen Tobin
2702 S Pagosa St
Aurora CO 80013

Rocky Mountain Rare Breed Club, The
Charles Petterson
11634 Community Center Drive #32
Northglenn CO 80233

Tennessee Rare Breed Assoc
Dick Dickerson
2706 Murfreesboro Pike
Nashville TN 37013
615/ 361-5348

West New York Rare Breed Club
Bonnie Cain
2015 Sherbourne Rd
Walworth NY 14568
315/ 597-9707

All of the clubs that did not fall into the other categories are listed in this chapter. They are generally a group of people interested in a certain type of dog although not a specific breed. Many times the clubs listed in this chapter have functions and shows that they sponsor for their type of dog. Like other clubs, they offer opportunities to meet with people who share a similar interest.

Canadian Sighthound Assoc
Susan Stewart
Box 1479
Ashcroft BC V0K 1 A0
604/ 453-2511

Canine All Breed Club
Lynn Arsenault
740 Atsion Rd
Atco NJ 08004
609/ 768-0955

Canine Collectibles Club of America
(dog memorabilia)
736 N Western Ave #314
Lake Forest IL 60045

Cold Nose Chow & Marching Society
(mixed-breed dog club)
102 W Sharon Rd
Glendale OH 45246
513/771-6367

Collie Information Center
Oaks Corner, Common Lane
Hemingford Abbots
Cambridge England PE 18 9AP

Federacion Canofila de Puerto Rico (FCPR)
Roberto Velez-Pico
Box 13898
Santurce Station
Santurce PR 00908
809/ 760-5104

French & Swiss Hounds
(Location of French &
Swiss Hound breeders)
E S Traverse
RT 1 Box 28
Castleton VT 05735
802/ 468-5484

Mixed-Breed Dog Club of America
Cheri Barnes
512 Menahen St
Napa CA 94559

Movie Dog Nostalgia Fan Club
Debbie Goldstein
Suite 390 - 3601 Plank Rd
Fredericksburg VA 22401

Mutts of America
Juanita Bednarz, "Crackers," president
PO Box 1716
260 Lathrop St
Kingston PA 18704
717/ 287-8726

National Working Breeds Society
Mrs A Davis
308 Hughenden Rd
High Wycombe, Bucks
England UK

New York City Coalition For Dogs
51 MacDougal St. #120
New York NY 10012
212/ 243-5460

Owner Handlers Assoc of America
RD 1 Box 755
Millerstown PA 17062
717/ 589-3098

Pet Care Savings Club
[benefits for resp pet care]
membership services dept
4501 Forbes Blvd
Lanham MD 20706
800/388-PETS

Responsible Dog Owners Assoc
[educating the public & anti-dog laws]
PO Box 173
Fountainville PA 18923
610/249-1377

Terrier Breeders Assoc of Canada
Sylvia Hamilton
RR #2
Rockwood ONT N0B 2K0
519/ 853-1456

USA Loves Dogs Club
2537 Wells Ave
Sarasota FL 34232
800/ 553-6475

If you cannot find the activity you're interested in, check under the organizations related to your breed. Many times the parent club of a breed of dog is involved in the sport or activity in which you are interested or will know whom to contact. For example, if you're interested in Terrier *go- to-ground* trials, you can write to the Jack Russell Terrier clubs. Other sources to consider are publications and registry organizations. If a publication or registry is even remotely connected with the activity you're seeking, they will offer you suggestions for contacts. Sometimes magazines will have a request for information in their publications that you can write to for more information.

All American Obedience Titles
New England Obedience News
35 Oakwood Dr
Portsmouth NH 03801-5779

American Coon Hunters Assoc
American Kennel Club
51 Madison Ave
New York NY 10010

American Mixed-Breed Obedience
Registration
Mona Marshall
205 1st St SW
New Prague MN 56071

American Working Collie Assoc Inc
Gail A Joy
2100 Fiero Ave
Schenectady NY 12303

American Working Dog Federation
Jim Engel
19007 Millstream Rd
Marengo IL 60152
815/568-5963

American Working Terrier Assoc
Karla Martin
RD 3 Box 165B
Columbia Crossroads PA 16914

Canadian German Shepherd
Schutzhund Club
Susan Lawrence
Box 3848
Leduc AB T9E 6M8

Canadian National Spaniel Field Trial Assoc
Jeannette Foran-White
2979 Old Windsor Hwy RR#4
Lr Sackville NS B4C 3B1
902/865-3026

Canadian Scent Hurdle Racing Assoc
Mrs Merle Milsom
154 Garland Crescent
Sherwood Park ALB T8A 2A6

Canine Search & Rescue, See *SAR Dog
Alert*, General Publications

Chow Chow Club Inc
(obedience & sports for Chows)
Sandra Voina
PO Box 148
Telford PA 18969

Clever Canine Companions
Jane Sohns-CSB
Working Regis/Titles for Pure and Mixed-
Breed Dogs
140 Weidler Lane
Rothsville PA 17543-3003
SASE required

Collie Carting Program
Kathy Stokey
5 Woodland Ct
Saratoga Springs NY 12866-1008

Come N Get It K-9 Frisbee Championships
(formerly Ashley Whippet Invitational)
Irv Lander
PO Box 16279
Encino CA 91416
818/780-4913; 800/423-3268

English Springer Spaniel Field Trial Assoc
Marie Andersen
2951Z 47th Ave S
Auburn WA 98001

Field Trial & Hunting Clubs
American Kennel Club
51 Madison Ave
New York NY 10010

Field Trial & Hunting Clubs
United Kennel Club
100 E Kilgore Rd
Kalamazoo MI 49001-5592
616/343-9020

Frisbee Contests, See General Publications,
Come N Get It

Greyhound Racing Federation of Canada
Linda M Reidt
RR 1
Baltimore ONT KOK1C0
416/342-3391

Hunting Retriever Club Inc
United Kennel Club
100 E Kilgore Rd
Kalamazoo MI 49001-5592
616/343-9020

Independent Work & Sport Dog Assoc
Schutzhund Events
PO Box 7272
Olympia WA 98507

International Weight Pulling Assoc
PO Box 994
Greeley CO 80632

Landersverband DVG America Inc
(Schutzhund)
PO Box 160399
Miami FL 33116

Mixed-Breed Dog Club of America
(Neut. Mix, Disabled, Rare-Breed Obed
Titles)
Phyllis Massa
1937 Seven Pines Dr
St Louis MO 63146-3717
314/878-8497

National Committee for Dog Agility
Charles "Bud" Kramer
401 Bluemont Circle
Manhattan KS 66502
913/537-7022

National Committee for Dog Agility
Virginia Isaac
5882 Woodleigh Dr
Carmichael CA 95608
916/966-5287

Newfoundland Club of America
Water Rescue Tests
Mr Halsey Frederick
530 Fishers Rd
Bryn Mawr PA 19010
215/525-3245

North American Flyball Assoc
Mike Randall
2553 Oaks Plantation Dr
Raleigh NC 27610-9329

North American Ring Assoc
Cheryl A Carlson
5325 W Mount Hope Rd
Lansing MI 48917
517/322-2221

Purina HiPro Dog Run
K-9 Promotions Inc (dogs and people race)
711 Pine Acres
Davenport IA 52803

Southwestern Ontario Schutzhund Club
Cor Vandermuren
RR5
Harrow ONT N0R 1G0
519/736-5931

Toronto Lure Coursers
Janice Preiss
Box 324
Beeton ONT LOG 1AO

Tri States Working Dog Assoc
PO Box 161
Newfield NY 14867

United Schutzhund Clubs of America Inc
3704 Lemoy Ferry Rd
St Louis MO 63125
314/894-3431

United States Dog Agility Assoc Inc
PO Box 850955
Richardson TX 75085-0955
214/231-9700

As more people become interested in herding, more organizations are formed that offer herding programs. These organizations will usually offer clinics as well as trials. This chapter lists organizations and clubs that offer herding activities. If the organization nearest to you is involved with a different breed from what you have, do not hesitate to contact them anyway. Often they will work with you or know someone you can contact. If you cannot find an organization near you, contact the registry for your breed and ask them who to contact. Another source would be some of the general herding groups, such as the American Herding Breed Association.

Livestock guarding programs offer the latest in research about livestock guarding dogs. Although the need for livestock guarding dogs is not as great as it was 100 years ago, these programs can provide information for the protection of livestock that would otherwise not be available. Livestock guarding dogs dramatically reduce the loss of livestock.

Alabama Stock Dog Assoc
PO Box 736
Tallassee AL 36078

Alaska Herding Club, Interior
Tolli Nelson
46 Lincolnwood Dr.
North Pole AK 99705
907/ 488-6347

Alberta Stock Dog Assoc
Box 26
Lone Pine ALB T0G 1M0

American Herding Breed Assoc
Linda Rorem
1548 Victoria Way
Pacifica CA 94044
415/ 355-9563

American Tending Breed Assoc, The
Carolyn Wilki
34 Bentley Ave
Jersey City NJ 07034
215/ 588-8349; 201/ 433-8897

Arizona Herding Assoc
Marianne Boich
8325 North 9th Ave
Phoeniz AZ 85021

Arkansas Stock Dog Assoc
Virginia Pearson
RR1 Box 155AA
Omaha AR 72662
501/ 426-3498

Australian Shepherd Club of New England
Marten Walter
59 Jackson St
Belchertown MA 01337

Big Valley All Breed Stockdog Club
PO Box 1224
Lockeford CA 95237

Blue Ridge ASC
Bruce Caldwell
RT 3 Box 318
Stauton VA 24401

Capitol Region Herding Club, The
Kathy Stokey-Dillon
578 Randall Road
Ballston Spa NY 12020
518/ 885-9906

Chien De La Ferme Herding Club
J S Rohrig
RFD 11 Bedford Rd
Carmel NY 10512
914/ 228-4413

Cooperative Sheep Herding Group
Kathy Freeman
11 Baker Hill Rd
Freeville NY 10368
607/ 277-7184

Dakota Stock Dog Assoc
Leroy Goetz
HC3 Box 3
Flasher ND 58535

Illinois Stock Dog Assoc, Central
Phyllis Shaw
RR2 Box 118
Cambridge IL 61238
309/937-2700

Iowa Herding Dog Assoc
Barbara Bergert
RR1 Box 128
Elberon IA 52225
319/ 444-3157

Kansas Stock Dog Assoc
Shirley Taylor
RT 1 Box 97
Burns KS 66840

Keystone ASA, The
Diana Oliver
RD 2 Box 205
Rome PA 18618

Livestock Guarding Dog Assoc
Hampshire College
PO Box FC
Amherst MA 01002
413/ 549-4600 x 487

Livestock Guarding Dog Program
USDA-ADC
12345 W Alameda Pkwy #313
Lakewood CO 80228
303/ 969-6560

Livestock Guarding Dog Project
Department of Fisheries & Wildlife
Oregon State University
Corvallis OR 97331
503/ 754-4531

Livestock Guarding Dog Project USDA
List of livestock guarding dog
resources/ Animal Plant Health
Inspection Service
Animal Damage Control
Bend OR 97702

Mid-Atlantic Herding Stock Dog Club
2201 Blacks School House Rd
Taneytown MD 21787

Mid-South Stock Dog Assoc
Debbie Dunn
6471 Chase Rd
Millington TN 38053
901/ 872-1234

Mid-States Stockdog Assoc
Kathy Knox
RT 5 Box 147
Butler MO 64730
816/ 679-5578

Minnesota Stock Dog Assoc
Carole Hall
RT 1 Box 5
Grove City MN 56243

Mississippi Stock Dog Assoc
Mrs Jere Gale
PO Box 176
Hernando MS 38632
601/ 368-6552

Missouri Stockdog Assoc
Judy Freeman
RT 2
Harville MO 65667

Montana Stock Dog Handlers Assoc
Noreen Lefeldt
Box 111
Lavina MT 59046
406/ 638-4081

Mountain & Plains Stockdog Assoc
Roger Culbreath
32485 Highway 37
Gill CO 80624

Nebraska Stock Dog Assoc
Chris Redding
RR 2 Box 123
Elgin NE 68636
402/ 843-2342

New England Stockdog Assoc
Ellen Squier
198 Rose Hill Rd
Portland CT 06840
203/ 342-4081

New Mexico Herding Dog Assoc
RT 2 Box 305F
Santa Fe NM 87505

New York, Working ASA of Upstate
Debra St Jacques
RD 1 Bain Rd
Argyle NY 12809

Northeast Stockdog Assoc
Jackie Rohrig
RFD 11 Bedford Rd
Carmel NY 10512
914/ 228-1206

Ohio Valley Stock Dog Assoc
Roy Locher
6331 Jack Hinton Rd
Philpot KY 43266

Oklahoma Herding Dog Assoc, Central
RT 1 Box 97
Burbank OK 74633
405/ 765-8817

Oklahoma Stockdog Assoc
Bob Hooker
6103 Hummingbird Cir
El Reno OK 73036
405/ 262-7870

Oregon Stock Dog Society
Kathy Brunetto
24990 S New Kirchner Rd
Oregon City OR 97048

San Diego County Stock Dog Club
Janet Sewery
6130 West Manor Dr
LaMesa CA 92042

Saskatchewan Stock Dog Assoc
Pam Gonnet
Box 43
Broderick SASK S0H 0L0

Southern California Working Sheep Dog
Assoc
Central Coast Chapter
Russell Drake
PO Box 1058
Buellton CA 93427

Southern California Working
Sheep Dog Assoc
Riverside Chapter
Candy Kennedy
10210 48th St
Mira Loma CA 91752

Stock Dog Fanciers of Colorado
Jo Ann Weller
155580 E. 144th
Brighton CO 80601

Tennessee Sheep Dog Assoc, East
Stan Moore
3335 Byington Solway Rd
Knoxville TN 37931
615/ 690-2044

Texas Sheep Dog Assoc
Francis Raley
RT 1 Box 14A
Crawford TX 76638
817/ 486-2500

Tri-State Working Stock Dog Assoc
Michele Fisher
RD 1 Box 116
Bedford PA 15522
814/ 623-7778

Wisconsin Working Stock Dog Assoc
Beth Miller
10748 Paterson Rd
Durand IL 61024
815/ 248-4228

Wyoming Stockdog Assoc
Lisa Keeler
PO Box 4053
Laramie WY 82071
307/ 745-8176

This chapter lists those clubs that are involved with dog sled racing. While most of the clubs are for the northern breeds, any type of dog can compete in dog sled races, including mixed breed dogs.

If there is no club listed near you, contact your local northern breed club which can be found through the parent club or the registering body.

Arctic Sled Dog Club of America
Dave Hickey
RD 1 Box 191
Middle Grove NY 12850
518/ 882-6485

Arctic Sled Dog Club of Ontario
Duane Ramsay
Inverary ONT K0H 1X0

Canadian American Sledders Inc
Laurie Reely
1154 W Washington St
Bradford PA 16701
814/ 362-2801

Cascade Sled Dog Club
Bob & Lee Hills
39275 SE Wildcat Mt Rd
Eagle Creek OR 97022
503/ 637-3134

Central NC Siberian Husky Club
Phil Moseley
2880 Old Coach Rd
Graham NC 27253
919/ 226-4353

Club Riviere du Nord
CP 1017
Ste Adele QUE J0R 1L0
514/ 438-8765

Connecticut Valley Siberian Husky Club
Joanne B Altieri
104 Williams St
Meriden CT 06450
203/ 238-2532

Eastern Shore Siberian Husky Club
Phyllis Maier
11 Oakwood Dr
Cinnaminson NJ 08077
609/ 829-3868

First State Sled Dog Club
LuWanna Krause
20 Sunny Bend
Newark DE 19702
302/ 368-0130

Garden State Siberian Husky Club
Hetty Lindeboom
PO Box 252
Port Republic NJ 08241
609/ 965-7230

Gateway Sled Dog Club
Jon Slaton
1025 George
Alton IL 62002
618/ 465-6257

Great Lakes Sled Dog Assoc
Rollo Garrison
1846 Hamilton Hwy
Adrian MI 49221
517/ 265-8711

Green Mountain Sled Dog Club
Andy Ripley
RD 1 Box 160
Waterbury VT 05676
802/ 244-8556

Hampton Roads Siberian Husky Assoc
Suzie Parsons
1010 Washington Dr
Chesapeake VA 23320

Inland Empire Sled Dog Assoc
Brendia Hentzelman
6831 Deer Valley Rd
Newport WA 99156
509/ 447-5744

International Federation of Sled Dog Sports
Glenda Walling
7118 N Beehive Rd
Pocatello ID 83201

International Sled Dog Racing Assoc
Donna Hawley
PO Box 446
Norman ID 83848-0446
208/ 443-3153

Jersey Sands Sled Dog Racing Assoc
Betty Carhart
Box 1453 RD 1 Warner Rd
Mt Holly NJ 08060
609/ 267-7680

Kanganark Mushers
Don & Brenda Rosebrock
PO Box 441
Farmington UT 84025
801/ 451-5710

Lake Erie Allegheny Siberian Husky Club
Beth Terella
10243 RT 98
Edinboro PA 16412
814/ 734-5028

Mason Dixon Sled Dog Racing Assoc
Bernie Rogers
101 Brookes Ave
Gaithersburg MD 20877
301/ 977-2409

Mid-Atlantic Sled Dog Racing Assoc
(MASDRA)
Herman Lindeboon
PO Box 252
Port Republic NJ 08241
609/ 965-7230

Mid-Union Sled Haulers
Ski-Jouring Race Rules
Monica Hole
18900 Dresden
Detroit MI 48205-2156
313/ 527-2291

Midwest Sled Dog Club
Jerry Winder
10910 Moate Rd
Duirand IL 61024

Mohawk Valley Sled Dog Club
Bab Walker
129 Ross Park
Syracuse NY 13208
315/ 474-2820

Nanabijou Sled Dog Club
88 Summit Ave
Thunder Bay ONT P7B 3N9

Naragansett Bay Sled Dog Club
Faye Philla
72 Hamlin St
Acushnet MA 02743

Nebraska Sled Dog Racers Assoc
Mike Kerby
RR 1 Box 40A
Valparaiso NE 68065

New England Sled Dog Club
Kathy Beliveau
RFD 4 Box 305B
Manchester NH 03100

New Jersey Sled Dog Club
Ruth Henningsen
153 Holland Mt Rd
Oak Ridge NJ 07438

North Star Sled Dog Club
Annette Johnson
1484 Cty Rd 142
Mahtowa MN 55762

Northwest Sled Dog Assoc
Merlene Sloan
3920 144th St NW
Gig Harbor WA 98335

Oregon Recreational Mushers
Kathy Moulton
1787 Oak St
North Bend OR 97459

Pennsylvania Sled Dog Club
Roberta McDonald
RD 1 Box 358
Phillipsburg PA 16866

Providing Responsible Info.
on Dog's Environment (PRIDE)
PO Box 84915
Fairbanks AK 99708

Rocky Mountain Sled Dog Club
Claude Wild
PO Box 858
Conifer CO 80433

Seneca Siberian Husky Club
Janet Triplett
1764 Baird Rd
Penfield NY 14526

Siberian Husky Club of Delaware Valley
J R Wendelgass
RD 2 Malehorn Rd
Chester Springs PA 19425
610/458-0174

Siberian Husky Club of Greater Canton, Inc
Brenda Wise
3517 Sandy Lake Rd
Ravenna OH 44266

Siberian Husky Club of Greater Cleveland
Inc
Patricia Mace
33800 Grafton Rd
Valley City OH 44280

Siberian Husky Club of Greater NY
Jim Genesee
1332 Udall Ave
West Islip NY 11795

Sierra Nevada Dog Drivers
Jacey Holden
3991 W Peltier Rd
Lodi CA 95242

Snow King Alaskan Malamute Fanciers
Jane Riffle
PO Box 1023
Graham WA 98338
206/ 847-4128

South Shore Siberian Husky Sled Dog Club
Caroline M Burke
Box 586
Norwell MA 02061

Trail Breakers Sled Dog Club
Karen Sundock
749 E 343rd St
Eastlake OH 44094

Wisconsin Trailblazers Sled Dog Club
Doris Lovrine
11032 Four Duck Lake Rd
Three Lakes WI 54562

Zia Sled Dog Club
Steve Estep
PO Box 557
Cedar Crest NM 87008-0557
505/ 294-8221

The rescue clubs are listed by breed, with the all-breed clubs listed first. If you do not find a club near you, contact the ones listed, the parent club of the breed you are interested in as well as the registry organizations. In many cases your local animal shelter will know of the breed rescue groups in your area.

Most parent clubs have members who are willing to rescue dogs of their breed; dogs can also be adopted through these organizations. In many cases, the dogs offered for adoption are good dogs an owner has had to give up. Many breeders request that any dogs they sell be returned in the event the owners cannot keep them any longer. The dog is then offered for sale or adoption. Those that have been rescued from shelters and pounds are usually screened before being placed in new homes. There are many advantages to adopting a dog that is not a puppy. The dog may be housebroken, or, if not, he will learn quicker because he is older. Older dogs have usually had some training as well. Many times the person who rescued the dog will have started working with the dog.

An invaluable source of information for all those interested in the rescue effort for dogs is *Project Breed Directory*, which gives detailed lists of rescue organizations for the United States and Canada. This directory also provides information about all aspects of rescuing dogs. It is available through:

Network for Ani-Males & Females, Inc.
18707 Curry Powder Lane
Germantown MD 20874

AFFENPINSCHER

Affenpinscher Club of America
Nancy Holmes, Rescue Chair
51 Weare Rd
New Boston NH 03070
603/ 487-2156

AFGHAN HOUND

Afghan Hound Assoc of Long Island
Pat Marinaccio
43 Chapel Hill Dr
Brentwood NY 11717
516/ 231-6457

Afghan Hound Club of America
Rescue Committee
Judith Fellton
219 Johnson Ferry Rd
Marietta GA 30068
404/ 971-1533

Afghan Hound Club of Northern NJ Rescue
Nancy Check
RD 2, 999 Walcutt
Basking Ridge NJ 07920
201/ 628-9166

Afghan Hound Club of Oklahoma City
Shari Mason
PO Box 155
Mustang OK 73064
405/ 376-2929

Afghan Rescue
Lin Hullen
5917 Montecito Blvd
Santa Rosa CA 95409
707/ 538-7570; 415/ 851-7812

Afghan Rescue
Kathy Schwartz
15 E Crown Terrace
Morrisville PA 19067
215/ 295-5823

AIREDALE TERRIER

Airedale Terrier Club of Greater Philadelphia
Ben McCarthy
1737 Division Hwy
Narvon PA 17555
717/ 354-7646; 717/ 656-9391

Airedale Terrier Club of Metro DC
Lou Swafford
13108 Greenmount Ave
Beltsville MD 20705
301/ 572-7116

Airedale Terrier Rescue and Adoption
Service
Sarah Bullock
201 West Hampshire Dr
Deptford NJ 08096
609/ 228-1496

Airedale Terrier Rescue and Adoption
Service
Joey Fineran
Box 122 Lonely Cottage Dr
Upper Black Eddy PA 18972
610/ 294-8028

Airedale Terrier Rescue and
Adoption Service
Lynn Jensen
1180 Hopewell Rd
Downingtown PA 19335
610/ 873-9054

Wisconsin Airedale Terrier Club
Myrtle Huffer
2863 N Humboldt Ave
Milwaukee WI 53212
414/ 562-4299

AKBASH DOG

Akbash Dog North American
Rescue Network
Debbie Dowling
749 Waasis Rd
Oromocto NB E2V 2N4
506/ 446-4297

Akbash Dog Rescue
Marsha Peterson
PO Box 31911
Richmond VA 23294
703/ 872-5293

AKITA

Delaware Valley Akita Rescue, Inc
Margie Rutbell
PO Box 103
Carversville PA 18915
215/ 297-5970

Delaware Valley Akita Rescue, Inc
Kathy DeWees
PO Box 578
Rancocas NJ 08073
609/ 877-5027

ALASKAN MALAMUTE

Alaskan Malamute Protection League
Virginia DeVaney
PO Box 170
Cedar Crest NM 87008
505/ 281-3961; 203/ 649-0079

Alaskan Malamute Rescue
Katherine White
53 Yale Ave
New Castle DE 19720
302/ 328-6093

Alaskan Malamute Rescue
Barbara Licata
603 King Row Rd
Oxford PA 19363
610/ 932-5128

Alaskan Malamute Rescue
Pat Paulding
RR 1 Box 13 Lows Hollow Rd
Stewartsville NJ 08886
908/ 454-9520

Alaskan Malamute Rescue of CA
Tina Dunn
5040 Barnard
Simi Valley CA 93063
805/ 583-8280

Alaskan Malamute Rescue
of Eastern Pennsylvania
Karen York
PO Box 1621
Southampton PA 18966
215/ 364-0390

Alaskan Malamute Rescue
of Eastern Pennsylvania
Cathie Mortland
2408 Beverly Rd
Cinnaminson NJ 08077
609/ 829-4941

AMERICAN COCKER SPANIEL

American Cocker Spaniel Rescue
Regina Baker
607 Jamestown Rd
Edgewater Park NJ 08010-1929
609/ 386-6026

AMERICAN PIT BULL TERRIER

Friends of Terriers
Jeanne Balsam
47 Union St #303
Mont Clair NJ 07042
201/ 746-5587

ANATOLIAN SHEPHERD

Anatolian Shepherd Dog Int'l Inc Rescue
Karen Sen
PO Box 56
Korbel CA 95550
707/ 668-5721

Anatolian Shepherd Rescue
Cathy Desjardins
3110 Nicole Rd
Clarkville TN 37040
615/ 647-0586

ARGENTINE DOGO

Argentine Dogo Club of America
Gabriel Moyette
Box 234 Blueberry Hill Rd
West Shokan NY 12494
914/ 657-8370

AUSTRALIAN CATTLE DOG

Australian Cattle Dog Rescue League
Judith Ransom
PO Box 222
Bethlehem GA 30620
404/ 307-0846

AUSTRALIAN SHEPHERD

Aussie Rescue Placement Hotline
ARPH
PO Box 732
Leonavalley CA 93551
800/ 892-2722

AUSTRALIAN TERRIER

Australian Terrier Rescue
Barbera Curtis
939 Lochness Ct
Ft Collins CO 80524

BASENJI

Basenji Rescue
Margaret Hoff, Chairman
191 Butterfield Rd
San Anselmo CA 94960
415/ 453-2510

Basenji Rescue
Sharon Sweeney
8704 Avondale
Baltimore MD 21234
301/ 665-8809

Basenji Rescue
Mark Baime
259 English Place
Basking Ridge NJ 07920
908/ 580-9212

BASSET HOUND

Emerald Empire Basset Hound Rescue
Sandi Baldwin
265 13th St
Lebanon OR 97335
503/ 258-3064

Pilgrim Basset Hound Club
Barbara Boudreau
21 Podunk Rd
Sturbridge MA 01566
508/ 347-3207

BEAGLE

Beagle Rescue and Adoption
Bill & Janet Nieland
7092 Kermore Ln
Stanton CA 90680

Blossom Valley Beagle Club
Mary Powell
1015 Reed Ave
Sunnyvale CA 94086
408/ 244-1840

BEARDED COLLIE

Bearded Collie Club of America
Rescue Program
Chantal Bailey
771 SW 121 St
Davie FL 33325
305/ 475-0095; 617/ 275-0637

Bearded Collie Rescue
Olivia Seligmann-Kelly
6 W Shore Dr
Vincentown NJ 08088
609/ 859-0956

Bearded Collie Rescue
Carli Bates
1184 Creek Rd
Glenmore PA 19343
610/ 942-2656

BEAUCERON

North American Beauceron Club
Claudia Batson
RT 2 Box 68
Charlottesville VA 22901
804/ 293-4037; 610/ 323-6725

BEDLINGTON TERRIER

Bedlington Terrier Club of the West
Judy Barton
508 Curtis Dr
Bakersfield CA 93307
805/ 871-8224; 805/ 837-8353

BELGIAN SHEEPDOG

Belgian Sheepdog Club of America
Roy Elliott
RT 2 Box 384
Buffalo MN 55313
612/ 682-7448

BELGIAN TERVUREN

American Belgian Tervuren Club Rescue
Miki Baiocchi
107 E 2nd
Georgetown TX 78626
512/ 863-9251; 512/ 869-3592

American Belgian Tervuren
Club Rescue
Cindy Simonsen
W359 S2546 Highway 67
Dousman WI 53118

Belgian Tervuren Club Rescue
P J Laursen
PO Box 314
Armada MI 48055
512/ 863-9251

BERNESE MOUNTAIN DOG

Bernese Mountain Dog Club
of Nashoba Valley
Maria Hennessey
South Lee Depot
Lee NH 03824
603/ 659-8339

Bernese Mountain Dog Rescue
Lillian Ostermiller
Green Acres
PO Box 504
Flemington NJ 08822
908/ 996-2576

BICHON FRISE

Bichon Frise Club of Greater Houston
Darlene Malower
10202 Scofield
Houston TX 77096

Bichon Frise Club of Northern New Jersey
Anne Baird
25 Hayes Ave
Millville NJ 08332
609/ 327-2544

Bichon Frise Club of San Diego
Betty Ribble
13035 Via Caballo Rojo
San Diego CA 92129
619/ 556-6578

Bichon Frise Rescue
Celeste Fleishman
PO Box 353
Gwynedd Valley PA 19437
215/ 646-2929

Bichon Rescue
Laura Fox-Meachen
1309 63rd Dr
Union Grove WI 53182
414/ 878-2880

Greater NY Bichon Frise Fanciers, Inc
Eleanor Grossick
41 Audrey Ave
Elmont NY 11003
516/ 561-9147

National Bichon Frise Rescue Trust
Nancy McDonald
14303 Spring Maple Ln
Houston TX 77001

BLOODHOUND

American Bloodhound Club Rescue
James Ryan
PO Box 185
Woodstown NJ 08098
201/ 898-0670; 609/ 451-9439

Bloodhound Rescue
Evelyn Boyer
181 Washington Valley Rd
Morristown NJ 07960
201/ 898-0670

Bloodhounds East
Phil & Sandi Park
RT 1 Box 140-P
Fredericksburg VA 22401
703/ 786-6958

Bloodhounds West
Susan LaCroix & Stacy Mattson
20372 Laguna Canyon Rd
Laguna Beach CA 92651
714/ 494-1076; 714/ 494-9506

BORDER COLLIE

Border Collie Rescue
Sharon Nunan
3329 Foulk Rd
Boothwyn PA 19061
610/ 497-4378

Border Collie Rescue
Patty Allison
RR 1 Box 665
Harrison ME 04040
207/ 363-2353

BORDER TERRIER

Border Terrier Rescue
Lois Languish
Box 246J RD 1
Bordentown NJ 08505
609/ 267-6920

North American Border Terrier Welfare
Pam Dyer
3685 Montee 4 ieme Rang
Ste Madeleine QUE J0H 1S0
US Phone 203/ 334-3025

BORZOI

Borzoi Club of Delaware Valley
Debbie Carsillo
1407 Rising Sun Ave
Parkland PA 19047
215/ 757-2487

Borzoi Rescue-Northern California, Inc
Jacqueline Gregory
PO Box 733, 2200 Wolfhound Rd
Somerset CA 95684
209/ 245-6994

Puget Sound Borzoi Club
Lita Bond
13106 SE 304th
Auburn WA 98002
206/ 833-5876

BOSTON TERRIER

Boston Terrier Club of Milwaukee
Dr Myles Notaro
2925 South 10th St
Milwaukee WI 53215
414/ 482-1633

Boston Terrier Club of Western
Pennsylvania
Linda Trader
Box 53
Mather PA 15346
412/ 883-2169

Boston Terrier Rescue
Halsey & Trophy Frederick
530 Fishers Rd
Bryn Mawr PA 19010
610/ 525-3245

BOUVIER DES FLANDRES

American Bouvier Rescue League
Jacqueline R. Crowe
1880 W 11800 S
South Jordan UT 84065
801/ 254-0462

NE Illinois Bouvier des Flandres Club
Candice Lutz
210 Hazelwood Dr
Lindenhurst IL 60046
708/ 356-0084; 708/ 546-1220

BOXER

Boxer Rescue
Carole Peck
607 Beaumont Blvd
Pacifica CA 94044

Boxer Rescue
Evie Olsen
915 Baylowell Dr
West Chester PA 19380
610/ 692-4687

Boxer Rescue Service Inc
Michele McArdle
57 Devil's Garden Rd
Norwalk CT 06854
203/ 853-9595; 914/ 331-3693

Boxer Rescue Service Inc
Kathleen McNulty
6868 Radbourne Rd
Upper Darby PA 19084
610/ 284-1780; 716/ 484-8085

Boxer Rescue Service Inc
Susan McIntere
17 East St
Middleton MA 01949
508/ 777-7822; 201/ 238-6045

Boxer Rescue Service, Inc
Jean Loubriel
90 Holland Ave
Demarest NJ 07627
201/ 768-6627; 609/ 234-2715

BRIARD

Briard Education, Aid and Rescue
 (BEAR)
Mary Bloom
53-07 Douglaston Parkway
Douglaston NY 11362
718/ 224-5275

BRITTANY SPANIEL

Aloha Brittany Club
Dimi Poser
PO Box 78
Wainanae HI 96792
808/ 696-5030

Brittany Spaniel Rescue
Ann Murphy
2110 Lanes Mill Rd
Brick NJ 08724
908/ 840-2169

Missouri Brittany Club
Dave White
12012 W 150th Circle
Olathe KS 66062
913/ 897-3822

BRUSSELS GRIFFON

Brussels Griffon Rescue
Marjorie Simon
25 Windermere
Houston TX 77063
713/ 783-8887

BULL TERRIER

Bull Terrier Club of America
Welfare Foundation
Bill Edwards
1526 Belleau Rd
Glendale CA 91201
818/956-1170

Bull Terrier Club of Metro Detroit
Sharon Whalen
7185 Gillette
Flushing MI 48433
313/ 659-5951

Bull Terrier Club of New England
Kathy Brosnan
PO Box 634
Kingston NH 03848
617/ 642-5355; 617/ 867-4017

Bull Terrier Rescue
Gail Leverint
38 Clearfield Ave
Norristown PA 19403
610/ 630-6222

Central NJ Bull Terrier Club
Corinne Gliozzi
31 Bloomfield Ave
Somerset NJ 08873
201/ 214-0170

Golden State Bull Terrier Club Rescue
Randy Bisgaard
4391 Sunset Blvd #177
Los Angeles CA 90029

BULLDOG

Bulldog Club of North California
Pat Ropp
132 Blueberry Hill
Los Gatos CA 95030
408/ 356-0039; 408/ 356-1762

Bulldog Club of Texas
Brandy Nunciato
17719 Heritige Creek Dr
Webster TX 77598

San Antonio Bulldog Club
Dr Jim Young & Diana Young
7508 Marbach Rd
San Antonio TX 78227
512/ 673-8020 ; 512/ 340-0055

BULLMASTIFF

American Bullmastiff Assoc
Rescue Committee
Mary Walsh
690 E 8th St
S Boston MA 02127
617/ 268-0359; 508/ 939-5300

CAIRN TERRIER

Cairn Terrier Club of America
Betty Marcum
RT 3 Box 78
Alvarado TX 76009
817/ 783-5979; 203/ 846-3345

Cairn Terrier Club of Northern California
Bobbie Walker
PO Box 2177
Mill Valley CA 94442
415/ 388-6708

Cairn Terrier Club of South California
Karen Smith
889 El Paisano Dr
Fallbrook CA 92028
619/ 728-7133

Cairn Terrier Rescue
Jeanne Simons
40 Indian Ann Trail
RD 2
Vincentown NJ 08088
609/ 268-2471; 609/ 265-1234

Potomac Cairn Terrier Club
Lynda Hammel
12027 Sugarland Valley Dr
Herndon VA 22070
703/ 471-7769

CARDIGAN WELSH CORGI

Cardigan Welsh Corgi Club of
America Rescue
H Pamela Allen
406 E Alexandria Ave
Alexandria VA 22301
703/ 836-1963

Cardigan Welsh Corgi Rescue
Jeanne Bishop
PO Box 337
Cookstown NJ 08511
609/ 758-8557

Cardigan Welsh Corgi Rescue
Denise McDougall
7528 Bingham St
Philadelphia PA 19111
215/ 745-6154

CAVALIER KING CHARLES SPANIEL

Cavalier King Charles Spaniel Rescue
Lenore Urban
5151 Huckleberry Rd
Orefield PA 18069
610/ 395-5539

Cavalier King Charles Spaniel Rescue
Babbs Murdock
Box 232
Cumberland Center ME 04021
207/ 829-4436

CHESAPEAKE BAY RETRIEVER

Chesapeake Bay Retriever Rescue
Nancy Hettinger
RD 4 Box 4317
Mohnton PA 19540
610/ 777-0389

CHINESE SHAR-PEI

Chinese Shar-Pei Club of America
Jerry Wallace
317 N Walnut
LaHabra CA 90631
213/ 694-4193

Chinese Shar-Pei Club of America
Bonnie Berney
521 Pioneer Rd
Sapulpa OK 74066
918/ 224-0824

Chinese Shar-Pei Club of America
Alice Lawler
PO Box 143
Cream Ridge NJ 08514
609/ 758-7603

Chinese Shar-Pei Club of the
NE Rescue
Cynthia Czarda-Black
#7 13th St
North Brunswick NJ 08902
908/ 846-5232

CHOW CHOW

Chow Chow Club—Greater Houston
Rescue League
Shirley Gooch
PO Box 1593
Houston TX 77251-1593
713/ 672-6533; 713/ 590-1619

Chow Welfare League of NPD Inc
Barbara Malone
PO Box 282
Leonardo NJ 07737
908/ 872-9253

Chow Welfare League of NPD Inc
Sandy Voina
PO Box 148
Telford PA 18969
Karen DeBoer
215/ 638-4455

Wisconsin Chow Chow Club, Inc
Vicki Rodenberg
9828 E Co A
Janesville WI 53546
608/ 756-2008

CLUMBER SPANIEL

Clumber Spaniel Rescue Committee
Janna Glasser
40 Crosshill Rd
Hartsdale NY 10530
914/ 428-4582

COCKER SPANIEL

Bay Cities Cocker Spaniel Club
Vera Sell, Secty
110 Yellowood Pl
Pittsburg CA 94565

COLLIE

Collie Club of America
Carol Zielke
205 NE 174th
Seattle WA 98155
206/ 367-6653

Collie Humane Care Inc
PO Box 633
Bath NY 14810
607/ 776-3225

Collie Rescue
LuAnn Palmer
RR 1 Box 1581
Hop Bottom PA 18824
717/ 289-4902

Collie Rescue
Mary Bryson
109 Otter Branch Dr
Magnolia NJ 08049
609/ 783-1071

Collie Rescue
Ginny Cuneo
PO Box 155
Westbrook CT 06498
203/ 399-7724

Collie Rescue League of Mass, Inc
PO Box 54
North Weymouth MA 02191
617/ 335-1856; 207/ 525-3590

Collie Rescue League—Metro Washington
17604 Parkridge Dr
Gaithersburg MD 20878
301/ 948-6849

Collie Rescue Ranch
Charlene Schroeder
19600 Pine Echo Rd
N Fort Myers FL 33917
813/ 543-2290

Collie Rescue of SE Pennsylvania
Linda Knouse
PO Box 1307
Willow Grove PA 19090
215/ 659-3331; 215/ 822-6341

Mason-Dixon Collie Rescue
Pam Catalano
608 Plymouth Rd 229
Baltimore MD 21229
301/ 747-0296

Toledo Collie Club
Kathy Foley
5434 Armada Dr
Toledo OH 43623
419/ 472-4638

Toledo Collie Club
Carol Lamb
14701 Tunnicliff Rd
Petersburg MI 49270
313/ 856-2072

Tucson Collie Club
Jean Malone
7066 Calle Centuri
Tucson AZ 85710
602/ 790-0317; 602/ 747-1621

DACHSHUND

Dachshund Rescue of
Monmouth/Ocean County
Jody Caizza
RD 9 Box 256
Jackson NJ 08527
908/ 928-9786

Northeast Dachshund Rescue
Joan
413/ 743-4400; 508/ 679-2529

DALMATIAN

DAL Rescue Service
Barb Gannage
20472 Purlingbrook
Livonia MI 48152
313/ 471-3487; 313/ 383-5483

Dalmatian Club of North California
Joe Immerman
639 Prentiss St
San Francisco CA 94110
415/ 282-6929

Delaware Valley Dalmatian Club
Dottsie Keith
Kettle Ln
Box 67
Furlong PA 19002
215/ 794-7173

DANDIE DINMONT TERRIER

Dandie Dinmont Terrier Rescue
Evelyn Ammerman
312 Hoffnagle St
Philadelphia PA 19111
215/ 728-6268; 215/ 742-6933

DOBERMAN PINSCHER

Alliance of Persons For Dobermans Inc
Ron F Fach
PO Box 9202
Ft Lauderdale FL 33310
305/ 486-0605

Animal Rescue Foundation Inc
Doberman Shelter
Joyce Whitehead
PO Box 297
High Ridge MO 63049
314/ 677-3736

Aztec Doberman Pinscher Club
of San Diego
Angie Monteleon
9821 Dunbar Ln
El Cajon CA 92065
619/ 443-8944

Berkshire Doberman Rescue League
Sandra LaBombard
HC 63 Box 342
Chester MA 01011
413/ 623-5394

Cabrillo Doberman Pinscher Club
Elizabeth S Smith
25510 Carmel Knolls
Carmel CA 93923
408/ 625-0366; 408/ 375-2221

DOBE Rescue & Adoption Society Inc
Lynn Ely
PO Box 3611
Baltimore MD 21214
410/ 444-4632

DPC Houston
Karen Byrd
4303 Ravine
Friendswood TX 77546
713/ 992-5846

DPC of Dallas
Nancy Wagner
802 Smith Ln
Seagoville TX 75238
214/ 287-3133

DPC of Memphis Inc
Cope & Rescue
Kimberly Kellum
1157 Lake Clara Dr
Eada TN 38028
901/ 386-9279; 901/ 867-3218

DPC of Memphis Inc
Cope & Rescue
Linda Herron
3972 Pikes Peak
Memphis TN 38108
901/ 377-2586

DPC of Michigan
Rescue Committee
Pam Hughes
10396 Horton Rd
Goodrich MI 48034
313/ 636-2133

Dobe Rescue
Susan Sternberg
254 W Mt Airy Rd
Croton-On-Hudson NY 10520
914/ 271-5470

Doberman Pinscher
Breeders Assoc—Penn/Jersey
Pat Adriano
40 Broad Ave
Edison NJ 08820
908/ 548-2308

Doberman Pinscher Club of America
Judith Fellton
219 Johnson Ferry Rd
Marietta GA 30067
404/ 971-1533

Doberman Pinscher Club of Michigan
Maggie Hilliard
496 Emmons Blvd
Wayndotte MI 48192
313/ 284-2549

Doberman Pinscher Club of Michigan
Rescue Committee
Daisy Doolittle
14300 Blackstone
Detroit MI 48223
313/ 531-3796

Doberman Pinscher Rescue
Valerie Christenson
1088 Colton Ave
Sunnyvale CA 90489
408/ 734-5834

Doberman Pinscher Rescue League
Norma Gurinskas, Director
PO Box 1911
Rochester NH 03867
207/ 457-1329; 603/ 357-3533

Doberman Pinscher Rescue
of Delaware Valley
Sharon Schiele
357 3rd Ave
Phoenixville PA 19460
610/ 935-0896

Doberman Pinscher Rescue of PA
Pam Gutenkunst
1 Melvin Rd
Phoenixville PA 19460
215/ 935-0822

Doberman Rescue
Jim Ladyman
149 Briarwood Dr
Vacaville CA 95688
707/ 448-3850

Doberman Rescue
Sandra J Bonnevier
8270 Berlington Rd
Mobile AL 36619
205/ 660-8579

Doberman Rescue
JoAnn P Oerline
22 Adobe Ct
Danville CA 94526
510/ 820-3852

Doberman Rescue
Lori Moss
10303 Spruce St
Beuflower CA 90706
310/ 925-3941

Doberman Rescue
Larralyn McKay
Unit 36-10 Esterbrocke Ave
Willowdale ONT M2J 2C2
416/ 493-6408

Doberman Rescue
Joanne Bugai
PO Box 618
Durham CT 06422
203/ 349-3788

Doberman Rescue
Elynor J Johnson
1191 Tate Dr
Columbus GA 31906-2126
404/ 323-8450

Doberman Rescue
Kathy McNulty
41 W 434 Barlow Dr
St Charles IL 60175
708/ 584-2683

Doberman Rescue
Mary Piper
2225 Catalina Ln
Springfield IL 62702
217/ 522-4348

Doberman Rescue
Storm Bergin
1279 E 300 N
Warsaw IN 46580
219/ 269-3818

Doberman Rescue
Chris Thomas
3690 Leonard Rd
Martinsville IN 46151
317/ 342-0449

Doberman Rescue
Mary Roach
700 W Ridgeway
Waterloo IA 50701
319/ 268-0645

Doberman Rescue
Marilyn Twigg
131 Vincent Rd
Waterloo IA 50701
319/ 233-1687

Doberman Rescue
Julie Kay Stade
12416 S Haven Rd
 Haven KS 67543
316/ 465-3657

Doberman Rescue
Tom Bator
PO Box 195
Catlettsburg KY 41129
606/ 327-6418; 606/ 324-8299

Doberman Rescue
Sandra Hammond
PO Box 331
Hanson KY 42413
502/ 825-9873

Doberman Rescue
Bunny Lanning
303 S 13th St
Murray KY 42071
502/ 753-5620

Doberman Rescue
Debbie Bellke
10145 Trail Ridge Dr
Shreveport LA 71106

Doberman Rescue
Margaret A. Zanville
2605 Village Ln
Silver Spring MD 20906
301/ 460-3869

Doberman Rescue
Maryann Zuckerman
3911 Chruch Rd
Mitchellville MD 20721
301/ 369-9086

Doberman Rescue
Kathy Valone
3 Olde Lyme Rd
Winchester MA 01890
617/ 729-6402

Doberman Rescue
Chris Durate
865 24th Ave SE
Minneapolis MN 55414
612/ 379-3389

Doberman Rescue
R Dian Barker
RT 3 Box 270A
Springfield MO 65804
417/ 994-2760

Doberman Rescue
Cathy L. Camden
RT 5 #5 Ewing Circle
Fulton MO 65251
314/ 642-2716

Doberman Rescue
Jean Haley
6341 N Hope
Kansas City MO 64151
816/ 741-7585

Doberman Rescue
Shirley Harris
RT 2 Box 2535
Ste Genevive MO 63670
314/ 883-7658

Doberman Rescue
Cheryl Hausechild
2126 Silver
Ashland NE 68003
402/ 944-2138; 402/ 465-7037

Doberman Rescue
Jo Coney
323 Arthur St
Freeport NY 11520
516/ 378-8569

Doberman Rescue
Jeanne Deevy
16 Beech St
Garden City NY 11530
516/ 248-1131

Doberman Rescue
Rose Anne Fierro
4115 Meadow Ln
Seaford NY 11783
516/ 799-6948

Doberman Rescue
Doreen Luongo
219 Stuart Ave
Syracuse NY 13207
315/ 425-7491

Doberman Rescue
Kay Martin
38 Village Ct
Brooklyn NY 11223-4729
718/ 376-0900; 212/ 339-5503

Doberman Rescue
Jennifer Aycock
3642 Brick Church Rd
Burlington NC 27215
919/ 449-0444

Doberman Rescue
Judith Bolinski
122 Lower Grassy Br Rd
Ashville NC 28505
704/ 298-0070

Doberman Rescue
Barbara Yeatman
4801 Indian Corn Trail
Castle Hayne NC 28429
919/ 675-7803

Doberman Rescue
Liz Gaulke
PO Box 163
Bowling Green OH 43402
419/ 352-7339; 419/ 353-6587

Doberman Rescue
Gary Holder
9902-C East 43rd St
Tulsa OK 74146
918/ 622-2364

Doberman Rescue
Debbie Hartzell
4255 Laurel Ridge Dr
Allison Park PA 15101
412/ 487-5177; 412/ 391-1571

Doberman Rescue
Lenore Smathers
112 1/2 West Main St
Clarion PA 16214
814/ 226-5524

Doberman Rescue
Bryan Cleveland
221 White Oak Rd
Greenville SC 29609
803/ 244-1027

Doberman Rescue
Paul Dugger
211 Hickory Hollow Rd
Tullahoma TN 37388
615/ 455-0700

Doberman Rescue
Ann Fisher
9051 Andersonville Pk
Powell TN 37849
615/ 922-0963

Doberman Rescue
Cheri Roop
5008 Brown Gap Rd
Knoxville TN 37918
615/ 688-9641

Doberman Rescue
Judy Trainor
RR #1 Box 387
Erin TN 37061
615/ 763-2060

Doberman Rescue
Lyle Wescott
RT 2 Box 234B1
Holly Springs MS 38635
601/ 851-7147

Doberman Rescue
Patricia Pearce
18924 Pipeline Rd
College Station TX 77845
409/ 690-1332

Doberman Rescue
M'Linda Taylor
Apt. 2002
8501 Capitol of TX Hwy N
Austin TX 78759
512/ 343-0759

Doberman Rescue
Traci Mulligan
PO Box 71
Arlington VT 05250
802/ 375-6121

Doberman Rescue
Sharon Hildebrand
517 Etheridge Rd
Chesapeake VA 23320
804/ 482-3762

Doberman Rescue
A.L. Foshee
PO Box 1343 Thrash Rd
Clanton AL 35048
205/ 342-9048

Doberman Rescue
Christine Kusyk
4021 Michael Blvd
Mobile AL 36609
205/ 342-9048

Doberman Rescue
Dorothy Lechuga
PO Box 12220
Scottsdale AZ 85267
602/ 951-1155

Doberman Rescue
Shannon Messina
Ashmore Cottage
171 Camino Pablo
Orinda CA 94563
510/ 253-1149

Doberman Rescue Concern, Inc
Birdie F Johnson
6250 Fairgreen Rd
West Palm Beach FL 33417
407/ 686-3871; 407/ 683-7753

Doberman Rescue League
Kurt Orlosky
PO Box 24065
Oakland Park FL 33307-4065
305/ 946-4100

Doberman Rescue Unlimited Inc
Claire Kontos
PO Box 184
North Billerica MA 01862
508/ 454-9791

Doberman Rescue of
Monmouth/Ocean
Jody Caizza
RD 9 Box 256
Jackson NJ 08527
908/ 928-9786

Doberman Resuce
Elaine Hopkins
34 Jackson St
Farmingdale NY 11735
516/ 752-7441

New England Doberman Rescue
PO Box 929
Northboro MA 01532
508/ 624-5455

New Hampshire Doberman
Rescue League, Inc
Ted Beltz
PO Box 4001
Windham NH 03087-4001
603/ 894-4520

Newtown Doberman Rescue
Patti & Henry Clark
227 Hattertown Rd
Newtown CT 06422
203/ 426-6535

Northeast Florida Doberman Rescue
3991 CR 210 W
Jacksonville FL 32259
904/ 287-1502

Northeast Florida Doberman Rescue
Yvonne Diaz
11401 SW 95th St
Miami FL 33176
305/ 662-6332

Northern Penna Dobe Rescue
Christopher Vervan
74 West Palm
Olyphant PA 18447
717/ 489-0357

Oregon Doberman Rescue
Pat McMillan
3123 SE 129th Ave
Portland OR 97236
503/ 761-2455

Puget Sound Doberman Pinscher Club
Julianne Ferado
PO Box 58455
Renton WA 98058
206/ 226-4810

Salt Lake DPC, The
Marsha Sheppard
1725 Fort Douglas Circle
Salt Lake City UT 84103-4451
801/ 582-3226; 801/ 975-7772

Salt Lake DPC, The
Jill Adams
432 North 560 West
American Fork UT 84003
801/ 756-9222

Salt Lake DPC. The
Ernie Moss
3418 Fillmore
Ogden UT 84403
801/ 394-8197

Southern Tier Dobe Rescue
Rebecca Roter
PO Box 3
Kingsley PA 18826
717/ 289-4790

Utah Doberman Rescue
Edie Schoepp
4356 S El Camino St
Taylorsville UT 84119
801/ 969-3264; 801/ 394-8197

ENGLISH COCKER SPANIEL

English Cocker Spaniel Rescue
Jody Nelson
PO Box 153
Stevensville MD 21666
301/ 224-5800 work; 301/ 643-5117 home

ENGLISH SETTER

Golden Gate English Setter Club
M A Samuelson
21680 Fortini Rd
San Jose CA 94025
408/ 997-2605; 408/ 354-7205

ENGLISH SPRINGER SPANIEL

English Springer Spaniel Rescue
PO Box 107
Dunstable MA 01827
617/ 237-4751

English Springer Spaniel Rescue
Vivian S Haberstadt
1112 Grinnell Rd
Wilmington DE 19803
302/ 478-6557

English Springer Spaniel Rescue
Mary Hovis
4922 Neshaminy Blvd
Bensalem PA 19020
215/ 752-3034

English Springer Spaniel Rescue
Terry Gucci
PO Box 702
Bellport NY 11713
516/ 286-0486

English Springer Spaniel Rescue
Doreen Naimo
RD 4 Box 417
Jackson NJ 08527
908/ 364-6387 home; 908/ 431-5100 work

FRENCH BULLDOG

French Bulldog Club of America
Rescue Network
Brenda Buckles
6111 Walnut St
Kansas City MO 64113
816/ 444-3363

GERMAN SHEPHERD DOG

German Shepherd Dog Rescue
Diane Reppy
PO Box 117
New Ringgold PA 17960
717/ 943-2055

German Shepherd Dog Rescue
Bonnie Johnson and Christa Burg
PO Box 670266
Chugiak AK 99567
907/ 688-2352

German Shepherd Dog Rescue
Charlotte Williams
RD #2 Box 307
New Ringgold PA 17960
717/ 943-2624

German Shepherd Dog Rescue
Wendell Larsen
RD 1 Box 415
Upper Black Eddy PA18972
610/ 294-9216

German Shepherd Dog Rescue
Nancy Aiosa
9192 Valley View Dr
Clarks Summit PA 18411
717/ 586-9064

German Shepherd Dog Rescue
RE #2 Box 196
Tunkhannock PA 18657
717/ 388-6959

German Shepherd Dog Rescue
Jennifer Buck
RD #2 2821P
Hamburg PA 19526
610 562-3775

German Shepherd Dog Rescue
Christy Shore
PO Box 243 High St
Leesburg NJ 08327
609/ 785-9728

German Shepherd Dog Rescue
Mary Cummings
810 East Main Rd
Johnson City NY 13790
607/ 729-2718

German Shepherd Dog Rescue
Elizabeth Stidham
PO Box 386
Eaton OH 45320
513/ 456-5393

German Shepherd Dog Rescue
Diane Wright
244 E Stimmel St
West Chicago IL 60185
708/ 293-4167

German Shepherd Dog Rescue
Bonnie Capron
Box 121 Old West Rd
Arlington VT 05250
802/ 375-6057

German Shepherd Dog Rescue
Rex Jones
126 Oak St
Rutland VT 05701
802/ 775-1704

German Shepherd Dog Rescue
Anne Mackey
6128 College
Kansas City MO 64130
816/ 363-0121

German Shepherd Rescue
Risa Stein
226 Broadway
Rocky Point NY 11778
516/ 744-3258

Lacey's Shepherd Rescue
Donna Petrosie
PO Box 903
Jackson NJ 08527
908/ 370-3795

GERMAN SHORTHAIRED POINTER

German Shorthaired Pointer Club
Orange City
Karen Detterich
PO Box 818
Mira Loma CA 91752
714/ 359-6960

German Shorthaired Pointer
Rescue Program
Alison J Lavitt
13532 Elgers St
Cerritos CA 90701
213/ 921-1345

German Shorthaired Pointer Rescue
of New Jersey
Marcia Steinmann
15 Moraine Rd
Edison NJ 08820
201/ 879-2378

German Shorthaired Pointer Rescue
of New Jersey
Eleanor Campbell
30 Cherry Tree Ln
Chester NJ 07930
201/ 879-2378

German Shorthaired Pointer Rescue
of New Jersey
Jane Ludwig
18 Rittenhouse Rd
Stockton NJ 08559
609/ 397-2016

German Shorthaired Pointer Rescue
of New Jersey
Judy Marden
53 Nedsland Ave
Titusville NJ 08560
609/ 737-1910

German Shorthaired Pointer Rescue
of New Jersey
Joan Tabor
10 Norman Rd
Upper MontClair NJ 07043
201/ 746-5986

German Shorthaired Pointer Rescue
of New Jersey
Nancy Washabaugh
97 Linvale Rd
Ringoes NJ 08551
609/ 466-2727

GERMAN WIREHAIRED POINTER

Seattle-Tacoma German Wirehaired
Pointer Club
Laura Myles
21526 W Lost Lake Rd
Snohomish WA 98290
206/ 481-3371

GIANT SCHNAUZER

Giant Schnauzer Rescue
John Taglarino
PO Box 496
Oldwick NJ 08858
908/ 439-3703

GOLDEN RETRIEVER

Golden Retriever Rescue
Robin Adams
PO Box 2195
Sinking Spring PA 19608
610/ 678-2640 (8-5pm)

Golden Retriever Rescue
Los Angeles County
Friends for Pets Foundation
7131 Owensmouth Ave #39A
Conoga Park CA 91303
818/ 701-0674; 213/ 377-2998

Golden Retriever Rescue of LA
Margo Smith
2112 E Oakdale St
Pasadena CA 91107
818/ 449-4262

Golden Retriever Rescue
Education/Training Inc
Kathy Carbone
PO Box 2070
Ellicott City MD 21043
301/ 442-2213

Golden Retriever Rescue
Education/Training Inc
Carol Windsor
PO Box 88
Severna Park MD 21146
301/ 647-8717

Retrieve A Golden of Minnesota
Jane & Henry Nygaard
7500 North St
St Louis Park MN 55426
612/ 933-1854

Sooner Golden Retriever Rescue
Bob Bornstein
9209 S Youngs Blvd
Oklahoma City OK 73159
405/ 691-4839

Triad Golden Retriever Club
of Central NC
Lynn Brogan
6709 West Friendly Ave
Greensboro NC 27410
919/ 292-9365

Yankee Golden Retriever Rescue
PO Box 104
North Reading MA 01864
508/ 975-4091

GORDON SETTER

Gordon Setter Club of America
Rescue Committee
Crystal Todor
47 Taylor Rd
W Jefferson OH 43162
614/ 879-8405

Gordon Setter Rescue
Lenore Urban
5151 Huckleberry Rd
Orefield PA 18069
610/ 395-5539

Gordon Setter Rescue
Dale Gersch
1288 Simons Rd
Castleton NY 12033
518/ 732-2816

TarTan Gordon Setter Club
Natalie Haberman
42 Edmunds Rd
Wellesly MA 02181
617/ 237-3027

GREAT DANE

Great Dane Club Mid-South
Darcy Quinlan
105 Merchants Square #343
Cummings GA 30130
404/ 887-4417

Great Dane Club of California
Florence Treseder
8660 Telfair
Sun Valley CA 91352
818/ 767-0756

Great Dane Club of El Paso
Esther Scoggins
6643 Westside Dr
El Paso TX 79932
915/ 877-2042

Great Dane Club
of Greater Anchorage
Toni Tadolini
3301 Cottle Loop Rd
Wasilla AK 99687
907/ 376-3915

Great Dane Club of Greater Houston
Georgia Thomas
14123 Panhandle Dr
Sugar Land TX77478
713/ 491-7625

Great Dane Club of Greater Kansas City
Glenda Burns
6321 Woodward
Shawnee Mission KS 66202
913/ 432-2518

Great Dane Club of Las Vegas, The
Mel Covert
6129 Edgewood Circle
Las Vegas NV 89107
702/ 878-2970

Great Dane Club of Mid-Florida
Kevin Kavanaugh
8800 Erie Ln
Parrish FL 34219
813/ 776-1094

Great Dane Rescue
Heidi Hoover
3226 Eisenhower Dr
Norristown PA 19403
610/ 584-5056

Great Dane Rescue Service
of New England
Arlene Koopman
50 Canton St
Sharon MA 02067
617/ 784-9093; 207/ 998-2231

Greater Cincinnati Great Dane Club
Donna Wright
18057 Laurel Rd
Connersville IN 47331
317/ 698-3869

Willamette Valley Great Dane Club
Mary Gaffney
RT 2 Box 460
Hillsboro OR 97123
503/ 628-3422

GREAT PYRENEES

Great Pyrenees Rescue
Florence Connerton
1923 Parkview Ave
Bristol PA 19007
215/ 781-8129

Great Pyrenees Rescue Service
Rhonda
New Jersey
201/ 738-8937; 207/ 666-8816

Great Pyrenees Rescue Service
Maureen
Pennsylvania
717/ 545-4477; 401/ 397-2851

Great Pyrenees Rescue Service
Flo
New York
914/ 225-2754

Heart of Ohio Great Pyrenees Club Rescue
Pat Wallace
301 - 21st St NW
Canton OH 44701

GREYHOUND

Greyhound Club of America Rescue
Cheryl Reynolds
4280 Carpenteria Ave
Carpenteria CA 93013

Greyhound Club of Northern CA
Marjorie Leider
1091 Batavia Ave
Livermore CA 94550
415/ 447-4502

Greyhound Friends
Louise Coleman
167 Saddle Hill Rd
Hopkinton MA 01748
508/ 435-5969; 617/ 333-4982

Greyhound Pets of America
800/ 366-1472

Greyhound Rescue
Susan Netboy
5 Ranch Rd
Woodside CA 94062
415/ 851-7812

IBIZAN HOUND

Ibizan Hound Rescue
Jo Bice
PO Box 737
Windsor CA 95492
916/ 487-9979

IRISH SETTER

Eastern Irish Setter Assoc
Evelyn Kearon
RD 2 Box 293A
Branchville NJ 07826
201/ 948-4921

Irish Setter Club of Ohio
Nonda B Jones
7578 River Rd
Olmsted Falls OH 44138
216/ 235-4197

Irish Setter Rescue
Anna Jones
42 Station St
Berkeley Heights NJ 07922
908/ 464-5720

IRISH TERRIER

Irish Terrier Club of N California
Diana Martin
189 San Luis Rd
Sonoma CA 95476
707/ 938-4698; 415/ 521-3246

Irish Terrier Club of S California
Nan Bruner
13431 Winthrope St
Santa Ana CA 92705
714/ 633-5156

IRISH WATER SPANIEL

Irish Water Spaniel Club of America
Mr Dan Sayers
7 Indian Park Rd
Levittown PA 19057

The Irish Water Spaniel Club of America
Elizabeth B Peterson
Winston-Salem NC
919/ 922-3934; 609/ 451-7480

The Irish Water Spaniel Club of America
Nona & Harlan Noel
Indiana
219/ 872-0775; 213/ 874-0944

The Irish Water Spaniel Club of America
Nancy Wiley
California
415/ 461-7533

IRISH WOLFHOUND

Irish Wolfhound Assoc
of the Delaware Valley
Jean A Minneir
316 Pricketts Mill Rd
Vincentown NJ 08088
609/ 268-9373

Irish Wolfhound Assoc
of New England
Marcia Frankel
New Ashford Rd
Williamstown MA 01267
413/ 458-3269

Irish Wolfhound Club of Puget Sound
Beverly Little
16252 Tiger Mountain Rd
Issaquah WA 98027
206/ 392-7241

Irish Wolfhound Trust
Pat Huntley
16513 Napa St
Sepulveda CA 91343
818/ 894-8988

Potomac Valley Irish Wolfhound Club
Herb Savage
RT 1 Box 711-D
Accokeek MD 20607
301/ 283-4474

ITALIAN GREYHOUND

Italian Greyhound Rescue
Leslie Parsons
925 Canton St NW
Palm Bay FL 32907
407/ 724-9170

Italian Greyhound Rescue
June Mastrocola
W137 N9332 HY 145
Menomonee Falls WI 53051
414/ 251-8347

Italian Greyhound Rescue
Lynn Poston
1483 Lake Placid Dr
San Bernardino CA 92407
714/ 880-1073

JACK RUSSELL TERRIER

Jack Russell Terrier Rescue
Catherine Brown
4757 Lakeville Rd
Geneseo NY 14454
716/ 243-0929

KEESHOND

Keeshond Rescue
Phyllis Noonan
643 N Lewis Rd
Royersford PA 19468
610/ 327-3562

Nor-Cal Keeshond Club, Inc
Ms Wayne Peters
430 Bay Rd
Menlo Park CA 94025
415/ 322-2246; 415/ 325-3947

Peak to Peak Keeshond Rescue
Sue Riegel
1878 Old Highway #52
Erie CO 80516

KOMONDOR

Komondor Club of America
Gordon Sheddy
5907 E Law Rd
Valley City OH 44280
216/ 483-4941

Komondor Rescue
Joy C Levy
102 Russell Rd
Princeton NJ 08540
609/ 924-0199

KUVASZ

Kuvasz Rescue
Linda Lloyd
PO Box 317
Shermans Dale PA 17090
717/ 957-4996

Kuvasz Rescue/Adoption
914/ 644-8104; 914/ 221-2066

LABRADOR RETRIEVER

Golden Gate Labrador Retriever Club
Paul and Anne Gamlin
762 Cedar St
San Carlos CA 94070
415/ 592-8394

Labrador Retriever Rescue, Inc
508/ 369-8736

Tri-State Labrador Retriever
Rescue League
Pam Heidom
63 E Hillcrest Ave
Chalfont PA 18914
215/ 822-8589

Tri-State Labrador Retriever
Rescue League
Mary Pat Ezzo
3 Woodside Dr
Richboro PA 18954
215/ 953-0147

Tri-State Labrador Retriever
Rescue League
Pat Henning
189 Graterford Rd
Schwenksville PA 19473
610/ 489-0710

LAKELAND TERRIER

US Lakeland Terrier Club
Harold Tatro
804 Quail Run, Nassau Bay II
Grandbury TX 76049
817/ 326-5525

LHASA APSO

Lhasa Apsos Rescue
Debbie Burke
317 Mill Rd
Oreland PA 19075
215/ 887-1770

Lhasa Apsos Rescue
Joan Kendall
1044 Cedar Ave
Bensalem PA 19020
215/ 245-6872

San Diego County Lhasa Apso Club
William & Shirley Benedict
11202 Promesa Dr
San Diego CA 92124
619/ 278-2482

MALTESE

Evergreen Maltese Club
Beverly Passe
6015 Rosedale St NW
Gig Harbor WA 98335
206/ 858-9266; 206/ 653-5918

MANCHESTER TERRIER

Evergreen Empire Manchester Terrier
Fanciers
Muriel Henkel
4961 NE 193rd St
Seattle WA 98155
206/ 365-0445

MASTIFF

Mastiff Club of America
Mary-Louise Owens
RD 1 Box 627 Phelps St
Gloversville NY 12078

Mastiff Club of America
Rescue Service
Phyllis Miller
PO Box 1670
La Jolla CA 92037
619/ 454-8984; 518/ 766-2336

Mastiff Rescue
Gerry Roach
5125 Woodbine Ave
Philadelphia PA 19131
215/ 473-4188

MINIATURE SCHNAUZER

Miniature Schnauzer Club of S California
Peggie Blakley, president
9761 11th St
Garden Grove CA 92644
714/ 531-7473

Miniature Schnauzer Club of S California
Ruth Ziegler
1018 Montego Dr
Los Angeles CA 90049
213/ 472-7993

Miniature Schnauzer Rescue
Milly Robertson
172 Kelton St
San Carlos CA 94070

Miniature Schnauzer Rescue
Johnnie Hart
3085 SW 107th Ave
Portland OR 97201
503/ 244-0145

Mt Vernon Miniature Schnauzer Club
Carol Patterson
800 N York Rd
Sterling VA 22170
703/ 450-4287

NEAPOLITAN MASTIFF

Neapolitan Mastiff Rescue
Carol Paulson
PO Box 43
Lawrenceville NY 12949
315/ 389-4028

NEWFOUNDLAND

Newfoundland Club of America
Mary L Price
1004 Hwy 78 South
Mt Horeb WI 53572
608/ 437-4553

Newfoundland Club of New England
Ellen
617/ 329-8157

Newfoundland Dog Club of the Twin Cities
Nancy Robinson
8338 12th Ave S
Bloomington MN 55425
612/ 854-6943; 612/ 822-6715

Newfoundland Rescue Service
Pat Macken
Box 2416 RD 2
Mt. Holly NJ 08060
609/ 265-9259

NORWEGIAN ELKHOUND

Norwegian Elkhound Club
of Potomac Valley
Mary Angevine
12010 Old Gunpowder Rd
Beltsville MD 20705
301/ 937-0014

NORWICH and NORFOLK TERRIERS

Norwich & Norfolk Terrier Rescue
Miss Anne G Ruocchio
336 Northfield Dr
Raleigh NC 27609

Norwich and Norfolk Terrier Rescue
Frances Wilmeth
294 Aquetong Rd
New Hope PA 18938
215/ 862-2453

OLD ENGLISH SHEEPDOG

Greater Pittsburgh Old English
Sheepdog Club
Chris Gaburri
457 Orchard Ave
Pittsburgh PA 15202
412/ 761-0493

New England Old English
Sheepdog Club
Annie Raker
Stonehedge
Lincoln MA 01773
617/ 259-8173; 603/ 889-2536

Old English Sheepdog Club
of America Rescue
Karen Murdock
410 The Portage
Ticonderoga NY 12883-1509
518/ 585-6953

Old English Sheepdog League
of N California
Pam Henry
2491 Darla Dr
Santa Rosa CA 95401
707/ 579-1848

Old English Sheepdog Rescue
Shelia Kenyon
4 Log Rd
Morristown NJ 07960
201/ 538-4129

OTTERHOUND

Otterhound Club of America Rescue
Betsy Conway
RD 1 Box 134A
Yorktown Heights NY 10598

PAPILLON

Metro Area Papillon Club
of Washington DC
Margaret Quarto
3650 Mill Creek Dr
Haymarket VA 22069
703/ 754-2557

Papillon Club of America
Diana Fuchs
Rt 7 Box 5310
Quincy FL 32351
904/ 875-1422

PEKINGESE

Pekingese Rescue
Louise Harden
8338 Woodland Rd
Pasadena MD 21122
301/ 255-2166

PEMBROKE WELSH CORGI

Cascade Pembroke Welsh Corgi Club
Marian Rivers
1022 166th Pl. NE
Bellevue WA 98008
206/ 746-0910

Golden Gate Pembroke
Welsh Corgi Fanciers
Debbie Oliver
11429 Clayton Rd
San Jose CA 94123
408/ 272-2715

Lakeshore Pembroke Welsh Corgi Club
Terri Swaim
135 Tall Pine Ln
Ortonville MI 48462
313/ 627-3723; 616/ 625-9007

Lakeshore Pembroke Welsh Corgi Club
Deanna B Kuhn
33956 N Fairfield Rd
Round Lake IL 60073
708/ 546-1739

Mayflower Pembroke Welsh Corgi Club
Deborah Beal
RD 3 Box 157A
Stonington CT 06378
203/ 535-3913; 508/ 378-9061

Pembroke Welsh Corgi Club of Florida
Jean Bates
3707 Edgewater Dr
Orlando FL 32804
303/ 343-4803; 203/ 379-0668

Pembroke Welsh Corgi Club of Florida
Bonnie Hansen
10993 - 124th Ave N
Largo FL 34640

Pembroke Welsh Corgi Club of Florida
Deborah Shindle
3906 Indian River Rd
Vero Beach FL 32960

Pembroke Welsh Corgi Club of the Rockies
Sue Newman
14065 E 26th Ave
Aurora CO 80011
303/ 343-4803

Pembroke Welsh Corgi
Rescue League
Hilda W Towery
91 Willard Dr
Marietta GA 30060

PHARAOH HOUND

Pharaoh Hound Rescue
Randall Bullard
16807 Samgerry Dr
Valinda CA 91744
818/ 336-0780 ; 714/ 636-1798

POODLE

Beresfords Poodle Rescue Service
Gladys Renaghan
492 Franklin St
Duxbury MA 02332
617/ 837-6742

Delaware Valley Poodle Rescue
Gail Hoaz
820 N Corinthian Ave
Philadelphia PA 19130
215/ 236-4329

Greater Pittsburgh Poodle Club
Mary Lou Patrick
RD 1 Box 195
Clinton PA 15469

Poodle Club of SE Michigan
Nancy Nastasi
41940 Quince Dr
Novi MI 48375
313/ 344-0181; 313/ 255-6334

Poodle Rescue Program
of Central California
Patricia Moulthrop
815 Las Trampas Rd
Lafayette CA 94549
415/ 295-1070

Poodle Rescue of New Jersey
Jackie Solondz
1543 Deer Path
Mountainside NJ 07092
908/ 232-7872

PORTUGUESE WATER DOG

PWDCA Rescue & Relocation
Jane Harding
20 Driftway Ln
Darien CT 06820
203/ 655-7258

PUG

Bluebonnet Pug Dog Club
Margaret Dunning
1107 Derbyshire Ln
Carrollton TX 75007
214/ 242-6175

Central Indiana Pug Dog Club
Roger Perry
3502 E 39th St
Indianapolis IN 46205
317/ 546-7815

City of Angels Pug Club
Blanche Roberts
22963 Hatteras
Woodland Hills CA 90068
818/ 703-5026

Greater Atlanta Pug Dog Club
Robin Tondra
1448 Corinth Rd
Newnan GA 30263
404/ 254-1349

Mid-Michigan Pug Club
Terry Smith
221 E Scott St
Grand Ledge MI 48837
517/ 627-5916

Pug Club of South FL
Judi Crowe
1520 SW South Ave
Pompano FL 33060
305/ 785-2515

Pug Dog Club of Greater NY
Cecilia Geary
50 Greenwich Ave Apt. 5C
New York NY 10011
212/ 929-6606; 718/ 762-7508

Pug Dog Club of MD
Mrs Billie Hitt
14249 Briarwood Terrace
Rockville MD 20853
301/ 871-8063

Pug Rescue
Susan Natoli
1624 Sunnyslope
Belmont CA 94002
415/ 592-0732

Pug Rescue
Jean Hazen
122 Ridge Rd
Browns Mills NJ 08015
609/ 893-5240

Pug Rescue
Ginnie Warner
216 Sinkler Dr
Radnor PA 19087
610/ 293-9585

Pug Rescue of New England
Doris Aldrich
17 Jones Rd
Pelham MA 01002
413/ 253-3006; 603/ 924-6026

Tampa Bay Pug Club
Elizabeth Page
3965 Richy Rd
Mims FL 32754
407/ 269-0555

Yankee Pug Dog Club
Debora Chamberland
183 Cedar St
Newington CT 06111
203/ 666-9280

PULI

Puli Adoption, Rescue & Referral
Mary
301/ 686-9219

RHODESIAN RIDGEBACK

Rhodesian Ridgeback Rescue
Priscilla Gabosch
735 Park Ave
Collingwood NJ 08108
609/ 858-6227

ROTTWEILER

Orange Coast Rottweiler Club Rescue
Roberta Banfield
PO Box 450
Lake Elsinore CA 92330
714/ 674-4849

Rottweiler Rescue
Lois Schwechtje
23 E Greenhill Rd
Broomall PA 19008
610/ 353-1662

Rottweiler Rescue
Robin Roncoroni
RR5 Box 4A
Califon NJ 07830
908/ 832-9154

Rottweiler Rescue
Mary Schlager
110 Bourndale Rd
Manhasset NY 11030
516/ 627-0131

SAINT BERNARD

Delaware Valley Saint Bernard Rescue
Rich and Shirley Crockett
11763 Colman Rd
Philadelphia PA 19154
215/ 637-3086

Greater Milwaukee Saint Bernard Club
Jan Much
924 E Michigan
Oak Creek WI 53154
414/ 764-0262

North Texas St Bernard Club
Gloria Wallin
1423 Hampton Rd
Grapevine TX 76051
214/ 727-3537

Saint Bernard Club of Puget Sound
Suzanne Schoot
20117 SE 152 St
Renton WA 98059
206/ 255-7301

Saint Bernard Club of the Pacific Coast
Penny Mahon
15244 Arnold Dr
Glen Ellen CA 95442
707/ 996-4319

Southern Maryland St Bernard Fanciers
Cathy Babins
RT 1 Box 123A
Waldorf MD 20601
301/ 843-6406; 301/ 934-3785

SALUKI

Saluki Club of Greater San Francisco
Susan Netboy
5 Ranch Rd
Woodside CA 94062
415/ 851-7812

Saluki Rescue
Cloris Costigan
7 Huntington Rd
East Brunswick NJ 08816
908/ 257-9134

Saluki Rescue
Jean Faulkner
RD 1 Box 430
Green Lane PA 18054
215/ 453-9045

SAMOYED

Delaware Valley Samoyed Rescue
Sandy Phifer
2091 Hendricks Station Rd
Harleysville PA 19438
215/ 234-8308

SCHIPPERKE

Schipperke Rescue and Adoption
Marie
508/ 476-2478

SCOTTISH DEERHOUND

Scottish Deerhound Rescue
Helmi Konderock
58 Monmouth Parkway
Monmouth Beach NJ 07757
201/ 222-0308; 201/ 542-4458

Scottish Deerhound Rescue
Norma Sellers
1691 W Strasburg Rd
West Chester PA 19382
610/ 692-7178; 610/ 692-5207

SCOTTISH TERRIER

Scottish Terrier Club of America
Mrs Diane Zollinger
PO Box 1893
Woodinville WA98072-1893

Scottish Terrier Club of America
Caryl Alten & Dennis Mileski
4601 Woodward Ave
Downers Grove IL 60515

Scottish Terrier Club of Greater Atlanta
Greg Bobbs
831 Derrydown Way
Decatur GA 30030
404/ 373-9526

Scottish Terrier Club of Greater New York
William Berry
3 Sagamore Rd
Parsippany NJ 07054
201/ 227-1871

Scottish Terrier Rescue
Marian Krupp
PO Box 408
Solebery PA18963
215/ 862-5837

SEALYHAM TERRIER

American Sealyham Terrier Club
Mrs Daryl Pakkala
4450 Morristown Dr
Riverside CA 92505
919/ 347-4772; 217/ 877-0245

SHETLAND SHEEPDOG

Evergreen State Shetland Sheepdog Club
Lynn Erckmann
4761 - 162nd Ave NE
Redmond WA 98052
206/ 885-0701

Interlocking Shetland
Sheepdog Club—Monee
Jane Naden
417 Arlington
Crete IL 60417
708/ 672-6030

Jacksonville Shetland Sheepdog Club
Darla Duffey
5204 Beige St
Jacksonville FL 32258
904/ 262-5420; 904/ 724-8866

Shetland Sheepdog Rescue
Penny Miche
5505 Potters Ln
Pipersville PA 18947
215/ 766-7348

Shetland Sheepdog Rescue
Diane Evans
547 Cedar St
Spring City PA 19475
610/ 948-9049

Shetland Sheepdog Rescue
Debbie Jones
3315 Barrington Rd
Baltimore MD 21215
410/ 466-7118

Shetland Sheepdog Rescue
Mary Boyce
122 Crabapple Ln
Franklin Park NJ 08823
908/ 821-1765

Shetland Sheepdog Rescue & Adoption
Deborah DeNardo
38 River Ln
Deep River CT 06417
203/ 526-4018

SIBERIAN HUSKY

Delaware Valley Siberian Husky Rescue
Lottie McEanery
2 Morris Ln
Bryn Mawr PA 19090
610/ 525-8597

Siberian Husky Rescue
Rose Mary Laubach
34 Desai Ct RD 2
Howell-Freehold NJ 07728
908/ 431-1169

Yankee Siberian Husky Rescue Service
Susan Herlihy
617/ 593-7331

SILKY TERRIER

Richard Hammond Silky Terrier Rescue
Mrs Lee Easton
18801 NE Willamson Rd
Newberg OR 97132

Richard Hammond Silky Terrier Rescue
Ivy Rogers
656 Santa Maria Rd
El Sobrante CA 94803

Silky Terrier Rescue
Peggy Spratt
376 Aubrey Rd
Wynnewood PA 19096
610/ 896-8407

SOFT-COATED WHEATEN TERRIER

Del Valley Soft-Coated Wheaten Terrier
Club
Richard Tomlinson
4428 Province Line Rd
Princeton NJ 08540
609/ 924-1453

Soft-Coated Wheaten Terrier Club of N CA
Sonya Urquhart
775 Wesley Dr
Vacaville CA 95688
707/ 446-7494

Soft-Coated Wheaten Terrier Club of N CA
Robyn Alexander
1819 Rose St
Berkeley CA 94703
510/ 526-7948

STANDARD SCHNAUZER

Standard Schnauzer Club of N California
Mary Lou Just
3758 Hachers Circle
Stockton CA 95219
209/ 473-0323

TIBETAN SPANIEL

Tibetan Spaniel Rescue
Sharon Paynter
313 Cherry Rd
Atco NJ 08004
609/ 768-2589

TOSA KEN

Tosa Ken Rescue
Anne Absey
11117 Fleetwood St
Sun Valley CA 91352

TOY FOX TERRIER

Wisconsin Toy Fox Terrier Assoc
Dr Myles Notaro
2925 South 10th St
Milwaukee WI 53215
414/ 482-1633

VIZSLA

Connecticut Valley Vizsla Club
John Morris
3 Promontory Dr
Cheshire CT 06410
203/ 272-8210

Tampa Bay Vizsla Club
Judy Heiser
3541 NW 14th Ave
Pompano Beach FL 33064
305/ 941-9392

Vizsla Club of America
Rick Davis
150 Stilla Har Dr
Westminster SC 29693

Vizsla Club of Greater NY
Elaine Panebianco
33 Whistler Hill Ln
Huntington NY 11743
516/ 266-1602

Vizsla Rescue
Don Tamerleau
RD 1 Box 214C
Lakewood Rd Rt 528
New Egypt NJ 08533
609/ 758-7348

WEIMARANER

Sacramento Valley Weimaraner Club
Kathy Dunn
13560 Skyline Blvd
Oakland CA 94619
415/ 635-3921

Southern California Weimaraner Rescue
Friends for Pets Foundation
7131 Owensmouth Ave #39A
Canoga Park CA 91303
818/ 701-0674; 213/ 377-2998

Weimaraner Club of Greater St Louis
Rebecca Weimer
324 Sundew Dr
Belleville IL 62221
618/ 236-1466

Weimaraner Club of South Florida
Susan Warner
6630 W 13th Ct
Hialeah FL 33012
305/ 821-1826

Western Washington Weimaraner Club
Debra Follensbee
3021 87th Ave Ct. E
Puyallup WA 98371
206/ 845-2464

WELSH TERRIER

Welsh Terrier Cares Rescue Service
Ward Morris
485 Overbrook Dr NW
Atlanta GA 30318
404/ 351-1330

WEST HIGHLAND WHITE TERRIER

West Highland White Terrier Club of CA
Susan Porter
156 S Martel Ave
Los Angeles CA 90036
213/ 938-3569

West Highland White Terrier Club/Baltimore
Joe and Naomi Engers
807 Prospect Mill Rd
Bel Air MD 21014
301/ 838-6489

West Highland White Terrier Rescue
Patricia Marks
501 E Moreland Rd
Willow Grove PA 19090
215/ 657-6085

WHIPPET

Southern CA Whippet Assoc
Tom & Ellen Hammatt
Star Route 1130
Orange CA 92667
714/ 649-2286

WOLF

Mission: Wolf
PO Box 79
Silver Cliff CO 81249

Wolf Haven
3111 Offut Lake Rd
Tenino WA 98589

YORKSHIRE TERRIER

Bluebonnet Yorkshire Terrier Club
Susan Griffin
2712 Dorrington
Dallas TX 75228
214/ 320-9469

Yorkie Rescue
1315 Briardale Ln NE
Atlanta GA 30306

MISCELLANEOUS

Abandoned Terrier Rescue Assoc Inc
Airedale, Fox, Welsh, Lakeland
Ruth Millington
PO Box 824
Somis CA 93066
805/ 386-3757

All Animal and Mixed-Breed Rescue
Animal Survival
PO Box 1680
Cherry Hill NJ 08034
609/ 663-9045

All Breed Rescue
Bay Area Canine Rescue
PO Box 277
San Carlos CA 94070

All Breed Rescue Alliance
Sharon Schiele
357 3rd Ave
Phoenixville PA 19460
610/ 935-0896

Alyeska Canine Trainers
Pat Bouschor
5201 Rabbit Creek Rd
Anchorage AK 99516
907/ 345-1506

Animals in Distress
PO Box 168
Catasauqua PA 18032
610/ 264-5554

Atlanta Kennel Club
Dolores Russell
2441 Old Field Rd NW
Atlanta GA 30327
404/ 296-7126

California Timbra Wolfdog Res of Amer
1041 N Main St #225
Manteca CA 95336
209/239-5966

Coalition of All Purebred Rescue/AZ
PO Box 7264
Phoenix AZ 85011
602/ 494-9567

Conyers Kennel Club of Georgia
Jackie Dilworth
570 Clubhouse Dr
Conyers GA 30208
404/ 922-4151

Friends for Pets Foundation
7131 Owensmouth Ave #39A
Canoga Park CA 91303
818/ 701-0674; 213/ 377-2998

Friends of Pets
4711 South Bragaw
Anchorage AK 99507
907/ 561-3677

Jacksonville DFA
Betty Jean Shuman
PO Box 1232
Jacksonville FL 32201
904/ 733-1907

Jeff's Companion Animal Shelter
c/o Sandoz Pharmaceuticals
59 Rt 10
E Hanover NJ 07936

K-9 Animal Rescue League
Michael & Patti Blasko
PO Box 1602
Waianae HI 96792
808/ 696-4357

Kona Coast Kennel Club
Kathy Miller
PO Box 1027
Kapaau HI 96755
808/ 889-5900

Lower Bucks Dog Training Club
Joe Egan
18 Quail Rd
Levittown PA 19057
215/ 949-1204

Mixed Breed Rescue
Ellen Emmett
4474 Carwithan Rd
Philadelphia PA 19136
215/ 332-3105

Mixed Breed Rescue
Debbie Williams
2030 Kennicott Rd
Baltimore MD 21207
410/ 298-7637

Mixed Breed Rescue
Mary Ann Radford
RR 10
238 English Creed Rd
McKee City NJ 08232
609/ 484-8098

Project HEART
(Help For Every Animal
Regardless of Type)
Suite 222
768 Walker Rd
Great Falls VA 22066

Purebred Rescue Assoc of Michigan
Megen Veen
5188 Winchester Pass
Lapeer MI 48446
313/ 664-9800

Rhode Island Kennel Club
120 Mirick Ave
Cranston RI 02920
401/ 944-5042

Seattle Purebred Dog Rescue
PO Box 3523
Redmond WA 98073-3523
206/ 467-0205

Sighthound Rescue
5 Ranch Rd
Woodside CA 94062
415/ 851-7812

Wherewolf Rescue
3112 E Danbury Rd
Phoenix AZ 85032
602/ 867-8968

Almost every breed club publishes a newsletter. If you do not find your breed listed or if you want a publication that is not listed, contact the parent club and/or the registry organization for your breed. Many clubs offer their newsletters to nonmembers for nominal fees. The breed clubs will know of any other publications that cover their breed and activities related to their breed.

Afghan Hound Review
Box 30430
Santa Barbara CA 93130

Akbash Sentinel, The
Orysia Dawydiak & David Sims
RR 3 Union Rd
Charlottetown PE I C1A 7J7

Akita World
Hoflin Publications
4401 Zephyr St
Wheat Ridge CO 80033-3299
303/ 420-2222

Alaskan Malamute Annual, The
Hoflin Publications Ltd
4401 Zephyr St
Wheat Ridge CO 80033-3299
303/420-2222

American Cocker Magazine
14531 Jefferson St
Midway City CA 92655

American Staffordshire Annual, The
Hoflin Publications Ltd
4401 Zephyr St
Wheat Ridge CO 80033-3299
303/ 420-2222

Aussie Times
Vicki Rand
40516 C.R. 669
Decatur MI 49045
616/ 423-8621

Basenji, The
789 Linton Hill Rd
Newtown PA 18940
215/ 860-8254

Beagle Reporter, The Show
Jean Fergus
1456- 14th St
Los Osos CA 93402

Beardie Bulletin
Cynthia Moorhead
8150 Fleener Rd
Bloomington IN 47408

Bichon Frise Reporter, The
Jean Fergus
1456 14th St
Los Osos CA 93402

Border Collie, The Working
14933 Kirkwood Rd
Sidney OH 45365
513/ 492-2215

Border Collie Monthly
Barbara Beaumont Swann
284 Earlsdon Avenue North
Coventry England CV 5 6EX

Border Collie News, American
PO Box 396
Lockwood CA 93932
805/ 472-2640; 408/ 385-6249

Borzoi Annual, The
Hoflin Publications Ltd
4401 Zephyr St
Wheat Ridge CO 80033-3299
303/ 420-2222

Borzoi International
Sue Vasick-Croley, Ed/Pub
33594 Overland Lane
Solon OH 44139

Borzoi Quarterly, The
Hoflin Publishing
4401 Zephyr St
Wheat Ridge CO 80033-3299
303/ 420-2222

Boston Quarterly
Hoflin Publishing
4401 Zephyr St
Wheat Ridge CO 80033-3299
303/ 420-2222

Bouvier's, The International Magazine on
Cobbystone Gazette
1 Cedar Dr
Deale MD 20751

Boxer Review, The
Kris Dahl
8760 Appian Way
Los Angeles CA 90046

Brittany World
Hoflin Publications Ltd
4401 Zephyr St
Wheat Ridge CO 80033-3299
303/ 420-2222

Bugler, The
[Basset Hound Magazine]
PO Box 698
McMinnville TN 37110

Bull Terrier Quarterly, The
Hoflin Publications Ltd
4401 Zephyr St
Wheat Ridge CO80033-3299
303/ 420-2222

Bullmastiff Assoc Club Magazine, American
ABA
133 Chase Ave
Ivyland PA 18974

Chase, The
The Chase Publishing Co
[Foxhound Magazine]
PO Box 55090
Lexington KY 40555-5090
606/ 254-4262

Choban Chatter
[Anatolian Shepherd Dog Newsletter]
PO Box 966
Clarksville TN 37041
615/ 647-0586

Chow Chow Reporter
PO Box 18081
Louisville KY 40218
502/ 499-2531

Chow Life
Carol Patterson
PO Box 1197Lane
Chester CA 96020-1197
714/ 681-1649

Clumber Spaniel Bulletin
Laura Hofman
365 Brantwood Rd
Snyder NY 14226

Cocker Spaniel Leader
Gene & Shirley Este
19700 Jersey Mill Rd NW
Pataskala OH 43062-9750
614/ 924-6004

Collie Review
Drucker Publications
8760 Appian Way
Los Angeles CA 90046

Collie Variety
Hoflin Publications Ltd
4401 Zephyr St
Wheat Ridge CO 80033-3299
303/ 420-2222

Cooner, American
Box 211-A
Sesser IL 62884
800/ 851-7507

Coonhound Bloodlines
United Kennel Club Inc
100 E Kilgore Rd
Kalamazoo MI 49001-5598
616/ 343-9020

Corgi Capers
18105 Kirkshire
Birmingham MI 48009

Corgi Quarterly, The
Hoflin Publications Ltd
4401 Zephyr St
Wheat Ridge CO80033-3299
303/ 420-2222

Courier, The
Jody Van Loan
[Portugese Water Dog Magazine]
99 Maple Ave
Greenwich CT 06830
203/ 661-9347

Dalmation Quarterly
Hoflin Publications Ltd
4401 Zephyr St
Wheat Ridge CO80033-3299
303/ 420-2222

Doberman Magazine
Southern Publishing
PO Box 20
Holly Hill FL 32117-0020

Doberman World
Hoflin Publications
4401 Zephyr St
Wheat Ridge CO 80033-3299
303/ 420-2222

Elkhound Quarterly
Hoflin Publications Ltd
4401 Zephyr St
Wheat Ridge CO 80033-3299
303/ 420-2222

English Cocker Quarterly, The
Hoflin Publications Ltd
4401 Zephyr St
Wheat Ridge CO 80033-3299
303/ 420-2222

French Bullytin, The
[French Bulldog Magazine]
PO Box 50680
Mendota MN 55150-0680
612/ 454-9510

German Shepherd Dog Review
30 Far View Rd
Chalfont PA 18914

German Shepherd Quarterly, The
Hoflin Publications Ltd
4401 Zephyr St
Wheat Ridge CO 80033-3299
303/ 420-2222

Giant
Sonnen Publications
[Giant Schnauzer Magazine]
PO Box 137
Cranfills Gap TX 76637-0137

Golden Retriever Review, The
Marilyn Sturz
12 Bay Path Court
Huntington NY 11743
516/ 421-1897

Golden Retriever World
Hoflin Publications Ltd
4401 Zephyr St
Wheat Ridge CO 80033-3299
303/ 420-2222

Gordon Quarterly
Hoflin Publications Ltd
4401 Zephyr St
Wheat Ridge CO 80033-3299
303/ 420-2222

Great Dane, The Southern
Tom Wright
9862 SW 74th Ave
Ocala FL 34476
904/ 854-6982

Great Dane Reporter
Marlo Publications
Box 5284
Beverly Hills CA 90209
213/ 859-3930

Great Pyrenees Annual, The
Hoflin Publications Ltd
4401 Zephyr St
Wheat Ridge CO 80033-3299
303/ 420-2222

Greyhound Review
National Greyhound Assoc
Gary Guccione
PO Box 543
Abilene KS 67410
913/ 263-4660

Gun Dog Supreme, The
Wirehaired Pointing Griffon
Club of America
11739 SW Beaverton Hwy 201
Beaverton OR 97005

Hounds and Hunting
[Field Trial Beagles]
Box 372
Bradford PA 16701
814/ 368-6154

Hunters Horn, The
George Slankard
Foxhound Magazine/
114-120 E Franklin Ave
PO Box 707
Sesser IL 62884
618/ 625-2711

Irish Wolfhound Quarterly
Hoflin Publications Ltd
4401 Zephyr St
Wheat Ridge CO 80033-3299
303/ 420-2222

Italian Greyhound, The
Joan M & William J Cooper
8414 Kingsgate Rd
Potomac MD 20854
301/ 299-6269

Keeshond Review
PO Box 280
Wilmington VT 05363
802/ 464-2631

Keezette International
Carol A Cash
[Keeshond Magazine]
15646 Creekwood Lane
Strongsville OH 44136
216/ 238-4549

Labrador Quarterly, The
Hoflin Publications Ltd
4401 Zephyr St
Wheat Ridge CO 80033-3299
303/ 420-2222

Labrador Review, The
Marilyn Sturz
12 Bay Path Court
Huntington NY 11743
516/ 421-1897

Leopard Tree Dog News
J Richard McDuffie
[Catahoula Leopard Cow
Hog Dog Magazine]
1179 Shaws Fork Rd
Aiken SC 29801
803/ 648-2573

Lhasas Unlimited
Jean Fergus
1456 14th St
Los Osos CA 93402

Louisiana Catahoula Leopard Dog
National Assoc/Louisiana Catahoulas, Inc
Box 1041
Denham Springs LA 70727
504/ 665-6082

Maltese Magazine
Jean Fergus
1456 14th St
Los Osos CA 93402

Norsk Elghund Quarterly
Cotton & Stan Silverman
[Norwegian Elkhound Magazine]
31 Peck St
Rehoboth MA 02769
508/ 252-3909

Orient Express, The
Doll-McGinnis Enterprises
[Pekingese Magazine]
8848 Beverly Hills
Lakeland FL 33809
813/ 858-3839

Pit Bull Terrier, American Gazette
PO Box 1771
Salt Lake City UT 84110

Pom Reader, The
Doll-McGinnis Enterprises
8848 Beverly Hills Rd
Lakeland FL 33809
813/ 858-3839

Pomeranian Let's Talk Pom Talk
4345 Rogers Lake Rd
Kannapolis NC 28081

Poodle Review
Del Hahl
4401 Zephyr St
Wheat Ridge CO 80033
303/ 420-2222

Poodle Variety
PO Box 30430
Santa Barbara CA 93130
805/ 683-1771

Pug Talk
Anna Marie Wilson
223 W Louisiana
Dallas TX 75224
214/ 946-7509

Puli News
Puli Club of America
Carolyn Nusbickel
8078 Goshen Rd RD 2
Malvern PA 19355
610/ 296-8425

Quackers
Anne Norton
[Nova Scotia Duck Tolling
Retriever Magazine]
10358 Taylor Hawks Rd
Heron MI 49744
517/ 379-3210

Rhodesian Ridgeback Quarterly, The
Hoflin Publications Ltd
4401 Zephyr Rd
Wheat Ridge CO 80033-3299
303/ 420-2222

Rottweiler Express, Der
Doll-McGinnis Publications
8848 Beverly Hills
Lakeland FL 33805
800/ 780-3624

Rottweiler Free Press, The
PO Box 225-W
Pioneertown CA 92268

Rottweiler Quarterly
PO Box 900
Aromas CA 95004

Saluki Quarterly, The
Hoflin Publications Ltd
4401 Zephyr St
Wheat Ridge CO 80033-3299
303/ 420-2222

Samoyed Quarterly, The
Hoflin Publications Ltd
4401 Zephyr St
Wheat Ridge CO 80033-3299
303/ 420-2222

Scottish Deerhound Annual, The
Hoflin Publications Ltd
4401 Zephyr St
Wheat Ridge CO 80033-3299
303/ 420-2222

Sheepdog News, Working
Delia Sturgeon
Arfryn 17, Tan-y-Bryn
Pwllglas, MR
Wales C1Wdd UK

Sheepdog Newsletter, Northeast
Nancy Hayes
38 Highland St
Hopedale MA 01747

Sheltie International
Jean Fergus
1456 14th St
Los Osos CA 93412

Sheltie Pacesetter
PO Box 3310
Palos Verdes CA 90274
213/ 541-7820

Shepherd's Dogge, The
Carole Presberg
Box 843
Ithaca NY 14851
607/ 659-5868

Shih Tzu Reporter, The
1456 14th St
Los Osos CA 93402

Siberian Quarterly, The
Hoflin Publications Ltd
4401 Zephyr St
Wheat Ridge CO 80033-3299
303/ 420-4444

Smooth Colliers
Becky LaSpina
6045 Timerleaf Way
Orangevale CA 95662
916/ 989-3885

Springer Companion
Hoflin Publications Ltd
4401 Zephyr St
Wheat Ridge CO 80033-3299
303/ 420-2222

Weimaraner Magazine
WC.A. Futurity Pro Weimaraner Club
PO Box 110708
Nashville TN 37222-0708

Yorkshire Terrier Annual
Hoflin Publications Ltd
4401 Zephyr St
Wheat Ridge CO 80033-3299
303/ 420-2222

Yorkshire Terrier Magazine
9051 Soquel Dr
Aptos CA 95003
408/ 662-3130

Publications that are not related to a specific breed of dog are listed in this chapter. Some of the publications listed, deal with specific topics, such as working dogs.

If you're not sure you'll like a magazine, write to the publisher and request a sample copy. In many cases, you'll be asked to pay for a single issue. If the main theme of the magazine is not obvious, a brief explanation is included on the second line in parentheses.

Some publications such as *Dog World* are available on the newstand, but most of the publications listed in this chapter are avaliable by subscription only.

American Dog
[the video magazine & dog trading cards]
PO Box 127
Montpelier IN 47359
317/ 728-2144

American Journal Veterinary Research
[AJVR]
930 N Meacham Rd
Schaumburg IL 60196

American Ring Federation Newsletter
5325 W Mt Hope Rd
Lansing MI 48917
517/ 322-2221

Animal Alternatives Research & Ed. Project
[newsletter on natural therapies]
PO Box 6364
Santa Fe NM 87502

Animal Tales
[stories about animals]
PO Box 2220
Rayson AZ 85547-2220
602/ 246-7144

Animals Voice, The
PO Box 16955
N Hollywood CA 91695-9931

Bloodlines Journal
[all-breed obedience & UKC breeds]
100 Kilgore Rd
Kalamazoo MI 29001

Bulletin on Companion Animal Behavior
ABCS Inc
2288 Manning Ave
Los Angeles CA 90064
213/ 474-3776

Canine Chronicle
605 Second Ave North #203
Columbus MS 39701
601/ 327-1124; FAX 601/327-9750

Canine Classified
Page Run
4422 Orange Grove Dr
Houston TX 77039

Canine News
[Doctors Foster & Smith newsletter]
2253 Air Park Road
PO Box 100
Rhinelander WI 54501-0100
800/ 826-7206

Chinese Shar-Pei/German Shepherd/
Rottweiler Magazine
2881 Carew Ave
Winter Park FL 32789
407/ 647-6507

Classified Canine
[dog collectibles]
8123 W Margaret Ln
Franklin WI 53132

Classified K-9 II, The
[collectibles]
The Ultimate Pet
28828 207th SE
Kent WA 98042

Cold Nose Chronicle
[the canine connection]
3774 Clichy Ln
Bridgeton MO 63044-3503
314/ 291-8770

Come N Get It Frisbee Training Manual
SASE, business-size
PO Box 16279
Encino CA 91416

Common Emergencies and Your Dog
free
PO Box 88988
Checkerboard Square
St Louis MO 63188

Cornell Animal Health Newsletter
PO Box 52817
Boulder CO 80321-2817

Crates and Dogs
SASE, business-size; free pamphlet
31 Davis Hill Rd, Dept. SB
Weston CT 06883

DVM, The News Magazine of Veterinary
Medicine
7500 Old Oak Blvd
Cleveland OH 44130
216/ 243-8100

Dog Care and Trivia
MSD AGVET
PO Box 931
Whippany NJ 07981-9990
SASE, business-size

Dog Fancy
PO Box 53264
Boulder CO 80322-3264
303/ 447-9330

Dog Industry Newsletter
511 Harbor View Circle
Charleston SC 29412
803/ 795-9555; 803/ 795-2930

Dog News
1115 Broadway
New York NY 10010

Dog Sports Magazine
[America's journal of the working dog]
PO Box 1000
Glenrock WY 82637
800/ 451-4477 or 307/ 436-5300

Dog Talk
[weekly audio magazine]
PO Box 127
Montpelier IN 47359
317/ 728-2144

Dog Watch
[a weekly newspaper]
11331 Ventura Blvd #301
Studio City CA 91604-3155
818/ 761-3647

Dog World
9 Tufton St
Ashford, Kent TN 23 1QN
England UK

Dog World Magazine
29 N Wacker Dr
Chicago IL 60606
312/ 726-2802

DogGone, newsletter for dogs
[and their owners]
PO Box 651155
Vero Beach FL 32965-1155

Dogs In Canada
43 Railside Rd
Don Mills ONT M3A 3L9

Fetch the Paper
[the magazine for folks whose dogs
are like family]
Pawprince Press
815 Clark Rd
Marblemount WA 98267
206/873-4333

Front & Finish
[dog trainers news]
PO Box 333
Galesburg IL 61402-0033

Fur, Fin & Feather News
World Pet Society
Box 570343
Tarzana CA 91357

Gaines Assorted Pamphlets
write for list
PO Box 9001
Chicago IL 60604-9001

Good Dog!
Ross Becker
511 Harbor View Cr
Charleston SC 29412
803/795-9555
800/968-1738
803/795-2930

Guide to the Scientific Literature
of Dog and Cat Behavior
ABCS
2288 Manning Ave
Los Angeles CA 90064

Guidelines for Disaster Planning
AKC, free
51 Madison Ave
New York NY 10010

Gun Dog
Stover Publications Co Inc
1901 Bell Ave #4
PO Box 35098
Des Moines IA 50315
515/243-2472, FAX
515/243-2472

Hound Dog Magazine
PO Box 20
Holly Hill FL 32117-0020

Hunters Whistle, The
AKC Pure-Bred Dogs Afield
51 Madison Ave
New York NY 10010

Hunting Retriever
100 E Kilgore Rd
Kalamazoo MI 49001-5598
616/343-9020

Ilio
[Hawaii's dog news]
261 Ohana St
Kailua HI 96734
808/262-6677
808/1068

Institute for Scientific Info
[research info avail:dog/cat behavior]
Philadelphia PA
215/386-0100

Internat'l Pet Industry Newsletter
511 Harbor View Cr
Charleston SC 29412
803/795-9555
803/795-2930

Internat'l Search & Rescue Trade Assoc
David Rider
4537 Foxhall Dr NE
Olympia WA 98506
206/352-5613
206/493-0949

Journal of Amer Veterinary Medical Assoc
930 N Meacham Rd
Schaumburg IL 60196

K-9 Enforcer
[internat'l publication for dog handlers]
PO Box 90849
Long Beach CA 90809
800/635-9399

K-9 Product News
PO Box 1000
Gelnrock WY 82637
800/451-4477
307/436-5300

Kennel Healthline
PO Box 6500
Chicago IL 60680

Livestock Guarding Dog Pubs
Livestock Guarding Dogs Wear
Sheep's Clothing
Smithsonian, 4-82 pp 65-73
Hampshire College
Amherst MA 01002

Livestock Guarding Dog Pubs
Protecting the Flock
Sheep, 7-81 pp 14-17
Hampshire College
Amherst MA 01002

Livestock Guarding Dog Pubs
50 cents a copy; *Range Journal*
New England Farm Center
Hampshire College
Amherst MA 01002

Livestock Guarding Dog Pubs
free
USDA Sheep Experiment Sta
Dobois ID 83423

Livestock Guarding Dog Pubs
free, Journal of Range Mgt, 1985
USDA Sheep Experiment Sta
Dobois ID 83423

Match Show Bulletin, The
East Coast
Box 214
Massapequa NY 11758
516/541-3442

Model Dog Lover's Journal, The
[dog figurine shows]
15 San Carlos
St Charles MO 63303-4117

Moosie's Musing
Feathers & Fur Talent Agcy
[dog newsletter]
PO Box 20816
Portland OR 97220

Mushing Magazine
[sled dog racing]
PO Box 149
Ester AK 99725
907/479-0454

Muttmatchers Messenger
W Washington edition
[pet placement newsletter]
PO Box 1165
Enumclaw WA 98022-1165
206/848-7741

Muttmatchers Messenger
Fillmore edition
PO Box 920
Fillmore CA 93016
805/534-4542

Muttmatchers Messenger
San Diego edition
PO Box 632785
San Diego CA 92163

Nat'l Bulldogger Magazine
Box 142
Patriot IN 47038

Nat'l Stockdog Magazine
PO Box 402
Butler IN 46721-0402

New England Obedience News
35 Oakwood Dr
Portsmouth NH 03801-5779

Off-Lead
[dog training magazine]
PO Drawer A
Clark Mills NY 13321

Our Dogs
5 Oxford Rd
Station Approach
England UK

Pet Behavior News
William E Campbell
PO Box 1658
Grants Pass OR 97526
503/476-5775
503/476-5523

Pet Business Magazine
5400 N W 84th Ave
Miami FL 33166
305/592-9890
305/592-9726

Pet Focus
1 Klimback Ct
West Caldwell NJ 07006-7508

Pet Forum
[health info re pets]
1613 E Millbrook Rd
Raleigh NC 27609

Pet Gazette
1309 N Halifax Ave
Daytona Beach FL 32018
904/255-6935

Pet Review & Natural Pet Newsletter, The
PO Box 22899
Melbourne FL 32902-2899
407/723-4183

Pet Talk
PO Box 302
Bensalem PA 19020
215/638-38385

Pets on the Go
free travel booklet
Box 4000
Lehigh Valley PA 18001

Pure-Bred Dogs/AKC Gazette
51 Madison Ave
New York NY 10010
212/696-8226

Purina's Kennel Tips
Checkerboard Square
St Louis MO 63164

Racing Siberian Husky, The
PO Box 3040
Pullman WA 99165-3040
509/334-1986

Ranch Dog Trainer, The
RT 2 Box 333
West Plains MO 65775

Rare Breed Quarterly
Box 446
Chardon OH 44024

SAR Dog Alert
search & rescue dogs
3310 Wren Ln
Eagan MN 55121-2324
612/452-4209

Scent Article, The
[search & rescue & K-9]
PO Box 126
Scoudouc NB EOA 1NO

Schutzhund Magazine
DVG America
PO Drawer P
Stanford FL 32772

Show Sight
Doll-McGinnis Pub
8848 Beverly Hills
Lakeland FL 33809-1604
813/853-DMCG
$90 yr, 1st class; $60 yr, book rate

Showtime South Magazine
Southeastern Dog Exhibitors
2197 McCollum-Sharpsburg Rd
Newnan GA 30263
404/251-1299

Sighthound Review
PO Box 30430
Santa Barbara CA 93130
805/966-7270

Spaniels
David & Charles Inc
North Pomfret VT 05053

Team & Trail
[the mushers monthly news]
PO Box 128 Sibley Rd
Center Harbor NH 03226
603/258-
603/-253-6265

Telltail Dispatch
[true stories about dogs]
PO Box 0721
Fremont CA 94537

Terrier & Toy Magazine
Southern Publishing
PO Box 85
Holly Hill FL 32125-0085

Today's Breeder
PO Box 3427
Cincinnati OH 45201

Top Notch Toys
8848 Beverly Hills
Lakeland FL 33809
813/858-3839

Topics in Veterinary Medicine
812 Springdale Dr
Exton PA 19341-2803

Various Free Pamphlets
585 Hawthorne Ct
Galesburg IL 61401

Veterinary Forum
ideas/service for & by practitioners
1610A Frederica Rd
St Simons Island GA 31522

Veterinary Industry Newsletter
PO Box 31292
Charleston SC 29417
800/968-1738

Windhound, The
4401 Zephyr St
Wheat Ridge CO 80033-3299
303/420-2222

WOLF!
PO Box 112
Clifton Heights PA 19018

Wolves & Related Canids
PO Box 1026
Agoura CA 91301

Working Sheepdog News
Arfryn, 17
Tan-y-Bryn
Pwllglas Mr Wales
United Kingdom

This chapter has the most foreign organizations listed. People who are involved with rare breeds, or those interested in contacting dog people in other countries will find the foreign registries helpful. When contacting a dog registry in a foreign country, it is best to have the letter written in the country's native language. If you do not know someone who speaks the language, contact your nearest college language department.

Some general and specific registry organizations in the United States are also listed. Generally, the specific registry organizations such as the National Stock Dog Registry, will register non-AKC breeds of stock dogs. The UKC also registers all types of breeds not recognized by the AKC. If you are looking for a registry for a rare breed, it is a good idea to consult the parent club for that breed since many of the rare breeds are registered by their parent club.

American Aigokai [kai] Ken
PO Box 217
Maximo OH 44650

American Border Collie Assoc
P Rogers
82 Rogers Rd
Perkinston MS 39573-8843
601/ 928-7551

American Intern'l Border Collie Registry Inc
1534 E 36th St
Des Mooines IA 50317

American Kennel Club
[exec, admn, dog &
   performance events only]
51 Madison Ave
New York NY 10010
212/696-8200

American Kennel Club
[registration and related services]
5580 Centerview Dr
Raleigh NC 27606
919/233-9767

Animal Research Foundation
[wolf hybrid registry]
PO Box 1480 Rt 2
Quinlan TX 75474

Aniwaya Wolf Club of Texas
[wolf & hybrid]
3509 Anderson-Gibson Rd
Grapevine TX 76051

Carolina Wolfers Assoc
[wolf & hybrid]
Rt 15 Box 408
Statesville NC 28677

Federation of Intern'l Canines
PO Box 25037
Montgomery AL 36125
205/284-4401

Global Kennel Club, Inc
1526 South 102nd St
Edwardsville KS 66111
913/441-1352

Iowolfer's Assoc
[wolf & hybrid]
RR 4 Box 215A
Mt Pleasant IA 52641

Livestock Guarding Dog Assoc
Dog Data
Hampshire College
Box FC
Amherst MA 01002
413/549-4600X487

Mixed-Breed Dog Club of America
[sterilized mixed breeds,
   rare breeds, disabled]
1937 Seven Pines Dr
St Louis MO 63146-3717
314/878-8497

National Stockdog Registry
PO Box 402
Butler IN 46721
219/868-2685

N Amer Australian Kelpie Registry, Inc
2656 Merino Ave
Oskaloosa IA 52577
515/673-7754

North American Sheepdog Society
Rossine Kirsch
RR 3
McLeansboro IL 62859
618/ 757-2238

Pride of the Pack
[wolf & wolf hybrid registry]
PO Box 451
Palmer TX 75152

Rare Breed Kennel Club
PO Box 727
Tujunga CA 91043-0727

States Kennel Club
PO Box 389
Hattiesburg MS 39403-0389

US Wolf Hybrid Assoc
RR 1 Box 341A
Canada Rd
Covington PA 16917

United Kennel Club
100 East Kilgore Rd
Kalamazoo MI 49001-5598
616/343-9020

Universal Kennel Club
[wolf hybrids]
PO Box 574
Nanuet NY 10954-0574
914/639-1313

ARGENTINA

Federacion Cinologica Agentina
Pte Luis Saenz Pena 281
111 - Capital - Buenos Aires Argentina
00 54/476 0631, 46-6106
FAX 0054/1814 0037

AUSTRALIA

Australian National Kennel Council
Royal Show Grounds
Epsom Rd, Ascot Vale 3032
Victoria Australia
0061/33 76 37 33
FAX 0061/3 376 29 73

AUSTRIA

Austrian Kennel Club
Osterreischischer Kynologenverband
Johann Teufelgasse 8
A-1238 Wien Austria
00 43 222/88 70 92/88 70 93
FAX 0222/88 92 621

BAHRAIN

Kennel Club of Bahrain
PO Box 28555 Rufa
State of Bahrain [Arabian Gulf]
Bahrain

BARBADOS

Barbados Kennel Club
Wraysbury
Bucks
St Thomas Barbados VI

BELGIUM

Belgian Kennel Club
Union Royale Cynologque Saint-Hubert
25 Avenue de l'Armee
Le Gerlaan 25
Brussels 4 Belgium
02/733 45 90, 02/734 31 60
FAX 032/02/732 40 05

BERMUDA

The Bermuda Kennel Club Inc
PO Box HM
1455 Hamilton HM FX
Bermuda

BOLIVIA

Kennel Club Boliviano
Edif. Alborada, piso 10, of. 1002
Loayez esq Juan de la Riva
Casilla 11030, La Paz Boliva
591/37 52 19
FAX 32 38 57

BRAZIL

Brazil Kennel Club
Confederacao Brasileria de Cinofilia
Rua Newton Prado no 74
Sao Cristovao
CP 20930 - Rio de Janeiro - RJ Brazil
0055/21 580 0812
FAX 0055/21 5808178

BULGARIA

Federation Cynologique Republican pres du
Counseil Central de l'Union
Dulgare des Chasseurs et des Pecheurs
31-33 Boulevard Vitoche
BG-1000 Sofia Bulgaria
00 359/88 00 12

BURMA

Burma Kennel Club
Room NO 10
342 Maha Bandoola St
Rangoon Burma

CANADA

Canadian Kennel Club
100-89 Skyway Ave
Etobicoke ONT
Canada M9W 6R4
416/675-5511
FAX 416/675-6506

National Kuvasz Registry
Darla Lofrance
RR 2
Acton ONT Canada L7J 2L8

CARIBBEAN

The Caribbean Kennel Club
PO Box 737
Port of Spain
Trinidad

CHILE

Kennel Club de Chile
Castilla 8043 Correo 2 Vina Del Mar Chili
0056/235 85 89 235 33 38
FAX 0056/2 235 85 89

COLOMBIA

Asociatcion Club Canino
Colombiano
Calle 121 A No: 52-23
Bogata De Zona 11 Colombia
00 57/2 26 47 07, 2 26 64 37

COSTA RICA

Asociacion Canofila Costarricense
Apartado 593 - 1002 Paseo do los
Estudiantes
San Jose Costa Rica
00 506/23 06 27, 21 50 80
FAX 00 506/22 27 80

CROATIA

Hrvatski Kinoloski Savez
Ilica 61
41000 Zagreb Croatia
041/426-448

CUBA

Federacion Cinologica de Cuba
Calle 28 no 308 entre 23 y 25
Vedado, Muncipio Plaza de la Revolucion
La Habana C.P. 12300
PO Box 6135 Habana 6 Cuba
32 3249-30-4956
FAX 53 7 62 5604 (5605)

CYPRUS

Cyprus Kennel Club
44, Vas. Voulgaroctonou St
Flat 3-4
Nicosia Cyprus
02-472803
FAX 02-457407

CZECH REPUBLIC

Federalni Vybor Mysliverckyen Svazu
Husova 7
CS-11525 Prague 1 Czech Republic
00 42/222 40 25, 222 40 28
FAX 00 42/2 235 3724

DENMARK

Dansk Kennel Klub
Parkvej 1
Jersie Strand
DK-2680 Solrad Strand Denmark
00 45 53/14 15 66
FAX 00 45 53/14 30 03

DOMINICAN REPUBLIC

Federacion Canina Dominicana
Ave Winston Churchill, no 75
Edif. Martinez, Apto 304
Santo Domingo, R. D. Dominican Republic
00 1/809 565 1404
FAX RCA-32 64 159

EAST AFRICA

East Africa Kennel Club
PO Box 14223 Westlands
Nairobi
Kenya East Africa

ECUADOR

Asociacion Canina Ecuatoriana
Casilla 8548, sucursal 8
Gaspard de Villareol 512 y Shyris
Quito Ecuador

ENGLAND

English Kennel Club
1 Clarges St Piccadilly
London W1Y 8AB England

ESTONIA

Esti Kennellit
Mesila 14
200009 Tallinn Estonia

FIJI

Fiji Kennel Club
8 Richards Rd
Suva Fiji

FINLAND

Suomen Kennellitto
Finske-Kennelklubben
Kamreerintie 8 Sf 02770
Espoo Finland
00 358/0 805 7722
FAX 00 358/0805 46 03

FRANCE

Societe Centrale Canine
Pour L'Amelioration
155 Ave Jean Jaures F 93535
Auberville
Cedex France
(1) 49 37 54 00
FAX (1) 49 37 01 20

GERMANY

Verband fur das
Deutsche Hundewesen
Westfalendamm 174
Postfach 10 41 54
D-4600 Dortmund 1 Germany
00-49-231/596096/97
FAX 0321/59 24 40

GIBRALTER

Gibralter Kennel Club
PO Box 492
33 Rosia Roaldi Gibralter
00 350/41791
FAX 350/43352

GREECE

Kennel Club of Greece
c/o Dr U Kongou
PO Box 52825 - 146 01 N Erythrea
Greece
0030-1-646 2083
FAX 00 30-1-644 9995

GUATAMALA

Asociacion Gualtemalteca de
Criatores de Perros [AGCP]
12 Calle 2-04, Zona 9
Edif. Plaza del Sol, 5o nivel, Of. 505
Ciudad Guatamala
00 502/31 26 87

GUERNSEY

Guernsey Dog Club
Myrtle Grove
St Jacques
Guernsey CI

HOLLAND

Holland Kennel Club
Raad van Deheer op
Kynologisch Gebied in Nederland
16 Emmalaan
Amsterdam 2 Holland
00 31/20 684 21
FAX 00 31/20 684 68 76

HONDURAS

Associacion Canofila de Honduras
PO Box 3330
Tegucigalpa Honduras
(504) 37 4078
FAX (504) 38 0141

HONG KONG

Hong Kong Kennel Club
3rd Floor
28B Stanley St Hong Kong
00 852/5 23 39 44

HUNGARY

Magyar Ebtenyesztok Orszagos
Egyesulete
Fadrusz utea 11/a
H-1114 Budapest Hungary
0036/11 661 463, 11 659 648
FAX 36 11 669 463

ICELAND

Iceland Kennel Club
Hundaraektarfelag Islands
Skipholti 50 B
105 Reykjavik Iceland
00 354 1 6252 756

INDIA

Kennel Club of India
9 Balyar Kalvi Nilayam Ave
of Ritherdon Rd
Purasawaltam
Madras 600   007 India

INDONESIA

Perkumpulan Kynologi Indonesia
[Perkin]
The All Indonesia Kennel Club
JLN Tanah Abang 111/19
Jakarta Pusat Indonesia
00 62/21 58 26 44

INTERNATIONAL

Federation Cynologique Internationale [FCI]
12 rue Leopold 11
14B-6530 Thuin
Belguim

International Sheep Dog Society
A Philip Hendry
Chesham House
47 Bromham Rd
Bedford MK40 2AA
England United Kingdom
(0234) 52672

IRELAND

Irish Kennel Club
4 Harcourt St
Dublin 2 Ireland
00 353/533300, 532309-532310

ISRAEL

Israel Kennel Club
PO Box 1015
Ramat Gan 52110 Israel
00 972/03 740 949

ITALY

Ente Nazionale Della
Cinofilia Italiana
Viale Permuda 21
1-20129 Milan Italy
00 39/2760 21 706
FAX (2) 78 31 27

JAMAICA

The Jamacian Kennel Club
8 Orchard St
Kingston 5
Jamaica W1

JAPAN

Japan Kennel Club
1-5 Kanda Suda-Cho
Chiyoda-Ku
Tokyo 101 Japan
00 81/3 32 511 651
FAX 00 81/3/32 511 659

JERSEY

Jersey Dog Club
La Huppa Riches Ave
St Savious
Jersey C1

KOREA

Korean Pet Animal Protection Assoc
275-5 Ulchi-ro 5-GA
[Dongshin Bldg no 203]
Jung-Su, Seoul Korea
278 0661 2
FAX 277 4073

LUXEMBOURG

Union Cynologique St Hubert du Grand
Duche du Luxembourg
Boite Postale 69
L-4901 Bascharage Luxembourg
00 352/502 866
FAX 00352/50 54 14

MADAGASCAR

Societe Canine de Madagascar
23, rue Raveloary-Isoraka
Boite Postale 8316
Antananarivo (101) Madagascar
346-83

MALAYSIA

Malasian Kennel Assoc
Persatua Kenel Anjing Malaysia
No 8 1st Fl
Jalan Tun Mohd Faud Dua
Taman Tun Dr Ismail
60000 Kuala Lumpur Malaysia
60/03 - 719 2027, 717 4839
FAX 60/03 - 718 2312

MALTA

Main Kennel Club
Misida Youth Centre
15 Rue de'Argens Str
Msida Malta GC

MEXICO

Federacion Canofila Mexicana
Apartado Postal 22-535
CP 14000 Mexico DF
(905) 655-1600

MONACO

Societe Canine de Monaco
Palais des Congres
Avenued'Ostende 12
MC-98000 Monte Carlo Monaco
00 33/93 50 55 14

MORROCO

Societe Cemtrale Canine Marocaine
Boite Postale 15941
Casablanca Principal Morroco

NEPAL

Nepal Kennel Club
PO Box 653
Kathmandu Nepal

NEW GUINEA

Papua New Guinea Kennel Assoc
PO Box 3361 Port Moresby
Papus New Guinea

NEW ZEALAND

New Zealand Kennel Club
Prosser Street Eldson
Private Bag
Porirua New Zealand
00 64/4 237 4489
FAX 00 64/4 237 4489

NORWAY

Norsk Kennelklub
Nils Hansens Vei 20
Box 163 Bryn
N-0611 Oslo Norway
00 47/2 65 60 00
FAX 02 - 720 474

PANAMA

Club Canino de Panama
Apartado 6-4791 El Dorado Panama
00 507/61 2895
FAX 00507/86 32 51

PAKISTAN

The Kennel Club of Pakistan
Fortress Stadium
Lahore West Pakistan

PARAGUAY

Paraguay Kennel Club
Coronel Bogado c/Antequers
Planta Alta
Asuncion Paraguay
Postal Address PO Box 1809
00 595/(21) 492 676
FAX 595 21 60 68 64

PERU

Kennel Club Peruano
Avenida Benavides 712, Oficina 202
Lima 18 Peru
51/44 16 28
FAX 51 (14) 44 16 28

PHILIPPINES

Philippines Canine Club
PO Box 649
Greenhills Post Office 3113 Philippines
632/721-7152

POLAND

Zwiazek Kynologiczny
W Polsze
Nowy-Swiat 35 PL-00-029
Warschau POLAND

PORTUGAL

Cluba Portuguese de Canicultura
Praca D Joao da Camara 4-3o ESQ
P1200
Lisbonne Portugal
00 351/19 32 14 78
FAX 00 351/13 47 86 17

PUERTO RICO

Federacion Canofila de Puerto Rico
[Borinquen Kennel Club, Inc]
PO Box 13898, Santurce Sta
Santurce 00908 Puerto Rico
00 809/7593654, 7605104, 7224040
FAX 00 809/7241430

ROMANIA

Asociatia Chinologica din Romania
Calea Mosilor, Nr. 128, Codul 30334
Of. Postal 37, sectorul 2
Bucarest Romania
40/15 45 23

SAN MARINO

Kennel Club San Marino
Via XXVIII Luglio, 197
RSM-47031 Tavolucci San Marino
00 39/549-903306

SAN SALVADOR

Asociacion Canofila San Salvadorena
[ASCANSAL]
Prolongacion Juan Pablo No 18
Residendial Escalon San Salvador

SCOTLAND

Scottish Kennel Club
6 Forres St
Edinburgh EH3 6BR Scotland UK

SINGAPORE

The Singapore Kennel Club
Suite 12-02, 12th Floor
BUKIT Timah Shopping Center
170, Upper Bukit Timah Rd
Singapore 2158
00 65/469 48 21
FAX 00 65/469 91 18

SLOVENIA

Kinofloska Sveza Slovenije
Hirska 27
61000 Ljubljana Slovenia
320-949, 315-474

SOUTH AFRICA

Kennel Union of Southern Africa
PO Box 2659
Cape Town 8000 South Africa
00 27/021 23 90 28/8
FAX 00 27/021 23 58 76

SPAIN

Real Sociedad Central de Fomento
de las Razas en Espana
Los Madrazo 20-26
E 28014 Madrid Spain
00 341/522 24 00, 00 341/521 84 19
FAX 0034/522 51 91

SRI LANKA

The Ladie's Kennel Assoc of Sri Lanka
19, Race Course Ave
Colombo 7 Sri Lanka
94/95 831

SWEDEN

Svenska Kennelklubben
Norrbyvagan 32
Box 11043
S-161 11 Bromma Sweden
(00-46) 08-795 30 00
FAX (00-46) 08-795 30 40

SWITZERLAND

Societe Cynologique Suisse
Langgasstrave 8
Case Postale 8216
Ch 3001 Berne Switzerland
00 41/31 23 58 19
FAX 031/24 02 15

TAIWAN

Kennel Club of the Republic of China [KCC]
61, Min Tsu 2nd Rd
Kaohsiung
Taiwan - Republic of China
00 886/07 2726765
FAX 00 886/07 723 2715

URUGUAY

Kennel Club Uruguayo
Avda Uruguay 864
11100 Montevideo Uruguay
00 598/92 04 84 u. 92 08 86
FAX 00 598/2 96 25 40

VENEZUELA

Federacion Canina De Venezuela
Calle Toborda, QTA Ramiaya, Urb,
San Roma Las Mercedes, Apartado 88665
Caracas 1080 A Venezuela
00 58/2 914 490 - 912 301

YUGOSLAVIA

Federation Cynologique de la Republique
Socialiste de Youguslavie
Rue Alekse nenadovica, 19-23
YU-11000 Belgrade Yugoslavia
00 38/11 437 652
FAX 00 38/11 437 652

ZAMBIA

Kennel Association of Zambia
PO Box 30662
Lusaka Zambia

ZIMBABWE

Zimbabwe Kennel Club
PO Box BE61
Belvedere Zimbabwe
260/72 38 35

The organizations listed in this chapter provide very specific services. The tattoo organizations offer a registry service for tattooed dogs. Each one works a little differently, so contact them for details. Tattooing your dog is a very important precaution to provide a safeguard against theft, as well as for identification. It is inexpensive and painless to have done. In many cases, dog clubs offer tattoo clinics. The tattoo organizations can give you the name of people who will tattoo your dog.

For those of you interested in nutrition for dogs, there is an excellent book available: *The Dog Food Book* by Nan Weitzman and Ross Becker can be ordered by calling 800/968-1738.

The Orthopedic Foundation for Animals (OFA) is a registry service that evaluates X-rays of your dog's hips to determine if he has hip dysplasia. For more information, write to the OFA or ask your veterinarian.

The Canine Eye Registration Inc. (CERF) registers your dog as having no hereditary eye disorders. The forms and examination must be obtained from a canine opthamologist. Write to CERF or contact your veterinarian for more information. Local breed clubs often offer eye clinics.

If you're not sure what an organization does, write for details.

Action 81 Inc
[stop pet theft]
Rt 3 Box 6000
Berryville VA 22611
703/ 955-1278

American Health Insurance Agency
PO Box 2657
Danbury CT 06813-2567
203/ 790-8980

American Pet Care Assoc
[pet health insurance]
54 W Hubbard St #400
Chicago IL 60610
312/321-1126
800/538-7387

American Temperament Test Society
PO Box 397
Fenton MO 63026
314/ 225-5346

Animal & Plant Health Insp Service
APHIS
[transportation tips, pamphlet]
6505 Belcrest Rd, Rm 613
Hyattsville MD 20782

Animal Health Foundation
pet CPR & first aid provider certf
PO Box 1527
Philadelphia PA 19105
215/521-5981
215/521-5985

Border Collie Eye Committee
Ed Gebauer
11216 Handlebar Rd
Reston VA 22091
703/476-0913

Breeders Action Board, Inc
Centralized Tattoo Registry
  Information Center
Betty Milea, Sec
26678 Palomino
Warren MI 48089
313/ 754-1249
313/ 285-1822

Canine Eye Registration Inc [CERF]
Veterinary Medical Data Program
South Campus Courts, Bldg C
Purdue Universtiy
West Lafayette IN 47907
317/ 494-8179

Cornell University
programs in professional educ
[animal helath programs]
School of Cont Educ & Summer Prog
B12 Ives Hall
Ithaca NY 14853-3901
607/255-7529
607/255-8942

DO-IT
[promote air-travel safety for dogs]
Bud Brownhill, Intern'l Chairman
2147 Avon Circle
Anaheim CA 92804
714/ 776-9970

DO-IT
promote air-travel safety for dogs/
Larry Beauchamp, Canadian Rep
RR 2
Lakeside ONT
Canada N0M 2G0

DO-IT
promote air-travel safety for dogs/
JoAnn Odegaard, Eastern US Rep
34 Gayboy Ct
Middleton NJ 08270

DO-IT
promote air-travel safety for dogs/
Edie Bishop, Western US Rep
3322 Gondar Ave
Long Beach CA 90808

DVM Insurance Agency
[health insur for your pet]
4175 E LaPalma Ave #100
Anaheim CA 92807-9903
800/USA-PETS

Find-A-Pet
[tattoo registry]
PO Box 691170
San Antonio TX 78269-1170
512/ 698-3441

Hemopet
W Jean Dodds, DVM
[national animal blood bank]
938 Stamford St
Santa Monica CA 90403
213/ 828-4804
213/ 828-8251

Herds Merchant Seman
artificial insemination/
7 N 330 Dunham Rd
Elgin IL 60120
708/ 741-1444

I D Pet Inc
tattoo service/
74 Hoyt St
Darien CT 06820
203/ 327-3157

International Canine Genetics [ICG]
[freeze, ship or store semen]
271 Great Valley Parkway
Malvern PA 19355
800/ 248-8099

International Canine Semen Bank, Inc
2611 W Northern Ave
Phoenix AZ 85051
602/ 995-0460

International Veterinary Acupuncture
  Society, The
Dr Meredith L Snyder
2140 Conestoga Rd
Chester Springs PA 19425
610/ 827-7245

K-9 Carts
[carts to support dogs who are crippled]
532 Newtown Rd
Berwyn PA 19312
610/ 644-6624

Mortality Insurance For Titled Dogs
Competitive Dogs
PO Box 12314
Silver Spring MD 20908-0314
800/ 767-3647

National Animal Poison Control Center
College of Veterinary Medicinetion Center
University of Illinois
2001 S Linclon Ave
Urbana IL 61801
800/ 548-2423
$25 per case

National Dog Registry
[tattoo registry]
Box 116
Woodstock NY 12498
800/ 637-3647

National Pet Disaster Fund
210 Walnut St
Harrisburg PA 17101

National Pet Protect Netwrk [CMI]
Katherine Wallies
PO Box 178922
San Diego CA 92177
619/483-5621

National Pet Protect Ntwrk
Pet Protection & Recovery
PO Box 50
Milford MA 01757
508/533-5520; 203/379-7843

Orthopedic Foundation for Animals Inc
[OFA]
University Missouri-Columbia
817 Virginia Ave
Columbia MO 65201
314/ 442-0418

Partners in Education,
Training and Sharing [PETS]
Susan Daniels
RR#6 Box 308A
Tunkhannock PA 18657
717/ 836-2753

PAWS
care for pets of AIDS victims/
PO Box 460489
San Francisco CA 94146-0489
415/ 824-4040

PAWS/LA
care for pets of AIDS victims/
8272 Sunset Blvd
W Hollywood CA 90046
213/ 650-PAWS

PAWS/Pets are Wonderful Support
Rex Yale
[cares for pets of AIDS patients]
1278 University, Box 178
San Diego CA 92103

Pet Health Campaign
[free public service tapes]
Sharon Stephen
Smith-Kline Beecham
 Animal Health
800/ 866-5210 X2464

Pet Loss and Human Bereavement
Judith A Pulse
8350 Broadmoor Rd
Mentor OH 44060
216/ 942-2594

PETS - Washington DC
[care for pets of AIDS victims]
 1747 Connecticut Ave NW
Washington DC 20009
202/ 234-PETS

POWARS, Inc
[care for pets of AIDS victims]
PO Box 1116
 Madison Square Sta
 New York NY 10159
 212/ 744-0842

Progressive Retinal Atrophy
 Research Fund
PO Box 15095
San Francisco CA 94115

Spayed Club, The
[dedicated to reducing pet
overpopulation]
PO Box 1145
Frazer PA 19355
610/275-7486

Tattoo-A-Pet
Emmons Ave Dept 1625
Brooklyn NY 11235
800/ 828-8667

Tellington Touches
[touch method for dogs]
TTEAM Office
PO Box 3793
Santa Fe NM 87501
505/ 455-2945

Temperament Test Associates
 of Canada, Inc
Sandie Bingley
Box 149
St Davids ONT
Canada L0S 1P0
416/ 468-3911
416/ 262-4682

Therapy Dogs Inc
[uses dogs as therapy for people]
Ann Butrick
2416 East Fox Farm Rd
Cheyenne, WY 82007
307/ 638-3223

Therapy Dogs International
[dogs used as therapy for people]
Ann Lettis
91 Wiman Ave
Staten Island NY 10308
718/ 317-5804

US Temperament Testing Assoc
William Burrell
PO Box 357
Sudbury MA 01776

Veterinary Pet Insurance
4175 E La Palma Ave #100
Anaheim CA 92807-1846
800/VPI-PETS; 800/USA-PETS

This chapter covers dog-show-related services. It offers photographers that specialize in dog shows, entry services, as well as dog show superintendents.

If you are interested in learning about the dog shows in your area, either to enter your dog or to attend dog shows, write to the superintendents nearest to you and request that your name be included on their mailing lists. Each superintendent will mail you flyers for the shows they sponsor. Dog show superintendents usually cover a specific geographical area. Some dog show superintendents sell ribbons for dog shows.

A match show is more or less a practice show that is conducted the same way as a point show and is sponsored by a local dog club. People will use a match show to practice with their dogs and to see how their dogs measure up against competition. You can pre-enter some of the match shows and almost all of them allow you to enter the morning of the show; however, you must pre-enter point shows. Generally, the rare-breed clubs use the match shows as their point shows.

There are a number of publications that list match shows, or you can contact a local dog club—either breed or obedience. Keep in mind that there are different types of match shows. Some allow mixed breeds to enter in obedience competitions while others do not.

CANINE SHOW SERVICES

Canine Show Services
RR 2 Maple Ave
West Brantford ONT
Canada N3T 5L5

DOG-SHOW-ENTRY SERVICES

Entries on Time, Inc
PO Box 431
Oregon City OR 97045
800/992-8955; FAX 503/650-4864

R & R Dog Show Entry Services
PO Box 4658
Federal Way WA 98063
206/547-1982

PHOTOGRAPHERS

Allen, Luke
4735 Hatchert Rd
San Angelo TX 76903
915/653-4135

Alverson, Diana
PO Box 5430
Fairlawn OH 44334
216/668-2002

Ashbey Photography, Inc
PO Box 249
Gilbert PA 18331
215/681-4968

Backstage Photo
Leslie Simis
5241 N Halifax Rd
Temple City CA 91780
818/ 350-4922

Bergman, Rich & Susan
11545 Wildcat Cyn Rd
Lakeside CA 92040
619/443-5688

Booth Photography, Inc
PO Box 308
Willianston MI 48895
517/655-4081

Callea Photo, Meg & Jim
E 200 Tramac Pl
Shelton WA 98584
206/426-2172

Cott, Wayne
PO Box 5260
Pueblo CO 81002
719/542-7007

Digiacomo, Tom
PO Box 146
Williston Park NY 11596
516/254-3686

Edwards, Jean C
RR #8 Box 36
Bridgeton NJ 08302
609/451-5207

Fox & Cook Photo
PO Box 1840
Aptos CA 95001-1840
408/688-7508

Graham, Inc, Earl
1908 S Ridge Ave Box 86
Kannapolis NC 28082
704/932-6159

Harkins, Bruce
3557 Centennial LN
Ellicot City MD 21043
410/461-3557

Holloway, Vicki
2525 Thayer Ct
Riversisde CA 92507
714/682-3164

Klein, Stephen
150-15 79th Ave
Flushing NY 11367

Kohler & Associates, Bill
2202 W Edgemont Ave
Phoenix AZ 85009
602/271-9953

Lindemaier, Carl
11850 SW Boones Ferry
Portland OR 97219
503/245-9341

Ludwig, Joan
1113 N Wetherly Dr
Hollywood CA 90069
213/276-9412

McNealy, Cheri
2913 Candleberry Wy
Fairfield CA 94533
707/429-3730

Meyer, Bill
PO Box 20618
St Louis MO 63139
314/647-5397

Mikron Photography
RR #2
Innisfail AB Canada TOM 1AO
403/227-4870

Mitchell, Mike
8915 River Valley Ct
Santee CA 92071
619/449-5421

Nugent, Sara
9002 Elsie Ln
Houston TX 77064

Pegini
Peggy Hemus
711 Glen Echo Ln
Houston TX 77024
713/461-3520

Perlmutter, Michele
RD 1 Box 279
Ghent NY 12075
518/392-9320

Petrulis, Don
PO Box 760
Granbury TX 76048

Rinehart, Joe
2301 Madera Dr
Sierra Vista AZ 85635
602/458-7742

Roberts, Lewis D
PO Box 4658
Federal Way WA 98063
206/839-1448

Robyn, Richard
2207 Parmer Ln
Austin TX 78727
512/835-9539

Ross, Steve
Box 1145
Chehalis WA 98532
206/864-4462

Rubin, Eddie
PO Box 24621
Los Angeles CA 90024
213/553-2249

Seltzer, Lloyd
RR 1 Box 52
Stewartsville NJ 08886
201/859-0151

Sequel, Ltd
RT 1 Box 62-C
Logansport LA 71049
318/858-3430

Sosa, Luis F
PO Box 8467
New Orleans LA 70182
504/244-8383

Tatham, Chuck
Box 268
Munsonville NH 03457
603/847-9040

Yuhl, Missy
14533 Tyler St
Sylmar CA 91342-2823
818/362-6767

DOG SHOW SUPERINTENDENTS

Antypas, William G
PO Box 7131
Pasadena CA 91109

Bradshaw, Jack
PO Box 7303
Los Angeles CA 90022

Brown, Margery
2242 London Ave
Redding CA 96001

Brown, Norman E
PO Box 2566
Spokane WA 99220

Crowe, Thomas J
PO Box 22107
Greensboro NC 27420

Houser, Helen
PO Box 420
Quakertown PA 18951

McNulty, Eileen
1745 Rt 78
Jana Center NY 14082-9610

Mathews, Ace H
PO Box 06150
Portland OR 97206

Onofrio, Jack
PO Box 25764
Oklahoma City OK 73125

Rau Enterprises, Jim
PO Box 6898
Reading PA 19611
800/523-8282

Reed, Robert
265-H Reservation Rd # 321
Marina CA 93933

Roberts, B Jeannie
PO Box 4658
Federal Way WA 98063

Saldivar, Elaine
4343 1/2 Burns Ave
Los Angeles CA 90029

Sleeper, Kenneth A
PO Box 828
Auburn IN 46706

Wilson, Nancy
8307 E Cameback Rd
Scottsville AZ 85251

TROPHIES

Camelot Specialties, Inc
1018 Lunt
Schaumburg IL 60193
708/893-8827; 708/893-8831

Purina Show & Field Material
PO Box 21982
Greensboro NC 27420
800/648-3022

Rau Enterprises, Jim
[dog show ribbons]
PO Box 6898
Reading PA 19611
800/523-8282

Rayco Dog Show Ribbons
1172 N Cowiche Rd
Tieton WA 98947
509/678-5060

Steinman Ribbon Co
1000 Lambs Bridge
S Fork PA 15956
800/648-3022

If the main product line of the supply catalog is not obvious and is intended for a specific type of product, the type of catalog is stated after the name of the company. For example:

Sea Meadow Products Company

K-9 Equipment

This tells you that the equipment used for police K-9, Schutzhund, etc., is the main line of this company. If the specific line is not obvious or mentioned on the second line, then it is a general catalog with a wide range of products.

A L C Inovators Inc
May Gillio
[diet supplements]
PO Box 2280
Darien CT 06820-0280
203/877-8526; FAX 203/877-9743

A R N Indus
A J AcAdoo
[general supplies]
907 Virginia St
Sioux City IA 51105
712/252-5685

ASU Pet Supplies
1620 S Lewis St
Anaheim CA 92805
800/283-4PET

Aaronco
[general supplies]
248 E 34th St
New York NY 10016
212/685-3776

Aben Engraving
Ben Goodman
[novelty items]
1581 Springfield Ave
Maplewood NJ 07040
201/761-1104

Acco Chain & Lifting Prod Div
Donna Williams
[leashes & collars]
76 Acco Dr
PO Box 792
York PA 17405
717/741-4863

Adams, John Q & Assoc, Inc
John Quincy Adams
[grooming supplies]
4004 Hickory Ave
Baltimore MD 21211
301/889-9072

Adanac Sled & Equipment
[dog sled equip]
4108 Hwy 93 N
Kalispell MT 59901
406/ 752-2929

Add-En-On Kennels
112 Pond Rd
Honeoye Falls NY 14472
716/ 624-1155

Adirondack Dog Sled Mfg
Marshall Fish
[dog sleds only, must pick up]
West Port NY 12993
518/ 962-4897

Agreeable Friends
  Antiques and Collectibles
PO Box 727
Gwynedd Valley PA 19437
215/ 646-8068

Airborne Custom Crates
PO Box 9011
Airport Station
Los Angeles CA 90009
213/ 649-3630

All West Pet Supply Co
4200 Monroe St
PO Box 16565
Denver CO 80216
800/748-2038

Allen Industrial Prod
[flea & tick prod]
3235 NW 37th St
Miami FL 33142
305/633-0627

Allerpet
[health products]
PO Box 1076
Lenox Hill Station
New York NY 10021
212/ 861-1134

Alpine Publications
[books]
225 S Madison Ave
Loveland CO 80537
303/ 667-2017

American Leather Specialties
87 34th St
Brooklyn NY 11232
718/ 965-3900

American Medical Indus
Dan Anderson
[vet supplies]
PO Box 725
Highland Park IL 60035-0725
708/433-2442

American Veterinary
  Identification Devices Inc
3179 Hammer #5
Norco CA 91760

Amherest/Moses Corp
[ice and water pet beds]
101-C Cumming Indust'l Pk Dr
Cumming GA 30130
800/ 621-6686

Anatomical Chart Co
[collectibles]
8221 Kimball Ave
Skokie IL 60076-2956
800/ 621-7500

Anderson Pet Memorials
[burial]
207 Park Ave
Carrollton KY 41008
502/ 732-5860

Andis Co
Jack Miller
[grooming supplies]
1718 Layaro Ave
Racine WI 53404
414/634-3356

Andoe, Inc
Anne Dobelle
[novelty items]
PO Box 1727
New City NY 10956
914/638-6915

Animal Town
A Brockmire
[general supplies]
1035 Pioneer Way #160
El Cajon CA 92020
619/441-8503

Animals by Popowitz
1601 W 131 St
Burnsville MN 55337
612/ 890-2112

Aqua Pet, Windborne Prod
Char Banoch
[pet life jackets]
114 Lincoln Dr
Sausalito CA 94965
415/331-3542

Arner Publications Inc
[books]
100 Bouck St
Rome NY 13440
315/ 339-2033

Art Studio Workshop
[dog rubber stamps]
518 Schilling
Forest Lake MN 55025

Artistic Creations
Mary M Livermore
[collectibles]
723 S Main
Princeton IN 47670
812/386-6767

Artistics in Miniature
Parker Dist Co of N A Inc
[novelty items]
410 43rd St W #A
Bradentondy FL 34209-2901

Ashland Barns
Jay Wallace
[general supplies]
990 Butler Creek Rd
Ashland OR 97520
503/488-1541

Atlantic Feed Supplements
Sylvia Boudreau
[supplies]
Richmond Indust Park
Louisdale
Canada BOE 1VO
902/345-2973

AverGraphics
[gifts]
PO Box 782
Sandusky OH 44870
419/ 625-8473

B & B Leather Co
Bob Balentine
[general supplies]
5518 Nevins Rd
Charlotte NC 28269
704/598-9080

B Brent Atwater Enter
B Brent
[general supplies]
PO Box 475
Southern Pines NC 28388-0475
919/723-8707; FAX 919/723-2522

B Elegant Prod
Hazel Trout
[general supplies]
1733 Victory Blvd
Glendale CA 91201
818/247-5252

BHB Veterinary Supply
L W Boyer, DVM
7117 S Westnedge
Portage MI 49002
800/253-0899; 800/632-9284

B J Miller Co
[pet bed, mattress, pillow &
bedding ensemble]
505 Forest Home Dr
Francis Creek WI 54214
414/684-3677

B L Prod
1106 Kenmore Ave
Buffalo NY 14216
800/ 465-5494
FAX 716/ 874-3774

Bach Remedies
[health aids]
644 Merrick Rd
Lynbrook NY 11563
516/ 593-2206

Bardwyn & Associates
Doug McLennan
[general supplies]
PO Box 5044
Westport CT 06881-5044
203/454-4300

Bargain Bones
Wayne Cohen
[toys]
160 Belmont Ave
Garfield NJ 07026
210/478-6903

Bark Ave Ltd
Marsha Feltingoff
[general supplies]
300 E 40th St #26A
New York NY 10016
212/949-0918

Barkleigh Publications
6 State St #113
Mechanicsburg PA 17055-7934

Baron Enterprises
Joel A Yagoda
[pet beds]
PO Box 8413
Coral Springs FL 33065
407/451-0721

Basilia Dobes
Guido Garcia
[novelty items]
27 Forest Ave
Lake Grove NY 11755
516/737-1484

Bass Kennel Equipment
PO Box 352
Monett MO 65708
800/ 798-0150

Bean, Inc
[pet deodorizer]
G GPO Drawer 638
Brunswick ME 04011
207/ 729-3708

BenePet Pet Care Prod
Pamela M Evans
[general supplies]
PO Box 8111
St Joseph MO 64506
800/825-0341; FAX 816/279-4725

Berolina Imports
118 NE 1st Ave
Hallandale FL 33009
305/ 456-0202

Best Friend Prod
Willy Ephraim
[general supplies]
826 N Easton Rd
Doylestown PA 18901
215/348-8700

Best N Show Pet Prod
M Harris
[general supplies]
PO Box 25502
Dallas TX 75225
214/783-8219

Bibliography of the Dog
[rare & out-of-print books]
PO Box 118
Churubusco NY 12923
514/ 827-2717

Bickmore Inc
P Ottowitz
[health aids]
Box 279
Hudson MA 01749
617/562-9172

Big Red Search Supplies
[search & rescue supplies]
12309 SE 164th
Renton WA 98058
206/ 255-6852

Bio Care
Tom Austin
[grooming supplies]
1976 Hartog Dr
San Jose CA 95131-2212

Bio Zyme Enterprises
Dennis Johnson
[food supplements]
1231 Alabama
St Joseph MO 64504

Biologic Pet
Mrs E M Roseig
[general supplies]
853 N Main St
Spring Valley NY 10977
914/354-2440

Birdsong
Marie Wooten
[grooming supplies]
PO Box 643
Coronado CA 92118
619/435-8892

Black Ice
[dog sled equipment]
11225 County Rd 20
Delano MN 55328

Black Sheep
[pets earth bed]
3220 W Gentry Pkwy
Tyler TX 75702
800/ 527-6762

Blue Ribbons, Inc
2475 Bellmore Ave
Bellmore NY 11710
516/ 785-0604

Boehringer Ingelheim Animal Health Inc
[flea & tick control prod]
2621 N Belt Hwy
St Joseph MO 64506-2002
800/821-7476; FAX 816/233-4767

Bombus Gifts
[dog rubber stamps]
121st Ave
Fennville MI 49408
616/ 543-4366

Bone I Fied Greetings
Deanna Atzinger
[novelty items]
3713 Millerton Ave
Pittsburg PA 15212
412/766-2338

Bone-Anza Specialities
Joan Tyrrell
[collectibles]
1313 SE 125 Ave
Vancouver WA 98684
206/892-0631

Books In Motion
[books on cassette tapes]
E 9212 Montgomery
Spokane WA 99206

Booth Studios, Rita
[dog rubber stamps]
732 Pierce
Milton-Freewater OR 97862-12435

Border Collies in Actiion
Dan & Geri Byrne
[gift items for stockdog owner]
Rte 2 Box 54D
Tulelake CA 96134
916/664-5871

Border Corner
Randy & Mary Ann Cummings
2317 Woodruff Ln
Marysville CA 95901
916/742-0202

Borwick Innovations, Inc
[pet doors]
PO Box 30345
Santa Barbara CA 93130
800/ 365-5657

Boulder Bluff, Inc
Charles Ridener
[sheepherding whistles]
1107 Young Ridge Rd
Greenwood AR 72936
501/996-4007

Boulder Brass Works, Inc
Bill Ray
[ID tags]
5421 Western Ave
Boulder CO 80301
303/443-3142

Boundary Waters Catalog, The
[wolf & wildlife items]
800/223-6565

Bows by Laura Lynne
Laura Lynne Garcia
[general supplies]
34 Mineral Spring
Passaic NJ 07055
201/473-0344

Bowsers
Trisha Hailperin
[gift items]
1301 Cool Spring Rd
Raleigh NC 27614
919/846-3756

Breakthrough Pubs Inc
[books]
Millwood NY 10546
800/ 824-5000

Breeders Equip Co
Dr Alfred Kissileff
[general supplies]
PO Box 177
Flourtown PA 19031
215/233-0799

Briarwood
609 Valley Bridge Rd
Chattanooga TN 37415
615/ 870-3938

Buck Stop Lure Co Inc
Phyllis Garbow
[general supplies]
3600 Grow Rd
Stanton MI 48888
517/762-5091

Caddis Manufacturing
[cedar-filled dog bed]
1040 Alpine Ave
McMinnivlle OR 97128
800/ 422-3347

Cal-Formed Plastics
[dog houses]
2050 E 48th St
Los Angeles CA 90058
800/ 772-7723

Calacritter Designs
Leslie Falteisek
[dog rubber stamps]
623 1/2 La Bore Rd
Little Canada MN 55117
612/483-0380

Campbell, William E
[pet behavior pamphlets/
puppy info pack]
PO Box 1658
Grants Pass OR 97526
503/476-5775; FAX 503/476-5523

Camelot Collectibles
[figurines, books, ephemera]
PO Box 148
Phillipsburg NJ 08865
908/ 454-3814

Camp 7 Sport Chalet
[back packs for dogs]
920 Foothill Blvd
LaCanada CA 91011
818/ 790-9800

Campbell Craft
[heirloom bed]
7101 Lavender Ln
Knoxville TN 37921
800/ 452-PETS

Canine Caterers
1305 Goshen Pkwy
West Chester PA 19380
610/696-6300; 800/228-3666

Canine Cushion Co
2936 Canton Rd
Marietta, GA 30066
800/ 743-6064
404/ 426-7015

Canine Keepsakes
Cheryl Robinson
14 Fawn Lake Rd
Stockholm NY 07460

Canine-Care-A-Van
[supplies for mobile animal units]
PO Box 6022
Thousand Oaks CA 91359
818/ 780-1955

Canvasback Training Equip Ltd
[dog, cat, horse supplies]
Box 398
Silkirk MAN
Canada R1A 2B3

Carriage Works, The
[carts]
707 South 5th
Klamath Falls OR 97601
503/ 882-0700

Cardinal Labs Inc
[general supplies]
710 S Ayon Ave
Azusa CA 91702
818/969-3797; FAX 818/969-5183

Care A Lot
Kimberly Young
[general supplies]
1617 Diamond Springs Rd
Virginia Beach VA 23455

Carol Butcher
[rare & out-of-print books]
3955 New Rd
Youngstown OH 44515
216/793-6832

Carson Tanner
[agility items, clothing, etc]
PO Box 244
Uwchland PA 19480
610/ 458-0150

Cat Nap
[heated cushions]
3020 Bridgeway #177
Sausalito CA 94965
415/ 331-5293

Cattus Ltd
David B Covey
[supplies]
RT 21 Box 1165
Conroe TX 77301
409/760-2287

Cedar River Labs
Bruce E Dietrich, DVM
[general supplies]
PO Box 1462
Mason City IA 50401
515/228-2212

Cedar-al Prod
[natural flea control prod]
RT 1 Box 6
Clallam Bay WA 98326

Central Florida Wire Prod Inc
Bill Mueller
[exercise pens]
9809 SE 176th Ct {RT 3}
Oklawaha FL 32179
904/288-2503

Central Metal Prod Inc
Sam Rush
[crates]
PO Box 396
Windfall IN 46076
317/945-7677

Charles Press
[books]
PO Box 15715
Philadelphia PA 19103
215/ 925-3995

Chem I Matic Inc
L C Cunningham
[supplies]
PO Box 920706
Houston TX 77292
713/686-1460

Cherish A Balls
Carolyn K Wolfe
[collectibles]
706 S Moss St
Leesburg FL 32748
904/787-8815

Cherished Pet Caskets
1321 NE 173rd St
North Miami Beach FL 33162
800/382-9619

Cherrybrook
PO Box 15 Rt 57
Broadway NJ 08808
201/ 689-7979

Childress & Co Pet Caskets
PO Box 35
Afton VA 22920
703/949-0527

Chimeara Wilkinson Ent
Kathy Wilkinson
[collectibles]
PO Box 33
Culbertson NE 69024
800/426-1324

Chipp
Paul Winston
[novelty items]
342 Madison Ave
New York NY 10173
212/687-0850

Chuck A Poo
[canine waste disposal equip]
PO Box 5357
Glendale CA 91221

City Dog Designed Co
[cool spot waterbed]
533 W 112 St #5-B
New York NY 10025
800/ CITY-DOG

City Dog Designed Co, Inc
[canine outerwear]
323 S Carlise St
Allentown PA 18103
215/433-5539; 215/433-5587

Clanin, Karen
[dog artwork]
9895 Santa Clara Ave
Atascadero CA 93422
905/466-3775

Clark Cages, Inc
[crates]
PO Box 555
North Bay ONT
Canada P18 1H0
705/ 474-8303

Classic Prod
Roz Migatz
[supplies]
1451 Vanguard Dr
Oxnard CA 93033
805/487-6227

Colby's Noiseless Treadmills
39 Pine Hill Rd
Newburyport MA 01950
508/ 462-9810

Comfortable Critters
[heated/cooled bed]
1321 Elysian Way NW
Atlanta GA 30327
404/ 352-3092

Companion Pet
5345 Bridge Rd
McNaughton WI 54543
800/442-7387

Complete Dog Story, The
[out-of-print books]
662 Franklin Ave #254
Garden City NY 11503
516/883-3262

Conagra Pet Prod
Trinette Bartman
[general supplies]
One Central Park Piz #700
Omaha NE 68102
402/449-7053

Concord Pet Prod
Lou Conner
[general supplies]
45 Boxwood Dr
Kings Park NY 11754
516/724-7666

Corgi Gift Shop, The
Ret 7 South Main St
Lanesboro MA 01237

Coulston Prod
[flea & tick prod]
PO Box 30
Easton PA 18044-0030

Country Pet Supply
5140 W Clifton St
Tampa Fl 33634-8035
813/889-7161; 800/277-PETS

Custom Marketing
3340 Land Dr
Fort Wayne IN 46809
800/967-7387

DJL Design Group
[breed-specific doghouses]
1420 Sherwood Rd
Linden NJ 07036
201/925-8220; 201/925-0647

Dabney Herbs
[natural flea-control prod]
Box 22061
Louisville KY 40222

Dandy Prod Co
[pooper scoopers]
PO Box 124
Hwy 23 West
Ripon WI 54971

DeckSlider of Florida
771 110th Ave N
Naples FL 33963
800/ 782-1474

Denlingers Publishers
[books]
Box 76
Fairvax VA 22030

Designs by Gary Beeber
[stationery]
322 E 94th St 3E
New York NY 10128
800/ 543-3470

Diamond Enter & Book Pubs
Box 537
Alexandria Bay NY 13607
613/ 475-1771

Direct Book Service
[in- & out-of-print books,
rare books, free book-
review service]
PO Box 3073
Wenatchee WA 98801
800/ 776-2665; FAX 509/ 662-7233

Dirty Business Deals, Inc
[canine waste disposal equip]
PO Box 1887
Bridgehampton NY 11932
516/537-2180

Discount Doctor
[pet supplies]
4626 Dahlman
PO Box 7086
Omaha NE 68107
800/ 874-2233

Disigner Doggie Ltd
[diapers for incontinent dogs]
PO Box 159
Browns Valley CA 95918
916/749-9310; FAX 916/749-0211
800/354-1064

Distinguished Animal Portraits
Barbara Walker
RT 2, Box 925-A
Adkins TX 78101
512/947-3767

Dog Breed Chart
Quaker Professional Service
Cycle Dog Chart
585 Hawthorne Ct
Galesvury IL 61401

Dog Guard
[electronic fence]
318 Delaware Ave
Main Square Plaza
Delmar NY 12054
518/439-0495

Dog House, The
[sheepdog supplies]
RT 1 Box 14A
Crawford TX 76638
817/486-2500

Dog Ink
Kathy Darling
46 Cooper Ln
Larchmont NY 10538
914/ 834-9029

Dog Notepaper
PO Box 974
Dover NJ 07801
201/ 361-8060

Dog Watch Hidden Fence Sys
[electronic fence]
13 Pelham Island Rd
Wayland MA 01778
508/358-2200

Dog-Gone Computers
[software]
251 Jackson Ave
Syosset NY 11791
516/ 921-1351

Dog-Tex
ConChemCo, Inc
[removes & deodorizes
liquid pet stains]
400 N Ashland
Chicago IL 60622

Doggone Books
[out of print]
2215 Motor Pkwy
Ronkonkoma NY 11779
516/ 981-5057

Doggone Pet Prod
15009 Manchester Rd #136
Ballwin MO 63011
314/ 576-9265

Dogloo Inc
[dog houses]
22845 NE 8th #314
Redmond WA 98053
206/ 391-3053

Dogloo
[pet bed]
1160 California Ave
Corona CA 91719
714/ 279-9560

Dogonit
PO Box 3376
Walnut Creek CA 94598
415/ 934-7167

Dogs Outfitter, The
1 Maplewood Dr
PO Box 2010
Hazleton PA 18201
717/384-5555

Dolt USA
[back packs for dogs]
2421 S 34th Pl
Tucson AZ 85713
800/ 367-3658
602/ 745-0024

Drake Design, Inc
[dog houses]
1700 Oak
Kansas City MO 64108
800/ 752- 5234

E-Z Post
[grooming products]
15122 Bellflower Blvd
Bellflower CA 90706

ERI Bookstore, Inc
[search & rescue pubs/videos]
4537 Foxhall Dr NE
Olympia WA 98506
206/491-7785; FAX 206/493-0949
509/782-4832

Eagle Creek Backpackers
REI Corp
[back packs for dogs]
1525 11th Ave
Seattle WA 98122
800/ 426-4840

EcoSafe Prod
PO Box 1177
St Augustine FL 32085
904/ 824-5884

Eliz Gilbert
[paints pets on fanny packs]
Ramblewood Farm
RD 8
York PA 17401

Elkins Kennel Manufacturing
490 Osage St
Denver CO 80204
303/ 893-9720

Embossing Arts
PO Box 626
Sweet Home OR 97386

Emerg Response Pubs
[SAR pubs/videos]
79 Exeter Rd
Okehampton
Devon England EX20 1QF
0837 53322

Engenuity Designs, Inc
[canine waste disposal equip]
10409 Nesbitt Ave
Bloomington MN 55437
612/884 1116

Epona Books
[rare]
302 Ferguson St
Atlanta GA 30307
404/ 222-9648

Esper's Canine Prod
PO Box 968
Oroville CA 95965
916/ 533-3640

Everlasting Stone Prod Co
[trophies, caskets, urns]
PO Box 995
Barre VT 05641
802/ 454-1050

Ewephoric Country Designs
14406 Mausbach Ave
Bakersfield CA 93312
805/ 589-7091

Explorer Dog Trailers of Ohio, Inc
[vehicle accessories]
4825 Columbus-Lancaster
Carroll OH 43112
614/ 756-7387

F O Berg Co
Bill Gabrio
[pet houses]
E 410 Trent Ave
Spokane WA 99202
509/624-8921

Faithful Friend Pet Caskets/Vaults
Div of McCord Prod Inc
1135 N Main St
PO Box 646
Bowling Green OH 43402
419/ 352-3691

Fazo Corp Prod Inc
[dog books]
PO Box 69007
Laval QUE
Canada H7X 3M2

Feed & Seed Center
5329 W Crenshaw St
Tampa FL 33634
813/884-6055; 800/969-6055

Flexi-Mat Corp
[pet beds]
2244 S Western Ave
Chicago IL 60608
312/ 376-5500

Foster & Smith
[includes vet supplies]
509 Shepard St
Rhinelander WI 54501
800/ 826-7206

Four-M Enterprises
[rare books]
1280 Pacific
Union City CA 94587
800/487-9867
FAX 510/489-8331

Free Spirit Sled Dog Outfitter
Bob & Pat Lugo
RR 3 Box 179
Malaca MN 56353
800/ 484-3647
612/ 983-3785

Freedom Fence
[electronic fence]
163 River Rd
North Adams MA 01247
413/662-2119

Fritz Pet Prod
230 Sam Houston
Mesquite TX 75149
214/ 285-5471

Frostline
[back packs for dogs]
2512 W Independent Ave
Grand Junction CO 81505
303/ 241-0155

Frosty Hill Farm
Beth Edge
[harness supplier]
4480 Hendershot NW
Grand Rapids MI 49504
616/ 784-2919

Future Tech Inc
[electronic fence]
2622 Billingsley Rd
Columbus OH 43235
614/798-0161

Garden State Pet Supplies
69 William St
Belleville NJ 07109
201/751-1416; FAX 201/751-0180

Gehringer, Pam
[gifts in wood]
86 Noble St
Kutztown PA 19530
610/683-7890

Gem-Line
[canine waste disposal equip]
PO Box 768
Setauket NY 11733
516/689-5770

General Cage Corp
238 N 29th St
Elwood IN 46036
317/ 552-5039; FAX 317/ 552-6962

General Store Pub House, Inc
#1 Main St
Burnstown ONT
Canada K0J 1G0
613/ 432-7697

George's Dog Chalet
20947 Avenue 245
Lindsay CA 93247
209/ 562-4460

Glassman Pet Casket Co
[caskets & urns]
41-15 Astoria Blvd
Long Island City NY 11105
718/274-5703

Gorman Enterprises
[canine waste disposal equip]
1409 Oakwood Dr
Modesto CA 95350-4850

Gray Cats
PO Box 3303
New York NY 10185

Gumbo Graphics
90 N Lawrence
Eugene OR 97401

Gun Dog House Door
RR 1
Sabin MN 56580
218/ 789-7128

Hale Security Pet Door
Bill Hale
5622 N 52nd Ave #4
Glendale AZ 85301
800/888-8914; FAX 602/242-8854

Handy Home Prod
[dog houses]
PO Box 548
Walled Lake MI 48390
800/ 221-1849

Happiness Is...
Paw Prints from the Gentry
Helen Gentry
[decals & bumperstickers]
11521 Marino Ave
Everett WA 98204
206/ 355-1011

Harbingers of a New Age
[vegetarian diet info for dogs/cats]
12100 Brighton St
Hayden Lake ID 83835
208/772-7753

Hi Ridge Farm
[sheepdog supplies]
RT 3
Napanee ONT
Canada K7R 3K8
613/ 354-4433

Highland Design Studio
[Border Collie T-shirts, etc.]
PO Box 323
Spencerport NY 14559-0323
716/352-4191

Hoegh Pet Casket
PO Box 311
Gladstone MI 49837-0311

Hoof Prints
[dog/horse/fox prints]
PO Box 1917
Lenox MA 01240-4917
413/637-4334

Hueter Toledo Inc
[canine waste disposal equip]
605 E Center St
Bellevue OH 44811
419/483-5608

Hulme Sporting Goods & Mfg Co
[hunting supplies]
PO Box 670
Paris TN 38242
800/ 843-9637

I'm Stuffed
Beverly Saul
[customized stuffed toy pets]
PO Box 432
Richboro PA 18954
215/322-8946

Ikon Outfitters Ltd
[sleds, backpacks, carting
   weight-pulling etc.]
7597 Latham Rd
Lodi WI 53555
608/ 592-4397

Inkadinkado Inc
[dog rubber stamps]
105 South St
Boston MA 02111

Inn The Doghouse
[dog houses]
PO Box 1648
Chino CA 91710
714/ 465-5747

Innotek
[electronic fence]
605 Landsford Dr
Fort Wayne IN 46825
219/489-1711

Innovative Pet Homes
[solar dog house plans]
PO Box 3576
Springfield MO 65808
417/ 732-2273

Innovative Sports Prod Grp
[leash attaches to belt]
PO Box 262
Hood River OR 97031
509/493-4088

International Gate Devices
[electronic fence]
Folsom Industrial Ctr
101 Sycamore Ave
Folsom PA 19033
800/331-6267

Invisible Fence Co
1525 B Ogden Ave
Downers Grove IL 60515
708/ 505-1092

Invisible Fencing
[electronic fence]
300 Berwyn Pk
Berwyn PA 19312
610/640-9700

Ivory Hound, The
[antique china/porcelain figurines]
Dogarty's
PO Box 244
Troy OH 45373
513/339-2037

J-B Wholesale Pet Supplies
289 Wagaraw Rd
Hawthorne NJ 07506
800/ 526-0388; FAX 201/ 423-1181

J J Prod Inc
Betty James
[general supplies]
PO Box 2396
Capistrano Beach CA 92624
714/493-6410

J & J Supplies
PO Box 1517
Galesburg IL 61402
800/ 642-2050

J M Brady Co, Inc
1361 South St
PO Box 307
Needham MA 02192
800/227-7746; 800/221-1693

J & M Stuart Co
M9 Claychester Dr
St Louis MO 63131
800/ 467-2669
314/ 822-4946

JEM Pet Signs
Jean Moore
41 Ridware Crescent
West Hill Toronto ONT
Canada M1C 3S1
416/284-4867; FAX 416/284-0041

JHP Enterprises
[photo pet urns]
12475 Central Ave
Box 311
Chino CA 91710
714/627-3739

James & Kenneth Publishers
2140 Shattuck Ave #2406
Berkeley CA 94704
510/ 658-8588

Jeffers Vet Supply
1452 Gibson
PO Box 948
West Plains MO 65775
417/ 256-2323

Jefferson State Prod
[dog houses]
PO Box 7778
Kalamath Falls OR 97602
503/ 883-3629

Jemar Kennel Supply
2433 Liberty Grove Rd
Colora MD 21917
301/ 658-6707

Jog-A-Dog
[exercisers]
PO Box 156
Genoa OH 43430
419/ 855-7337

Johnson Pet-Dor, Inc
320 N Graves Ave
Oxnard CA 93030-5134
805/988-4800; FAX 805/988-2400

June Enterprises
[auto seatbelt sys/dogs]
Box 180
1658 Matterson Rd
Errington BC
Canada VOR 1VO
604/248-7345

K-2 Enterprises
[electronic fence]
104 Freeman Ave
Solway NY 13209
315/468-3596

K-9 Sulkys
2406 N Wood Ct
Claremont CA 91711
714/ 621-7511

K-Kollar, The
Klein Design Inc
PO Box 417
Glenshaw PA 15116
412/486-3094; 800/442-5565

K-D Wood Prod
[dog houses]
PO Box 645
Lander Ave
Bingham ME 04920
207/ 672-4333

K-II Enterprises
Keith Tupper
[pet-agree]
PO Box 306
Camillus NY 13031
315/ 468-3596; FAX 315/ 468-0454

K Rais
[rare books]
3901 Conshohocken Ave # 2310
Philadelphia PA 19131

K O S Indus
[canine waste disposal equip]
400 W Dundee
Buffalo Grove IL 60089
708/634-8778

Kanine Kola
Terveen Enterprises, Ltd
[vitamin-enriched beef-
flavored drink]
PO Box 175
Emery SD 57332
800/477-2479

Katgo
[flushable cedar cat litter]
69 North 6th St
Brooklyn NY 11211
718/388-7510

Kathie Comerford Kanine Collectibles
Box 271
Stonybrook NY 11790
516/751-2805

Kay-Nine Designs
[collectibles]
RT 3 Box 78
Cleveland OK 74020
918/243-5932

Kennel Komfort
[dog mats]
5525   19th Ave
Kenosha WI 53140
800/ 558-4040

Kennel Vet Corp
1811 Newbridge
PO Box 835
Bellmore NY 11710
516/ 783-5400; 516/ 783-7516

Kennel-Aire Inc
[dog crates & supplies]
6651 Hwy 7
Minneapolis MN 55426
800/ 346-0134

Khiva Outfitters
[dog-pack equip]
1256C Poplar Ave
Sunnyvale CA 94086-8619

King Books, John K
PO Box 33363
Detroit MI 48232-5363
313/ 961-0622

Konari Outfitters Ltd
[dog sled equipment]
52 Seymour St
PO Box 752
Middlebury VT 05753
802/ 388-7447

Kondos Outfitters
[dog sled equipment]
SR 1 Box 3108
Ely MN 55731
218/ 365-4189

Kuranda USA
[trampoline bed for pets]
1001 Paca Ln
Annapolis MD 21403
800/ 752-5308

L L Bean
[dog beds]
Freeport ME 04033-0001
800/221-4221

L A Stampworks
5432 Cahuenga Blvd Ste B
North Hollywood CA 91601

LaCrosse Stitch Designs
N 1555 Hagen Rd
LaCrosse WI 54601
608/ 788-3785

Lakeshore Artisans, Inc.
PO Box 160
Belgium WI 53004-0160
414/ 285-3160

Lazy Pet Prod
2521 N Loma Ave
El Monte CA 91733-1417
800/622-1288

Lettershop, The
[dog rubber stamps]
Box 3335
Early TX 76803

Linda Coffey
[general supplies]
4244 Linden Hills Blvd
Minneapolis MN 55410
800/448-4738; FAX 612/922-7603

Livingstone
[dog sculptures]
PO Box 5476
Chula Vista CA 91912
619/ 661-1292; 619/ 661-1764

Logee's Greenhouse
[natural flea-control prod]
55 North St
Danielson CT 06239

Long Environmental Systems
PO Box 187
Gambrills MD 21054
301/ 793-0600

Loveland Pet Prod
7160 Industrial Row Dr
Mason OH 45040
800/999-1930

Lucky Dog Equip
18342 Redmond Way
Redmond WA 98052
206/ 881-1781

M & M Training Supplies
Mike M Schragel
2726 Strong St
Highland IN 46322
219/ 923-9454

Maplewood Kennel
Kathy Simonette
[sweaters farm designs]
Star Rt 27
Meadville PA 16335

Marine Bio Prod
[food supplements]
333 W First St
Boston MA 02127
617/ 268-0758

Mark August Collection
Mark E West
[jewelry]
PO Box 782
Cambridge MA 02238
617/876-7753

Marks of Distinction
5442 S Dorchester Ave
Chicago IL 60615

Master Animal Care
PO Box 2010
Hazelton PA 18201-0676
800/ 346-0749

Matthews Mfg Co
8617 Old Hwy 87
Orange TX 77630
409/746-7129

Mel's Custom Harness
Mel Fishback Riley
PO Box 365
Kila MT 59920-0365
406/755-0312

Merion Station Mail Order Co Inc
[fireman alert sign for dogs]
PO Box 6
Merion Station PA 19066-0006

Montana Etc
[dog houses]
PO Box 3704
Great Falls MT 59403
406/ 452-0896

Mountain Ridge Pet Supply
49 Harbor Ave
Nashua NH 03060
603/ 883-9877

Mountain Smith
[dog-pack equip]
West 7th Ave Unit A
Golden CO 80401

Mt Tam Sports
Steve Nash
[1st responder mobile medical
fanny pack]
Box 111
Kentfield CA 94914-0111
415/461-8111

My Pet
[granite memorials]
Box 160
Carlton GA 30627
800/524-3054

Name Service
PO Box 156
Walkersville MD 21793-0156

National Scent Co
PO Box 667
San Jacinto CA 92383
800/ 338-8993

Natural Pet Care Catalog, The
2713 E Madison
Seattle WA 98112
800/962-8266

Nature Impressions
1007 Leneve Pl
El Cerrito CA 94530

New England Serum Co
US Rt 1
Topsfield MA 01983
800/ 637-3786; FAX 508/ 887-8499

Nicholas Garden Nursery
[natural flea-control prod]
1190 N Pacific Hwy
Albany OR 97321-4598

Nordkyn Outfitters
[dog sled supplies]
Box 1023
Graham WA 98338-1023
206/ 847-4128

Northcoast K-9 &
 Leather Equipment
901 Columbus Ave
Sandusky OH 44870
419/ 627-0151; 419/ 929-0909

Northern Hydraulics
[electronic fence]
PO Box 1219
2800 Southcross Dr W
Burnsville MN 55337
612/894-9510

O'Hagin's Inc
[canine waste disposal equip]
PO Box 126
Sebastopol CA 95473-0126
707/823-4762

Odormaster Canada
[grooming supplies]
994 Westport Crescent
Mississauga ONT
Canada L5T 1G1
416/ 671-1010

Omaha Vaccine Co
3030 L St
Omaha NE 68107
402/ 731-9600

Orient Publications, Inc
PO Box 6468
Arlington VA 22206
703/ 671-0645

Original Duke's Dog Fashions, The
12195 SW Douglas
Portland OR 97225
503/626-8184

Orvis Co
[dog nest]
1711 Blue Hills Dr
Roanoke VA 24179
800/ 541-3541

Our Best Friends
79 Albertson Ave
Albertson NY 11507
516/ 742-7400

Ozark Shores Pet Prod
PO Box 101
Windsor MO 65360
816/ 647-5971

Ozelis, Linda P
[Border Collie items]
1866 Albermarle Ave
East Meadow NY 11554
516/794-8644

POCO
Poodle Corral Inc
[collectibles]
3707 Edgewater Dr
Orlando FL 32804
407/298-1945

P T P Marketing
[collectibles]
32 Chruch Drive
E Keswick Leeds
England LS17 9EP
0-937-573080; FAX 0-937-573080

Patrick Communications Ltd
Susan Pearce
[list of hotels accepting pets]
43 Railside Rd
Don Mills ONT
Canada M3A 3L9
416/441-3228; FAX 416/441-3212

Pawmarks
Debbie Burke
[colored elastic bands for dogs]
317 Mill Rd
Oreland PA 19075
215/887-1770

Penn Herb Co
[natural flea-control prod]
603 North 2nd St
Philadelphia PA 19123-3098

Pet Alert
[safety devices]
7057 Lanewood Ave #305
Los Angeles CA 90028-7011

Pet Book Shop, The
PO Box 507
Oyster Bay NY 11771
516/922-1169

Pet Castle Co
PO Box 1059
Brownwood TX 76804
800/ 351-1363

Pet Doors USA
4523 30th St W
Bradenton FL 34207
813/ 753-7492

Pet Feeding Dishes
PO Box 1246
Arlington TX 76004-1246
817/467-5116; FAX 817/472-9810

Pet Food Express
PO Box 16370
Rumford RI 02916
401/431-1PET; 800/637-7338

Pet Goods Mfg & Imports
30941 Agoura Rd #310
Westlake Village CA 91361-4618
818/ 889-4768

Pet Groom Prod
Div Veeco Mfg Co
1217 W Washington Blvd
Chicago IL 60607
312/ 666-0902

Pet Heaven
[indoor pet memorial plaques]
133 W 19th St
New York NY 10011
212/243-1488; FAX 212/645-0279

Pet Love Prod
PO Box 71001
Reno NV 89570
800/ 637-LOVE

Pet Memorials, Inc
PO Box 110
Elberton GA 30635
404/ 283-6600

Pet Perimeters
[electronic fence]
PO Box 530
Hudson OH 44236
800/ 934-PETS

Pet Pouch
[carriers]
PO Box 797144
Dallas TX 75379
214/ 931-6534

Pet Stones
Heater's Hill
PO Box 57
Matamoras PA 18336-0057
800/323-3551

Pet Stuff
825 Barsby St
Vista CA 92084

Pet Supply House, The
593 Main St E
Milton ONT
Canada L9T 3J2
416/876-1577; 800/268-3716

Pet Supply Wholesale
2912 Bristol Hwy
Johnson City TN 37601
800/ 543-7387

Pet Warehouse
PO Box 20250
Dayton OH 45420
800/ 443-1160

Pet-Agreeables
Rizka Baltz
412 Garfield
Middletown OH 45044
513/ 424-3131

Petra
[grave markers]
PO Box 153
Lewistown MO 63452
314/497-2202; 800/553-9708

Pets Remembered
[slate grave markers]
1533 N Kellog St
Galesburg IL 61401
309/342-1964

Photograph Memorials, Inc
3856 N Main St
Fall River MA 02720
508/ 679-8244

Pik-Up Mfg
[canine waste disposal equip]
PO Box 31732
Chicago IL 60631-0732
312/763-1400

Pines 'N Birches
[dog rubber stamps]
Osgood Ave N
Stillwater MN 55082

Piranha Shop, The
Paul T Wettlaufer
[gifts, supplies, books]
1550 Avenue Rd
Toronto ONT
Canada M5M 3X5
416/789-3512

Pointer Specialties
[SAR & hunting coats for dogs]
PO Box 156
Wellsville PA 17365
717/ 292-4776; 717/292-0440

Poop Scoops
[canine waste disposal equip]
43 N Federal Hwy
Pompano Beach FL 33062
305/946-4867

Premier Pet Prod
Sharon Bennett
[wholesale leashes and collars]
2406 Krossridge Rd
Richmond VA 23236
804/ 276-7741

Premier Sheep Supplies, Ltd
[sheep and sheep dog supplies]
Box 8
Washington IA 52353
319/ 653-6631; 319/ 653-3128

Quality Prod
[pet sympathy cards]
PO Box 1132-D
Pittston PA 18640-5118
717/655-1330

R & M Marketing
[auto mister for insect control]
6825 Jimmy Carter Blvd #1630
Norcross GA 30071

R C Steele
[supplies]
1989 Transit Way
Box 910
Brockport NY 14420-0910
800/872-3773; 800/424-2205

RCI Software
1117 Redwood Dr
Loveland CO
800/735-2848

Raceway Prod Corp
[carting supplies]
2708 N Walnut St
Muncie IN 47303
317/ 289-2244

Radar Rex Corp
[flea & tick prod for carpet]
2520 N W 16th Ln # 13
Pompano Beach FL 33064
800/771-9955

Radio Fence
[electronic fence]
5008 National Dr
Knoxville TN 37914
800/858-0485

Rae's Harness Shop
[dog sled equipment]
1524 E Dowling Rd #6
Anchorage AK 99507
907/ 563-3411; 800/770-1177

Ramsey Outdoor Store
[back packs for dogs, etc]
226 Rt 17
Paramus NJ 07653
201/ 261-5000

Rarities
[rare-breed notepaper]
PO Box 1891
Snoqualmie WA 98065-1891
206/888-4552

Rawcliffe
[jewelry]
155 Public St
Providence RI 02903
800/343-1811; FAX 401/751-8545

Ray Allen Mfg Co
975 Ford St
Colorado Springs CO 80915-3760
719/ 380-0404

Rescue 3 East Inc
[full body K-9 rappeling harness]
17 Terril Ave
Mercerville NJ 08619-1328
609/586-8356; 609/586-8985, FAX

Resha Sled Dog Equipment
SR # 1
Lewis Run PA 16738
814/ 362-3048

Rex Granite Co
[granite pet memorials]
PO Box 924
St Cloud MN 56302-0924

Robertson Fence Company
10732 Schaedl Rd SE
Mt Sterling OH 43143
800/ 742-3467

Romark Indust Inc
[canine waste disposal equip]
20800 Center Ridge Rd #100
Cleveland OH 44116
216/333-0027

Rosemary House, The
[natural flea-control prod]
120 S Market St
Mechanicsburg PA 17055

Roughhouse
[rare books]
7751 Cooley Rd
Ravenna OH 44266

Rover Vinyl-Tech Indust
20 Kiji Dava
Sun Dog Industrial Park
Prescott AZ 86301
800/658-5925
FAX 602/776-7001

Ruff Rider Granite Gear
[back packs for dogs]
PO Box 278
Two Harbors MN 55616
218/ 834-6157

Ryter Corp
[canine waste disposal equip]
29 Estes Ave NW
Madelia MN 56062
507/642-8529

Sawtooth Mt Sled Works Inc
Rt 3 Box 693
Grand Marais MN 55604
218/ 387-2106

Scoop A Doo
[canine waste disposal equip]
3532 Corona Del Mar
Las Vegas NV 89108
702/645-7824

Sea Meadows Prod Co
[K-9 equipment]
627 Jennings Ave
Vallejo CA 94591-6535

Seven Gables
[dog books]
313 Washington
Northfield MN 55057
507/645-8572

Sheepman Supply Co
[sheep and sheep dog supplies]
PO Box 100
Barvoursville VA 22923
800/ 336-3005

Sinus Saver Indus Inc
[canine waste disposal equip]
1395 Angler St
Merritt Island FL 32952-5707
800/338-2678

Smart Dog Prod
215 7th St
PO Box 1036
Picayune MS 39466
601/ 798-9263

Smoky Point Monuments
7237 Lakeside Rd
Ontario NY 14519
315/ 524-9593

Soulou Enterprises of Florida
[pet beds]
RR 1 Box 588
High Springs FL 32643-9801
407/ 952-2063

Specialpets
PO Box 7481
Louisville KY 40257
502/ 893-9652

Stamp Francisco
466 8th St #1
San Francisco CA 94103-4428

Stamp Happy Rubber Stamps
PO Box 114
Hermosa Beach CA 90254

Stampberry Farms
1952 Everett St
North Valley Stream, NY 11580

Stone Brothers
[figurines]
PO Box 1002
Thousand Oaks CA 91358
805/ 495-3251

Stormrunner Outfitters
[dog sled equipment]
42 Cooper St
Agawam MA 01001
413/ 789-2000

Style Designer Pet Prod Inc
1324 Southeast 12th Wy
Fort Lauderdale FL 33316
305/525-0606; FAX 305/525-0607

Sunland Pet Supplies
4010 E Broadway Rd #210
Phoenix AZ 85040
602/437-4418; 800/444-4418

Talon Pet Supply
903 Naamans Creek Rd
Chadds Ford PA 19317
610/ 459-5421

Tarmans Books
[rare books]
10 Dunover Ct
Hummelstown PA 17036
717/566-9843

Thornell Corp
[skunk odor eliminator]
160 Wheelock Rd
Penfield NY 14526

Time-N-Type
[rare & out-of-print books]
5122 Vines Rd
Howell MI 48843

Togs for Dogs & Cats Too!
48 Darcy Ave
San Mateo CA 94403
415/ 574-5364

Tongie Vet & Feed Supply
17604 198th St
Tonganoxie KS 66086
800/642-9116

Town and Country Dogs
[grooming supplies]
22 Pheasant Dr
Fairmont WV 26554
304/ 366-6343

Trophy Pet Care
2796 Helen St
Pensacola FL 32504
904/ 476-7087; FAX 904/ 476-7087

Truly Nolen of America Inc
[flea & tick control prod]
232 N Orange Blossom Tr
Orlando FL 32805
800/771-6423

Tun-Dra Outfitters
[dog sled equipment]
16438 96th Ave
Nunica MI 49448
616/ 837-9726

Ultra Lite Animal Enclosures
6074 Corte Del Cedro
Carlsbad CA 92009
619/ 431-7887

United Pet Supplies, Inc
17251 W 12 Mile Rd #201
Southfield MI 48076
313/ 569-6040

UPCO
Dept CSB
Box 969
St Joseph MO 64502
816/ 233-8800

Up-Country Collars & Leads
9 Newman Ave
Rumford RI 02916
800/541-5909

Valley Vet Supply
[general supplies]
East Hwy 36
PO Box 504
Marysville KS 66508-0504

Vet Express Inc
655 Washington
PO Box 1168
Rhinelander WI 54501
800/ 458-7656

Veterinarian's Best
[general supplies]
Box 4459
Santa Barbara CA 93103
800/866-PETS

Von Russ Giants
[carting supplies]
123 Yeager Ave
Forty Fort PA 18704
717/ 288-0735

Walter Rigdon
[cigarettes & postcards]
136 Stony Hollow Rd
Greenlawn NY 11740

Well-Sweep Herb Farm
[natural flea-control prod]
217 Mt Bethel Rd
Port Murray NJ 07865

Wenaha Dog Packs
[back packs for dogs]
4518 Maltby Rd
Bothell WA 98012
206/ 481-1205

West Winds Trading Co
[dog weathervanes/dinner bells/
nameplates]
3540 76th St SE
Caledonia MI 49316
616/698-0800

Whiskering Heights
PO Box 8038
Rego Park NY 11374-8038
718/ 459-3690

Whitehouse Designs
[igloo pet bed]
Rt 2 Box 321
Marietta OK 73448
405/ 276-4040

Wholesale Kennel Supply
PO Box 745 W
Siler City NC 27344
919/ 742-2515

Wild Wings
[prints and gift items]
S US Hwy 61
PO Box 451
Lake City MN 55041-0451
800/ 445-4833

Willowwitch Kennel & Pet Supply
S 5408 Grove Rd
Spokane WA 99204
509/ 328-6959

Will's Woodshed
81142 Mt 83
Bigfork MT 59911
406/837-1129

Wondereye Farm
Richard & Linda Karrasch
[sheepherding supplies]
Rt 1 Box 42
Vandiver AL 35176

Wood Miniatures
Sandra Alexander
[handcarved dogs in wood]
405 N New Hampshire Dr
Webster NH 03303

Wooden Illusions
[dog door stops]
OS509 Cornell
Villa Park IL 60181
708/ 834-0592

Working Breeds, Etc
4739 Bonnie Branch Rd
Ellicott City MD 21043
301/ 788-6149

Wysong Corp, The
[vegetarian diet info for dogs/cats]
1880 N Eastman
Midland MI 48640-8838
517/631-0009

Yesterdays
[collectibles]
PO Box 296
New York NY 10956
914/ 634-8456

Those organizations that are professional associations related to the canine industry are listed in this chapter. If you are seeking information about a career in a canine-related profession, the association related to that career can give you good advice on where to go or whom to contact. They usually set the standards of quality for their professions.

Also listed in this chapter are those groups that did not fall within the dog club category.

American Animal Hospital Assoc
PO Box 150899
Denver CO 80215-0899
303/ 279-2500

American Assoc of Veterinary Nutritionists
Frank W Kingsbury, DVM
Extension Veterinarian
RDH 1 Box 316
Glen Gardner NJ 08126

American Boarding Kennels Assoc
4575 Galley Rd #400A
Colorado Springs CO 80915
719/ 591-1113

American Canine Sports Med Assoc
[ACSMA]
[medical, surgical, nutrit programs]
12062 SW 117th Ct # 146
Miami FL 33142
305/633-2402

American Dog Owners Assoc
[works on anti-dog legislation]
1654 Columbia TPK
Cast leton NY 12033
518/ 477-8469

American Grooming Shop Assoc
4575 Galley Rd #400-A
Colorado Springs CO 80915
719/ 570-7788
FAX 719/ 597-0006

American Holistic Vet Medical Assoc
2214 Old Emmorton Rd
Bel Air MD 21014

American Humane Assoc
Susan W Halberstadt
9725 E Hampden Ave
Denver CO 80231
303/ 695-0811

American Pet Boarding Assoc
PO Box 931
Wheeling IL 60090
312/ 634-9447

American Professional Pet Dist Inc
[APPDI]
440 Pineburr Ln
Stone Mountain GA 30087
404/498-5984

American Veterinary Medical Assoc
930 N Meacham Rd
Schaumburg IL 60196
800/ 233-2862 in IL
800/ 248-2862 other states

American Veterinary Society,
Animal Behavior
Department of Urban Practice
College of Veterinary Medicine
University of Tennessee
Nashville TN 37901
615/ 546-9240

Animal Vues
RD 2 Box 71
Bloomsburg PA 17815
717/ 784-0374

Assoc of American Vet Medical Colleges
1023 15th St NW, 3rd Floor
Washington DC 20005

Assoc of Small Animal Professionals
178 Peachtree St #299
Atlanta GA 30303
800-PRO-0748

Canadian Pet Industry Assoc
[CPIA]
PO Box 460
Brighton ONT
Canada K0K 1H0
613/ 475-2174

Canadian Veterinary Medical Assoc
339 Booth St
Ottawa ONT
Canada K1R 7K1
613/ 236-1162

Continental Dog Assoc
Alan Alford
PO Box 357-C
Sudbury MA 01176
508/ 443-8387

Delta Society
[human/animal bond]
PO Box 1080
Renton WA 98057-1080
206/ 226-7357

Dog Writers' Assoc of America
Mary Ellen Tarman
10 Dunover Ct
Hummelstown PA 17036
717/566-9843

Federation of Dog Clubs & Breeders
For an updated list contact:
American Kennel Club,
Communication Dept
Stephanie Robinson
51Madison Ave
New York NY 10010
212/ 696-8336

Federation of Dog Clubs & Breeders
Arizona Dog Council
Mildred Gleeson
10642 N 68th Pl
Scottsdale AZ 85254
602/948-6904

Federation of Dog Clubs and Breeders
Assoc Dog Clubs of New York State
Gordon Carvill
RD 1 Miller Rd
East Greenbush NY 12061
518/477-5266; 518/477-9555

Federation of Dog Clubs & Breeders
Assoc Dog Clubs of Texas
Steve Schmidt
1713 Ross
Carrollton TX 75006
214/242-1078; 214/358-3362

Federation of Dog Clubs & Breeders
Colorado Dog Fanciers Assoc
Mickey Rubin
1856 S Columbine
Denver CO 80210
303/722-0161

Federation of Dog Clubs & Breeders
Confederacy of Tail Waggers
Steve Wallis
6000 High Bluff Ct
Raleigh NC 27612
919/ 782-2558

Federation of Dog Clubs & Breeders
Connecticut Dog Federation Inc
Diane Taylor
43 Umpawaug Rd
W Redding CT 06896
203/938-3152

Federation of Dog Clubs and Breeders
Dog Federation of Wisconsin
Don Heibler
4231 N 87th St
Milwaukee WI 53222
414/ 463-2614; 414/ 965-3649 info.

Federation of Dog Clubs and Breeders
Florida Assoc of Kennel Clubs
Diane Albers
401 Cardinal Oaks Ct
Lake Mary FL 32746
407/ 322-8980; 407/ 323-8696

Federation of Dog Clubs and Breeders
Georgia Coalition of Dog Clubs
Cindy Goodman
3939 Pate Rd
Loganville GA 30249
404/985-6769; 404/365-1908

Federation of Dog Clubs and Breeders
Granite State Federation of Dog Clubs
Jan Mullen-Stewart
165 Dover Point Rd
Dover NH 03820
603/ 742-0205

Federation of Dog Clubs and Breeders
Illinois Dog Clubs and Breeders Assoc
Sandra Bamberger
532 65th St
Clarendon Hill IL 60514
708/971-2364

Federation of Dog Clubs and Breeders
Maine Federation of Dog Clubs
Nola Soper
PO Box 577
Bucksport ME 04416
207/469-3852

Federation of Dog Clubs and Breeders
Michigan Assoc for Pure-Bred Dogs
Richard McClure
122 South St
Bellville MI 48111
313/697-1181

Federation of Dog Clubs and Breeders
Michigan Federation of Dog Clubs
Stephanie Katz
1701 Strathcona Dr
Detroit MI 48203
313/ 368-3123

Federation of Dog Clubs and Breeders
New Jersey Federation of Dog Clubs
Diane Rau
PO Box 4348
Warren NJ 07059-0348
908/469-1754

Federation of Dog Clubs & Breeders
Oklahoma K-9 Legislative Alliance
Wendy Musgrove
700 NW 22nd St
Oklahoma City OK 73103

Federation of Dog Clubs & Breeders
Oklahoma Dog Fanciers Coalition
Donna Danner
PO Box 27691
Tulsa OK 74149
918/587-3811

Federation of Dog Clubs and Breeders
Pennsylvania Federation of Dog Clubs
Dotsie Keith
PO Box 67
Furlong PA 18925
215/842-2407

Federation of Dog Clubs & Breeders
Responsible Animal Owners of Tennessee
Donna Malone
3327 Lockmeade
Memphis TN 38127
901/353-1805

Federation of Dog Clubs & Breeders
Responsible Dog Breeders Assoc of Oregon
Patti Strand
4141 SE 141st Ave
Portland OR 97236
503/761-8962

Federation of Dog Clubs & Breeders
Responsible Dog Owners Assoc of New
York
Ann Lettis
91 Wiman Ave
Staten Island NY 10308
718/317-5804

Federation of Dog Clubs and Breeders
Responsible Dog Owners of Louisiana
Donald Kirsch
PO Box 9196
Metairie LA 70055-9196
504/ 837-7038

Federation of Dog Clubs and Breeders
Responsible Dog Owners of Ohio
Dr Alan Riga
6325 Aldenham Dr
Mayfield Heights OH 44143
216/ 449-3662

Federation of Dog Clubs & Breeders
Responsible Dog Owners of the
Golden State [California]
Kevin Belcastro
2400 Darwin St
Sacramento CA 95825-0106
916/321-3742

Federation of Dog Clubs and Breeders
Responsible Pet Owners Alliance
Mary Beth Duerler
14350 Marin Hollow
Helotes TX 78023
210/695-3388

Federation of Dog Clubs and Breeders
South Carolina Federation of Dog Clubs
Don Wilson
908 Cedar Springs Rd
Blythewood SC 29016
803/ 754-4880

Federation of Dog Clubs & Breeders
Tennessee Dog Federation
MaryAnne Armbruster Smith
536 Paragon Mills Rd
Nashville TN 37211

Federation of Dog Clubs & Breeders
Texas Coalition of Responsible Animal
Owners
Robert Rohr
PO Box 294914
Lewisville TX 75029-4914

Federation of Dog Clubs & Breeders
Utah Dog Fanciers Assoc
Evelyn Bohac
384 East 200th North
Lindon UT 84042
801/ 785-1750

Federation of Dog Clubs & Breeders
Vermont Federation of Dog Clubs
Ann Thornhill
RD 1 Box 80
North Ferrisburg VT 05473

Federation of Dog Clubs & Breeders
Virginia Federation of Dog Clubs & Breeders
June Zink
6031 Woodpecker Rd
Chesterfield VA 23832
804/590-1811

Human Animal Bond Assoc of Canada
PO Box 1088
Smith Falls ONT
Canada K7A 5B4

Independent Pet & Animal Trans Assoc
Cherie Derouin
RT 1 Box 747
Big Sandy TX 75755
903/769-2847; 903/769-2867 FAX

Internat'l Assoc of Home Pet Care Services
38 Sunset Dr
Kensington CA 94707
415/ 524-0451

Internat'l Assoc of Pet Cemeteries
PO Box 1346
South Bend IN 46624
219/ 277-1115

Internat'l Pet Trade Organization [IPTO]
PO Box 504
3800 AM Amersfoort
Netherlands
31/ 33-635-828

Japan Pet Products Mfg Assoc
[JPPMA]
2-30-8 Higashi-Tamagawa
Setegayaku Tokyo
Japan 158
81/ 2-726-7747

Livestock Guard Dog Assoc
Hampshire College
Box FC
Amherst MA 01002

Morris Animal Foundation
45 Inverness Dr E
Englewood CO 80112-5480
303/ 790-2345

Nat'l Animal Control Assoc
Mike Burgwin
PO Box 154
Indianola WA 98342

Nat'l Assoc for Humane and Environ Educ
67 Salem Rd
East Haddam CT 06423

Nat' Assoc for SAR [NASAR]
PO Box 3709
Fairfax VA 22038
703/ 352-1349

Nat'l Assoc of Dog Obed Instructors
NADOI/
2286 E Steel Rd
St Johns MI 48879

Nat'l Assoc of Wholesale Distr [NAW]
1725 K St NW
Washington DC 20006
202/ 872-0885

Nat'l Dog Groomers Assoc of America
[NDGAA]
Box 101
Clark PA 16113
412/ 962-2711

Nat'l War Dog Memorial Project
407 S 6th Ave
Jacksonville Beach FL 32250
904/249-0924

N Amer Veterinary Technician Assoc Inc
PO Box 224
Battle Ground IN 47920

Northwest Professional Groomers Assoc
10220   29th St E # 5
Puyallup WA 98372
206/ 841-2544

Ohio Humane Education Assoc
Terry Bowman
PO Box 546
Grove City OH 43123

Pet Foundation Institute [PFI]
1101 Connecticut Ave NW #700
Washington DC 20036
202/ 857-1120

Pet Industry Distr Assoc [PIDA]
5024-R Campbell Rd
Baltimore MD 21236
301/ 256-8100

Pet Industry Joint Advisory Council
[PIJAC]
1710 Rhode Island Ave NW
Washington DC 20036
202/ 452-1525; 800/ 555-7387

Pet Industry Joint Advisory Council
[PIJAC]
7 King St E #1601
Toronto ONT
Canada M5C1A2
416/364-9317

Poodle Club of America Foundation
Mrs Michael J Wahlig
2945 Jamestown Rd
Long Lake MN 55356

Professional Assoc of Pet Industries
[PAPI]
4311 Treat Blvd
Concord CA 94521
415/ 674-0500

Professional Dog Groomers Assoc/Canada
Diane Sparham
182 Province St
Hamilton ONT
Canada L8H 4H8
416/ 549-4135

Rare Breed Judges Assoc
Dee Gannon
PO Box 832
Willingboro NJ 08046
609/ 877-8598

Royal Society Prevention of Cruelty to
Animals
The Causeway
Horsham, West Sussex RH12 1HQ
England UK

Senior Conformation Judges Assoc
Lt Col Wallace H Pede
7200 Tanager St
Springfield VA 22150
703/ 451-5656

Single Doglovers Assoc
PO Box 454
Slippery Rock PA 16057-0454

Society of N American Dog Trainers
ASPCA Companion Animal Services
441 E 92nd St
New York NY 10128
212/ 243-5460, 2-9pm

US Border Collie Handlers Assoc
Bud Boudrean
HC 78 Box 25A
Marcus SD 57757
618/ 233-0513

Veterinary Homeopathy Prof Course
1283 Lincoln St
Eugene OR 97401

Western Humane Educators Assoc
Micki Zeldes
Marin Humane Society
171 Bel Marin Keys Blvd
Novato CA 94947

Western World Pet Supply Assoc
[WWPSA]
PO Box 1337
South Pasadena CA 91030
818/ 799-7182

Working Breeds Assoc of Wales
Mrs G Mogford
Gwynfa, Pontymason Lane
Rogerstone Newport
Gwent Wales
UK

Some contests and awards are offered annually and some are a one-time event. Many times, contests are not widely publicized. If you are interested in learning about contests and awards that may not be listed in this chapter, write to all of the major dog food and pet product companies asking if they sponsor any awards or contests. Another place to check are any major publications, such as *Dog World* or *Dog Fancy.*

If you are interested in learning more about any of the award programs in this chapter, write to the organization listed.

AMBOR Hero Nominees
[mixed-breed heroes]
205 First St SW
New Prague MN 56071

American Animal Hospital Award/
Assistance Animal Award
Delta Society
PO Box 1080
Renton WA 98057

Annual Purina Award
Field Trial Beagle
Robert C Baumgartner
4 RPL Ralston Purina Co
Checkerboard Square
St Louis MO 63164

Annual Purina Award
Field Trial Herding Dog
Robert C Baumgartner
4 RPL Ralston Purina Co
Checkerborad Square
St. Louis MO 63164

Annual Purina Award
Field Trial Retriever
Robert C Baumgartner
4 RPL Ralston Purina Co
Checkerboard Square
St Louis MO 63164

Annual Purina Award
Honors Outstanding Coonhound
Robert C Baumgartner
4 RPL Ralston Purina Co
Checkerboard Square
St Louis MO 63164

Annual Purina Award
Top Field Trial Bird Dog
Robert C Baumgartner
4 RPL Ralston Purina Co
Checkerboard Square
St Louis MO 63164

Award of Canine Distinction
& Outstanding Service
Dog World Magazine
29 North Wacker Dr
Chicago IL 60606

Cycle Dog Obed Championships
PO Box 049001 # 23-1
Chicago IL 60604-9001
312/222-8792; FAX 312/222-8313

Dog Hero of the Year Contest
PO Box 1370
Barrington IL 60011

Dog Writers Assoc of America, Inc
Susan Jeffries, writing contest chair
2813 Lexham Rd
Louisville KY 40220-2856
502/ 499-7184

Dog Writers Educ Trust Scholar
Berta I Pickett
PO Box 2220
Payson AZ 85547

Dogs USA
Photo Contest
PO Box 6050
Mission Viejo CA 92690

Good Dog Award
[dogs who do positive acts]
511 Harbor View Cir
Charleston SC 29412

Grants to College Students
Mrs Robert Futh
47 Keilwasser Rd
Washington Depot CT 06794
SASE

Ken-L Ration
Suite 23-1
PO Box 9001
Chicago IL 60604-9001
312/ 222-7894

Most Outstanding Pet Contest
Pet Care Savings Club
Publications Dept
4501 Forbes Blvd
Lanham MD 20705
301/459-8020 X 2233

New England Anti-Vivisection Society
333 Washington St #850
Boston MA 02180

Pedigree Awards
[Canadian awards for areas
of the dog fancy]
2 Bloor St W # 100
PO Box 224
Toronto ONT
Canada M4W 3E2

Society Art Competition
Stephanie West
53 W Jackson Blvd #1552
Chicago IL 60604
312/427-6065

Listed in this chapter are interesting dog-related places to visit. Often, there will be special events taking place in the area you may be planning to visit. One way to find out about these events is to check with the national and local clubs that sponsor the type of events in which you're interested. It is always a good idea to check the local newspapers as they usually list special events for the area.

Also included in this chapter are some interesting places to go for a vacation that offer dog-related activities.

Algonquin Canoe Routes
[dog-sledding trips]
PO Box 187
Whitney ONT
Canada K0J 2M0
705/ 637-2699

Backcountry Alaska
[dog-sledding trips]
PO Box 2544
Palmer AK 99645-2544
907/ 746-3011

Bird Dog Museum
Bird Dog Foundation Inc
PO Box 774M
Grand Junction TN 38039
901/ 764-2058

Borton Overseas
[dog-sledding trips]
5516 Lyndale Ave S
Minneapolis MN 55419
800/ 843-0602

Camp Gone To The Dogs
Honey Joring
RR 1 Box 958
Putney VT 05346
802/ 387-5673

Denali Dog Tours
[dog-sledding trips]
PO Box 1
McKinley Park AK 99755
907/ 683-2321

Dog Museum, The
Queeny Park
1721 S Mason
St Louis MO 63131
314/ 821-3647; 314/821-7381

Dog Museum of America, The
William Secord Gallery Inc
52 E 76th St
New York NY
212/ 929-5793

Gould's Maple Farm
[working sheep dogs]
Edgar Gould
RFD 1 Cooper Ln
Shelburne Falls MA 01370
413/ 625-6170

Hartsdale Canine Cemetery, The
War Dog Memorial [1923]
Westchester County NY
914/ 949-2583

Hibbs, Don
[dog sled trips]
PO Box 80121
Fairbanks AK 99708
907/ 488-6787

Hundemuseum, The
[dog museum]
ALT Blankenburg Strasse #33
Germany

Key Underwood
   Coon Dog Cemetery
Tuscumbia AL 35674

Leeds Castle
[display of dog collars
 dating back 300 years]
Kent England

Lungholm Ulvepark
[wolf museum]
Freddy W Christiansen
Rodbyveg 20
DK-4980 Rodby
Denmark

Memorial Wall for Dogs [NEADS]
PO Box 213
W Boylston MA 01583
508/835-3304

North Country Travelers
[dog-sledding trips]
PO Box 14
Atlin BC
Canada V0W 1A0
2M-5017 White MT CH

Outer Edge Expeditions
[dog-sledding trips]
45500 W Pontiac Tr
Walled Lake MI 48390

Purina Farms
Gray Summit MO 63039
314/ 982-3232

Saint Bernard Hospice Museum
Switzerland

Trails North Tours
[dog sledding]
PO Box 923
Seward AK 99664
907/ 224-3587

Wilderness Inquiry Trips
[dog-sled trips]
1313 Fifth St SE #327
Minneapolis MN 55414
612/ 379-3858

Wolf Park Woods
Denver Zoo
Wolf Pack Profile
Denver Zoological Foundation
City Park
Denver CO 80205-4899
303/ 331-4100

Zoological Museum, The
[dogs of the last 100 years]
Annex of the British Museum
  of Natural History
Tring England

This chapter lists most major colleges that offer degrees in veterinary medicine. When writing for information or an application for admission, address your letter to the Admissions Office. While it is not the purpose of this book to offer a "how-to-pick-a-college guide," it is a good idea to carefully research a college before you select one. Costs and requirements can vary considerably.

For a list of the Veterinary Colleges of the World, American and Canadian Colleges offering programs in Animal Technology, specialized veterinary groups and services, you can consult the:

American Veterinary Medical Association Directory
930 N Meacham Rd
Schaumburg IL 60196-1074
312/885-8070

CANADA

Atlantic Veterinary College
University of Prince Edward Island
Charlottetown PEI C1A 4P3

Faculty of Veterinary Medicine
University of Montreal
Saint Hyacinthe QUE J2S 7C6

Western College of Veterinary Medicine
University of Saskatchewan
Saskatoon SAS S7N 0W0

UNITED STATES

ALABAMA

College of Veterinary Medicine
Auburn University
203 Martin Hall
Auburn AL 36803

School of Veterinary Medicine
Tuskegee Institute
Tuskegee Institute AL 36088

CALIFORNIA

School of Veterinary Medicine
University of California Davis
175 Mrak Hall
Davis CA 95616

COLORADO

College of Veterinary Medicine/
Biomedical Studies
Colorado State University
Administration Annex
Fort Collins CO 80523

FLORIDA

College of Veterinary Medicine
University of Florida
Gainesville FL 32611

GEORGIA

College of Veterinary Medicine
University of Georgia
Academic Building
Athens GA 30602

ILLINOIS

College of Veterinary Medicine
University of Illinois at Urbana-Champaign
10 Administration Building
2001 S Lincoln
Urbana IL 61801

INDIANA

College of Veterinary Medicine
Purdue University
Hovde Hall
West Lafayette IN 47907

IOWA
College of Veterinary Medicine
Iowa State University
7 Beardshear Hall
Ames IA 50011

KANSAS

College of Veterinary Medicine
Kansas State University
Manhattan KS 66506

LOUISIANA

School of Veterinary Medicine
Louisiana State Univ
Agricultural & Mechanical Coll
110 T Boyd Hall
Baton Rouge LA 70803

MASSACHUSETTS

School of Veterinary Medicine
Tufts University
200 Westboro Rd
N Grafton MA 01536

MICHIGAN

College of Veterinary Medicine
Michigan State University
250 Administration Building
East Lansing MI 48824

MINNESOTA

College of Veterinary Medicine
University of Minnesota: Twin Cities
230 Williamson Hall
Minneapolis MN 55455

MISSISSIPPI

College of Veterinary Medicine
Mississippi State University
PO Drawer 5268
Mississippi State MS 39762

MISSOURI

College of Veterinary Medicine
University of Missouri: Columbia
228 Jesse Hall
Columbia MO 65211

NEW YORK

College of Veterinary Medicine
Cornell University
410 Thurston Ave
Ithaca NY 14850

NORTH CAROLINA

School of Veterinary Medicine
North Carolina State University
Raleigh NC 27606

OKLAHOMA

College of Veterinary Medicine
Oklahoma State University
Stillwater OK 74074

OREGON

College of Veterinary Medicine
Oregon State University
Corvallis OR 97331

PENNSYLVANIA

School of Veterinary Medicine
University of Pennsylvania
1 College Hall
Philadelphia PA 19104

TENNESSEE

College of Veterinary Medicine
University of Tennessee: Knoxville
320 Student Services Building
Knoxville TN 37916

TEXAS

College of Veterinary Medicine
Southwest Texas State University
San Marcos TX 78666

College of Veterinary Medicine
Texas A&M University
College Station TX 77843

VIRGINIA

State University
Virginia Polytechnic Institute &
Virginia-Maryland Regional College of
Veterinary Medicine
Blacksburg VA 24061

WASHINGTON

College of Veterinary Medicine
Washington State University
Pullman WA 99164

WISCONSIN

School of Veterinary Medicine
University of Wisconsin-Madison
Madison WI 53706

Canine Search and Rescue (SAR) units are involved in using dogs to find lost people in various situations including wilderness, disaster, water, avalanche, and urban situations. The different types of training are airscenting, tracking/trailing and water rescue work. Some units are limited to dogs trained for certain types of rescue work as well as specific breeds while other units employ all breeds and types.

Those who are involved in SAR work find it to be very rewarding, challenging and fun.

Two toll free numbers are available for fire, police, rescue and emergency personnel to use to contact mission-ready search and rescue dog teams throughout the US.

Scott AFB (Air Force Rescue Coordination Center)
800/851-3051

Alaska: Call Elmendorf AFB

Canada: 800/661-6166

CANADA

Canadian SAR Dogs
Bill Grimmer
PO Box 126
993 Scoudouc Rd
Scoudouc NB E0A 1N0
Information 506/ 532-4988
Call Out 506/ 532-6691

Central NOVA Man-Trailers
Darrell Mills
RR 2
Stewiak NS B0N 2I0
Information & Call Out 902/ 673-2987
 or 455-4647

New Brunswick Ground SAR Assoc
Box 536
Hartland NB E0J 1N0

Nova Scotia Ground SAR Assoc
W L McLaughlin
PO Box 1502
Halifax NS B3J 2Y3

Provincial Emergency Program
Erin Wilson
7464 149-A
Surrey BC V3S 3H6
Information 604/ 597-6182

Sauvetage Canada Rescue
Art Galarneau
PO Box 145
Pierrefonds QUE H9H 4K0
Information 514/ 434-2735
Call Out 514/ 331-6100 X 4872

SAR Dog Assoc of Alberta
Kevin George
7120 91st
Edmonton AB T6E 2Z7
Information 403/ 469-6509
Call Out 800/ 272-9600

Timmins SAR
RR #2 Kraft Creek Rd
Timmins ONT P4N 7C3

West NOVA SAR Dog Assoc
Susan Tabor
PO Box 70
Cambridge Station NS B0P 1G0
Information 902/ 538-7919
Call Out 902/ 538-7919

UNITED STATES NATIONAL UNITS

International Mantrailing Bloodhound
Network
Bill Butler
31951 Lodgepole Dr
Evergreen CO 80439
Information 303/ 674-8317

International Rescue Dog Org
Caroline Hebard
104 Ballantine Rd
Bernardsville NJ 07924
908/766-7125

National Police Bloodhound Assoc
Becky Shaffer
PO Box 43
Dewart PA 17730

North American Search Dog Network
Joyce Phares
RR 2 Box 32
Urbana IL 61801
Information 217/ 367-5752

SAR Dogs of the United States, Inc
PO Box 11411
Denver CO 80211

SAR K-9 Service
PO Box 32621
Fridley MN 55432

ALASKA

Alaska SAR Dogs
Bill Tai
200 W 34th Ave # 665
Anchorage AK 99503
Information 907/ 344-7436
Call Out 907/ 269-5711

PAWS
Cathie Harms
PO Box 84388
Fairbanks AK 99708
Information 907/ 457-8210
Call Out 907/ 479-2016
or 907/ 452- 9256

SEADOGS
Bruce Bowler
PO Box 244
Juneau AK 99802
Information 907/ 465-2985
or 789-2582
Call Out 907/ 789-2161

Search Dogs Valdez
Box 2552
Valdez AK 99686

Sitka Volunteer Fire Dept
Rescue K-9's
Susan Royce
209 Lake St
Sitka AK 99835
Information 907/ 747-6064
Call Out 907/ 747-3233

ARIZONA

Cochise County Sheriff
SAR Dog Unit #1
Richard Chenlfant
NCR Box 335 c
Pierce AZ 85625
Information 602/ 824-3653
Call Out 800/ 362-0812

ARKANSAS

Arkansas SAR Dog Team
Tanya Cross
RT 3 Box 207
Lonoke AR 72036
Information 501/ 676-5078
Call Out 501/ 988-5141

Benton County SAR
David Comstock
12784 WC 28
Prairie Grove AR 72753
Information 501/ 846-2314
Call Out 501/ 271-1004

CALIFORNIA

Bay Area Rescue K-9
Linda Spangler
2211 Westchester Dr
San Jose CA 95124
Information 408/ 356-6519
Call Out 408/ 356-6519

Calif-Swiss Search Dog Assoc
Willy Grundherr
PO Box 66262
Scotts Valley CA 95066
Information 408/ 425-7661
Call Out 805/ 324-6551

California Rescue Dog Assoc
Shirley Hammond
1062 Metro Circle
Palo Alto CA 94303
Information 415/ 856-9669
Call Out 916/ 988-5542
or 916/ 989-4989

Contra Costa County Bloodhounds
Judy Robb
421 La Vista Rd
Walnut Creek CA 94598
Information 415/ 939-9279
Call Out 415/ 646-2441

Los Angeles Search Dogs
Jerry Newcomb
3224 N Mount Curve
Altadena CA 91001
Information 818/ 798-7616
Call Out 213/ 264-7084

Orange County Sheriff's
SAR Reserve
Larry Harris
1807 Highland Dr
Newport Beach CA 92660
Information 714/ 665-1612
Call Out 714/ 647-1850

Sierra Madre SAR Team
Arnold Gaffrey
9527 Wedgewood
Temple City CA 91780
Information 818/ 286-8053 or 355-8000
Call Out 818/ 355-1414

WOOF Search Dogs
Marin County Sheriff's Dept
Civic Center
San Rafael CA 94903
Information 415/ 499-7243
Call Out 415/ 499-7243

COLORADO

Black Paws Search, Rescue
& Avalanche Dogs
Marie Cloughesy
13050 Black Forest Rd
Colorado Springs CO 80908
Information 719/ 495-3287
Call Out 800/ 851-3051

Front Range Rescue Dogs
Ann Wichmann
417 Sherman
Longmont CO 80501
Information 303/ 441-3408
or 776-3957
Call Out 303/ 441-4444

Larimer County SAR
and SAR Dogs of Colorado
Fran Lieser
4216 Glade Rd
Loveland CO 80537
Information 303/ 667-9931
Call Out 303/ 221-7141

Moffat County SAR K-9 Unit
Dennis Craig
221 W Victory Way
Craig CO 81625
Information 303/ 824-4495
Call Out 303/ 824-4495

United Search Dogs
Dixie Ferrick
26061 Co Rd H
Cortez CO 81321
Information 303/ 565-4593
Call Out 303/ 565-8441

CONNECTICUT

Connecticut State Police
Tpr K Rodino
Hartford Rd
Colchester CT 06415
Information 203/ 238-6026
Call Out 203/ 566-4240

Stafford PD
Lewis Fletcher
22 Chruch St
Stafford Springs CT 06076
Information & Call Out 203/ 684-4926

FLORIDA

Central Florida SAR Team
Carolyn Wheelis
PO Box 875
Eustis FL 32727-0875

ESAR/PAC
[Special Response Team]
Mike Turner
2923 Whirlaway
Tall FL 32308
Information 904/ 386-8850
Call Out 904/ 576-2709

FASTER K-9 Division
Lucy Walburn
PO Box 727
Chiefland FL 32626-0727
Information 904/ 493-0282
or 493-6181
Call Out 800/ 945-3278

Florida Disaster Dog
Search Team, Inc
Judy A Davis
PO Box 292
Plymouth FL 32768
Information 407/ 298-0901
or 886-0260
Call Out 407/ 872-8099
or 263-2338

Florida Independent Dog
Handler Organization
Bill Frodl
PO Box 667
Astatula FL 34705
Information 904/ 343-0766
Call Out 800/ 241-4653

Florida Search Dog Assoc
Jennifer Tooker
Rte 2 Box 725-8
Micanopy FL 32667
Information 904/ 466-3090
Call Out 904/ 336-2413

Metro-Dade SAR Dogs
19570 Holiday Rd
Miami FL 33157
Information 305/ 255-0998
Call Out 305/ 596-8571

NW Florida SAR Squad
Nancy Jones
PO Box 257
Alford FL 32420
Info. & Call Out 904/ 579-4132
or 482-9669

South West Florida K-9 SAR
Charlene Schroder
19600 Pine Echo Rd
North Ft Meyers FL 33917
Information 813/ 543-2290

Special Response Team-A,
Florida Wing CAP
Lt Col E Wolff
PO Box 10581
Pompano Beach FL 33061
Information 305/ 943-0116
Call Out 800/ 255-1749

GEORGIA

Georgia K-9 Rescue Assoc
Sandra Crain
PO Box 12
Cusseta GA 31805
Information 404/ 989-3464
or 989-3648
Call Out 404/ 571-4939

Hamilton County STARS
Jim Poplin
114 Valley Breeze Trail
Roseville GA 30741
Information 404/ 861-1730
Call Out 615/ 757-2905

SAR Dogs of Gerogia
[SARDOG]
Allen or Karen Padgett
PO Box 662
Lafayette GA 30728
Information 706/ 638-4144
Call Out 706/ 865-3855

IDAHO

Intermountain SAR Dogs
Bob Langendoen
PO Box 1143
Ketchum ID 83340
Information 208/ 726-1842
Call Out 208/ 788-5555

Mountain West Rescue Dogs
Michael Anderson
509 Spokane St
Coeur d'Alene ID 83814
Information 208/ 664-5691
or 773-9437
Call Out 208/ 664-1511

ILLINOIS

Forest Preserve,
Du Page County Dog Unit
PO Box 2339
Glen Ellyn IL 60138
Information 708/ 920-1664
Call Out 708/ 790-4900 x 201

Hamilton County SAR
McLeansboro Fire Dept
209 E Brdway
McLeansboro IL 62859
Information 618/ 643-3829
Call Out 618/ 643-2233

Illini SAR Service
Mike Wiedel
24 W 640 Ohio St
Naperville IL 60540
Information 708/ 357-1271
Call Out 708/ 640-0102

Illinois/Wisconsin SAR Dogs
Patti Gibson
446 Porter Ave
Crystal Lake IL 60014
Information 815/ 459-6523
or 459-6442
Call Out 815/ 338-2143

RESAR
Bill Renaker
Box 425
Ingleside IL 60041
Information 708/ 587-2561
Call Out 708/ 587-3100

Springfield SAR K-9
Kay Watt
222 E Hazel Dell Ln
Springfield IL 62707
Information 529/ 7349

INDIANA

Indiana K-9 SAR
Don Rabe
94 Ashbourne
Noblesville IN 46060

SMART
Jeff Howell
PO Box 788
New Albany IN 47151
Information 812/ 945-4676
Call Out 812/ 948-5400

KANSAS

Black Paws Search & Rescue Dogs
Nicolette Dobson
515 E 10th St
Pittsburg KS 66762
Information 316/ 232-7010
Call Out 316/ 231-5377 pager

Lenexa Canine Unit
Pat Hinkle
12500 W 87th St
Lenexa KS 66205
Information & Call Out 913/ 888-4110

KENTUCKY

Jefferson Co EMS K-9 Unit
Jefferson Co EMS
7201 Outer Loop
Louisville KY 40228
Information 502/ 239-7110
Call Out 502/ 625-3636

Kentucky Search Dog Assoc
Patty Petzinger
R#4 Box 153
Owenton KY 40359
Information 502/ 484-3755
or 484-3417
Call Out 800/ 255-2587

LOUISIANA

LASAR-SAR Dogs
Dee Wild
PO Box 2477
Slidell LA 70459
Information 504/ 641-9769
Call Out 504/ 892-8181

MAINE

Maine SAR Dogs
Jennifer Applegate
80 Ledgelawn Ave
Bar Harbor ME 04609
Information 207/ 288-3882
Call Out 207/ 941-4440

Maine State Prison
Bloodhound Search Unit
Sgt John A Struk
Box A
Thomaston MA 04861
Information & Call Out 207/ 354-2535

Search Dogs Northeast
Perry Hopkins
PO Box 438
Alfred ME 04002
Information 207/ 324-3221
Call Out 800/ 585-6121

MARYLAND

Baltimore County Fire Dept
SAR Dog Unit
Lt Daniel Kluge
700 East Joppa Rd
Towson MD 21204
Information 301/ 378-4522 or 887-8100
Call Out 301/ 887-4592 or 887-2769

Mid-Atlantic DOGS Inc
Marian Hardy
4 Orchard Way North
Rockville MD 20854
Information 301/ 762-7217
Call Out 301/ 217-4644

SAR Dogs of Maryland
[ARDA-MD]
Bob Snyder
PO Box 545
White Plains MD 20695
Information 301/ 843-1609
Call Out 301/ 705-3546 pager

Southern Maryland SAR Dogs
Scott Earhart
365 Jones Wharf Rd
Hollywood MD 20636
Information 301/ 373-8259
Call Out 301/ 475-8016

MASSACHUSETTS

MASS Air Scenting K-9s
559 Peter Shan Rd
Athol MA 01331-9401
Information 508/ 249-6143
Call Out 508/ 355-4991

Martha's Vineyard K-9 Unit, Inc
Gina Hodges
PO Box 2277
17 Oklahoma Ave
Vineyard Haven MA 02568
Info. & Call Out 609/ 723-2760 or 508/ 693-7299

Mass Bay SAR Dogs
Donna Johnson
236 High St
Ipswich MA 01938
Information 508/ 356-7222

MICHIGAN

DOGS-North
Sally Santeford
RT 1 Box 332
Houghton MI 49931
Information 906/ 482-5135
Call Out 906/ 482-4411

Mid-Michigan Canine SAR Team
Mark Michalek
11512 Hazel Ave
Grand Blanc MI 48439
Information 313/ 695-2268
Call Out 313/ 257-3423

MINNESOTA

Arrowhead Search Dogs
Bill Mitchell
PO Box 468
Tower MN 55790
Information 218/ 365-2111
Call Out 218/ 741-7408

Minnesota SAR Dog Assoc
Kathy Newman
7335-223rd Ave NW
Elk River MN 55330
Information 612/ 441-3734
Call Out 612/ 427-1212

Northstar SAR Dog Assoc
Hans Erdman
PO Box 29134
Minneapolis MN 55429
Information 612/ 566-6236
Call Out 218/ 749-6010

Search Dogs Inc
Mary Jane Dyer
3310 Wren Ln
Eagan MN 55121
Information 612/ 452-4209

Southern Minnesota Canine SAR
Kathy Schroeder
28 7th St NE
Rochester MN 55904
Information 507/ 533-8015

MISSISSIPPI

DeSoto Co. Emergency
Management K-9
T H Walker
247 Losher
Hernando MS 38632
Information 601/ 429-1359
Call Out 601/ 429-1350

Gulf Coast SAR
Carlos Redmon
12397 N Oaklawn Ln
Biloxi MS 39532
Information 601/ 392-5419
Call Out 601/ 435-6150

MISSOURI

Black Paws Search, Rescue
& Avalanche Dogs
Richardson
16740 John's Cabin Rd
Glencoe MO 63038
Information 314/ 458-3248
Call Out 314/ 434-5500

Mid-America Rescue Dog Assoc
Karen Brown
HCR 77 Box 17-1
Sunrise Beach MO 65079
Information & Call Out 314/ 374-6388

Missouri SAR K-9
Irene Korotev
8307 Winchester
Kansas City MO 64138
Information 816/ 356-9097
Call Out 814/ 524-4300

Odessa VFD Bloodhounds
Orville Day
809 W Pleasant
Odessa MO 64076
Information 816/ 633-5396

Rainbow Mission SAR
Joyce Tolle
5865 Highway V
St Charles MO 63301
Information 314/ 258-3077
Call Out 314/ 949-3023

MONTANA

Absaroka Search Dogs
Vikki Fenton Bowman
2312 Pine St
Billings MT 59101
Information 406/ 245-7335
Call Out 406/ 322-5326

Black Paws SAR
Susie Foley
PO Box 684
Bigfork MT 59911
Information 406/ 837-5547
Call Out 406/ 883-4321

Lewis & Clark SAR Assoc
Ralph DeCunzo
PO Box 473
Helena MT 59624
Information 406/ 933-5962
Call Out 406/ 442-7880

Montana PAWS K-9 SAR
Kim Gilmore
PO Box 2081
Whitefish MT 59937-2081
Information 406/ 771-0139
Call Out 406/ 721-4516

Rivalli County SAR
Mary Jo Holmgren
PO Box 456
Stevensville MT 59870
Information 406/ 363-6312
Call Out 406/ 363-3033

Search Dogs North
Debbie Tirmenstein
PO Box 5254
Missoula MT 59806
Information 406/ 721-7256
Call Out 406/ 523-6044

NEW HAMPSHIRE

Granite State Search Dogs
Lisa Walpole
PO Box 126
Windham NH 03087
Information 603/ 434-3210

Granite State Search Dogs
Bill Peterson
PO Box 126
Windham NH 03087
Information 603/ 434-3210
Call Out 603/ 564-4521

New England K-9 SAR
Jo Ann Clark
RR 3 Box 38
St Johnsbury VT 05819
Information 802/ 748-6546
Call Out 603/ 352-3210

Strafford County Sheriff's
Bloodhound Unit
Penny Schroeder
RD 2 Box 726
Center Barnstead NH 03225
Information 603/ 269-5461
Call Out 603/ 742-4960

NEW JERSEY

Cape May County Sheriff's Dept
Col William Donohue
Crest Haven Complex
Cape May Court House NJ 08210
Information 609/ 889-6560
Call Out 609/ 465-1237

Palisades SAR Dog Assoc
April Pampalone
291 Main St
Milburn NJ 07041
Information 201/ 376-7377
Call Out 201/ 993-7868 pager

Ramapo Rescue Dog Assoc
Penny Sullivan
Goose Pond Mountain State Park
PO Box 151
Chester NY 10918
Information 914/ 469-4173
Call Out 201/ 664-1111

Watchung Mountain K-9 SAR
Barry Orange
1091 Raritan Rd
Clark NJ 07066
Information 908/ 381-3182
Call Out 800/ 631-3444

West Jersey Canine SAR
PO Box 205
Pittstown NJ 08867
Information 908/ 236-2387
Call Out 908/ 788-1202

NEW MEXICO

Albuquerque Rescue Dog Assoc
Diana Pappan
1037 Stuart Rd NW
Albuquerque NM 87114

Cibola SAR
Bruce Berry
10725 Edith NE
Albuquerque NM 87113
Information 505/ 897-3652
Call Out 505/ 827-9226

Four Corners SAR
Ed Hoog
PO Box 1921
Farmington NM 87499
Information 505/ 632-8525

Mountain Canine Corps
Terry DuBois
2896-B Walnut
Los Alamos NM 87544
Information 505/ 662-9605
Call Out 505/ 827-9226

New Mexico Bloodhound Assoc
Bill Bailey
801 Quincy NE
Albuquerque NM 87110
Information 505/ 255-7745
Call Out 505/ 827-9226

New Mexico Rescue Dogs
Bob Foster
80 Raven Rd
Tijeras NM 87059
Information 505/ 281-3975
Call Out 505/ 827-9226

NEW YORK

American/Adirondack Rescue Dog Assoc
Marilyn Green
5028 Juniper Ln
Schenectady NY 12303
Information 518/ 356-2431
Call Out 518/ 462-6964

Amigo K-9 SAR Team
Ed Rivera
RD 2 Box 77B Janke Rd
Delhi NY 13753
Information & Call Out 607/ 746-3647

Heritage K-9 Search &
Rescue Tracking Service
Pat & Tim Karas
216 Rumsey Hill
Van Etten NY 14889
Information 607/ 589-4246
Call Out 607/ 776-2165

Massassauga SAR Team
Larry Fleming
PO Box 518
Fairport NY 14450
Information 716/ 461-9470
Call Out 716/ 343-2200

Rensselaer County SAR Team
David Onderdonk
Onderdonk Ave
Rensselaer NY 12144
Information 518/ 477-9267
Call Out 518/ 479-1212

Wilderness SAR Team
Rick Reardon
202 Lynhurst Ave
N Syracuse NY 13212
Information 315/ 458-7509
Call Out 315/ 425-3333

Yates County Sheriff's Dept
Sheriff Jan Scofield
106 Seneca St Box 116
Dundee NY 14527
Information 607/ 243-7501
Call Out 315/ 536-4438

NORTH CAROLINA

Blue Ridge SAR Dogs
Brenda Davis
225 Stewart Rd
Waynesville NC 28786

Burke County Rescue Squad
Michael Metcalf
PO Box 371
Morganton NC 28655
Information 704/ 584-1387
Call Out 704/ 437-1911

North Carolina SAR Assoc
Denver Holder
Clyde NC 28721
Information 704/ 648-3851
Call Out 704/ 255-5631

Piney Grove Search Team
Capt Ken Young
1109 Piney Grove Rd
Kernersville NC 27284
Information 919/ 996-4244
Call Out 919/ 727-2222

Raleigh Fire Dept
Ray Bradford
1305 Broken Br Ct
Raleigh NC 27610
Information 919/ 231-1938
Call Out 919/ 831-6331

Safeway SAR
Wayne May
PO Box 691
Coats NC 27521
Information 919/ 897-3197

Search Dog Services Inc
Mac McClure
177 Chiles Ave
Asheville NC 28803
Information & Call Out 704/ 252-3291

NORTH DAKOTA

Black Paws Search, Rescue
& Avalanche Dogs
David Oehike
PO Box 823
Devils Lake ND 58301
Information 701/ 662-8587
Call Out 701/ 662-5323

OHIO

Athens Search, Track & Rescue
Jon Tobin
74 E State St
Athens OH 45701
Information 614/ 592-4630
Call Out 594-2261

Marblehead K-9 Unit, Inc
Jim Zarifis
PO Box 3
Marblehead OH 43440
Information & Call Out 419/ 798-4942

Ohio K-9 Search Team, Inc
Donna Stusek
PO Box 02200
Columbus OH 43202
Information 614/ 569-4855

Stonehill Mantrailers
Donna Stone
2146 Eden Rd
Hamersville OH 45130
Information 513/ 379-9301
Call Out 513/ 249-3572 pager

Tri-Star SAR
Donna Stone
2146 Eden Rd
Hammerville OH 45130
Information 513/ 379-9301

OKLAHOMA

Oklahoma K-9 SAR
Mike Nozer
4808 S Elwood
Tulsa OK 74101
Information 918/ 445-2291
Call Out 918/ 596-5601

Rescue Dogs of NE Oklahoma
Sharon Kyle
8544 E 11th
Tulsa OK 74112

SAR Dogs of Oklahoma
Tracy Fox
4119 E Zion St
Tulsa OK 74115
Information 918/ 836-7139
Call Out 918/ 596-5657

Western Ozark Bloodhound Team
Elsa Gann
RT 2 Box 162
Collinsville OK 74021

OREGON

Independent SAR Dog Assoc
David Graf
PO Box 1646
Tualatin OR 97062

Mountain Wilderness Search Dogs
Harry Oakes
PO Box 30364
Portland OR 97230
Information 503/ 650-1904
Call Out 503/ 650-1904

Search One SAR Dogs
Bill Ridings
7981 SW Nyberg Rd
Tualatin OR 97062
Info & Call Out 503/ 297-5540
or 231-2056

PENNSYLVANIA

Black Paws Search, Rescue
& Avalanche Dogs
Curtis Settle
RR2 Box 324
Portage PA 15946
Information 814/ 696-4112

Dept of Environmental Resources
SAR Unit
Ken Boyles
1599 Doubling Gap Rd
Newville PA 17241
Information 717/ 776-7949
Call Out 717/ 776-5272 pager

Dog Team 200
Joe Thrash
RD 1 Box 75
Fridens PA 15541
Information 814/ 445-4762
Call Out 814/ 445-4133

Friendship Fire Co K-9
SAR Unit
Susan & Larry Bulanda
106 Halteman Rd
Pottstown PA 19464
Information 610/ 323-8022
Call Out 610/ 469-7617 pager

Greensburg Fire Dept
Bloodhound Team
Edward Hutchinson
318 Alexander Ave
Greensburg PA 15601
Information 412/ 834-7365
Call Out 412/ 834-7007

Northeast SAR
Bruce Barton
PO Box 162
Stroudsburg PA 18360
Information 717/ 424-1883
Call Out 800/ 426-3647

Red Rose K-9 SAR Team
Allen & Patti Means
431 Weaver Rd
Strasburg PA 17579
Information 717/ 293-4432
Call Out 717/ 687-8873

Rescue 40
Patty Depp
21 Norwich Ave
Pittsburg PA 15229
Information 412/ 931-0590
Call Out 216/ 775-0880

STRIKE K-9
Carol Prosseda
PO Box 61
West Milton PA 17886
Information 717/ 742-8555
Call Out 717/ 742-8771

Thornhurst Volunteer Fire Rescue
Jim Howley
HC Box 119
Thornhurst PA 18424
Information 717/ 842-9412
Call Out 717/ 342-9111

Tri-County SAR K-9 Unit
Linda Good
RR# 1 Box 488
Mill Hall PA 17751
Information 717/ 726-4714

White Deer SAR
John & Kim Carr
PO Box 93
New Columbia PA 17856
Information 717/ 568-0567
Call Out 717/ 568-0567

SOUTH CAROLINA

Cross Creek Training Academy
Dondi Hydrick
PO Box 7368
North Augusta SC 29841
Information 803/ 279-8716

SOUTH DAKOTA

Dakota SAR Dog Team
Dick Ness
204 S 4th Ave
Brandon SD 57005-1248
Information605/ 745-4600
Call Out 605/ 339-2335

Nancy Dineen
110 E Van Duren
Rapid City SD 57701
Information 605/ 348-8515

TENNESSEE

Morristown Emergency
& Rescue Squad
Jackye Byrd
420 N Jackson St
Morristown TN 37814
Information 615/ 581-4469
Call Out 615/ 586-1314

TEXAS

CESAR
Tim Samsill
4704 Susan Lee Ln
North Richland Hills TX 76180
Information 817/ 577-2055
Call Out 817/ 581-4313

Law Enforcement Training Specialist
Sgt Billy Smith
1803 FM 656 Box C-1
Rosharon TX 77583
Information 713/ 595-3276
Call Out 713/ 595-2590

North Texas Volunteer Mantrailers
Teri Anglim
3805 Misty Meadow
Ft Worth TX 76133
Information 817/ 294-8740
Call Out 817/ 469-3976

San Angelo Rescue Dogs
Eddie Howard
3818 Deerfield Rd
San Angelo TX 76904
Information 915/ 944-1288
or 800/ 627-8916
Call Out 915/ 657-4356
or 915/ 658-8111

Search One
David Brownell
555 Northridge Dr
Allen TX 75002

South Texas SAR K-9 Unit
Juan Gonzaba
2105 Lemon Tree Court
Edinburg TX 78539
Information 512/ 381-8080
Call Out 512/ 383-8114

Starr County Sheriff K-9 Unit
Eugenio Falcon Jr
Starr County Courthouse
Rio Grande City TX 78582
Call Out 512/ 487-5571

Texas EMT Dog Unit/TEXSSAR
Ron Perry
3010 Sierra Dr
San Angelo TX 76904
Information 915/ 944-2139
Call Out 915/ 657-4356

Texas Search Dogs Assoc
Bobby Farquhar
2617 Oakwood Terr
Ft. Worth TX 76117
Information 817/ 838-3198
Call Out 817/ 432-5423

UTAH

American Search Dogs
Bob Ellis
4939 Ben Lomond Ave
South Ogden UT 84403
Information 801/ 476-9544
Call Out 801/ 451-3555

Rocky Mountain Rescue Dogs
Barbara Altum
3353 S Main St #122
Salt Lake City UT 84115-4457
Information 801/ 742-2469
Call Out 801/ 535-5855

VERMONT

Vermont SAR Dog Service
Mary Anne Gummere
PO Box 4
Barton VT 05822
Information 802/ 525-6253
Call Out 802/ 748-8141 x 436

VIRGINIA

Blue & Gray SAR Dogs
Vicki Michael
RT 3 Box 272-1
Dayton VA 22821
Information 703/ 869-1520
Call Out 703/ 879-9684 pager

Colonial Heights SAR Unit
Willie Jenkins
903 Kensington Ave
Colonial Heights VA 23834
Information 804/ 520-2056
Call Out 804/ 520-9300

DOGS East
Ed Johnson
136 Indiantown Rd
King George VA 22485
Information 703/ 775-9568
Call Out 800/ 468-8892

K-9 Alert SAR Dogs
Winnie Pennington
2732 Grantwood Rd
Richmond VA 23225
Information 804/ 320-8052
Call Out 804/ 674-2400

Search Services America, Inc
Cody Perry
PO Box 159
Goldvein VA 22720
Information 703/ 752-2394
Call Out 804/ 674-2400

Sussex County Sheriff's Dept Office
Philip Andrews
RT 2 Box 172A
Disputanta VA 23842
Information 804/ 834-3528
Call Out 804/ 246-5361

Tazewell County Sheriff's Dept
Clarence Tatum
RT 2 Box 21A
Cedar Bluff VA 24609
Information 703/ 964-4859

Tidewater Trail SAR Team
Ginger Branyon
111 Creek Circle
Seaford VA 23696
Information 804/ 898-7118
Call Out 800/ 468-8892

Virginia Bloodhound SAR Assoc
PO Box 229
Leesburg VA 22075

Virginia SAR Dogs
Alice Stanley
RT 1 Box 1508
Woodford VA 22580
Information 703/ 582-5708
Call Out 703/ 659-4133

WASHINGTON

Black Paws Search, Rescue
& Avalanche Dogs
Cynthia Baker
17907 26th St Ct
E Summer WA 98390
Information 206/ 393-0900
Call Out 206/ 862-1825

Cascade Dogs
Rich & Kathy Fifer
129 Wiatrak Rd
Morton WA 98356
Information 206/ 496-5184
Call Out 800/ 562-5620

Clark County SAR
10810 NE 67th St
Vancouver WA 98662
Information & Call Out 206/ 892-1386

Dog Alert Rescue Team
Lori Matlock
327 S Main
Colville WA 99114
Information 509/ 684-4481
Call Out 509/ 684-2555

German Shepherd Search Dogs
of Washington State
Bruce Cheshier
3202 Burnett Ave N
Renton WA 98056
Information 206/ 228-3278
Call Out 206/ 432-5855

Justice Search Dogs
Jan Tweedie
12309 SE 164th
Renton WA 98058
Information 206/ 255-6852
Call Out 206/ 969-2584

Mantrackers and Search Dogs
Alice Webber
10810 NE 67th St
Vancouver WA 98662
Information 206/ 892-5842
Call Out 509/ 427-8076

Northwest Bloodhounds SAR
Jan Tweedie
12309 SE 164th
Renton WA 98058
Information 206/ 255-6852

Pacific Rim Disaster Team
Marcia Koening
1155 North 130th St #420
Seattle WA 98133
Information 206/ 823-6030
Call Out 206/ 367-7712 pager or
206/ 995-2202

Sandpoint Cadet Squadron
Bloodhound Team
Tim Vik
7309 Sandpoint Wy NE 838
Seattle WA 98115
Information 206/ 526-0332

West Coast Search Dogs
Terre Reeson
512 W 5th St
Hoquiam WA 98550
Information 206/ 533-2790
Call Out 206/ 249-3911

WEST VIRGINIA

West Virginia K-9 SAR
Jack Coon
2489 Dudden Fork
Kenna WV 25248
Information 304/ 988-9775
Call Out 304/ 348-5380

WISCONSIN

Badgerland Search Dogs
Robert Streich
957 Lawrence St
Madison WI 53715

Dane County Sheriff K-9 Unit
Carl Koehler
626 Eagle Watch Dr
De Forest WI 53532-3044
Information 608/ 249-0208
Call Out 608/ 266-4948

Headwaters SAR Dog Assoc
Jill Lemke
441 Mian St
Sayner WI 54560
Information 715/ 545-3837
Call Out 715/ 479-4441

Minocqua Police Dept
Bloodhound Unit
Gerry Frigge
PO Box 636
Woodruff WI 54568
Information 715/ 356-9318
Call Out 715/ 356-3234

RescuMed Dog Assoc
Lori Wick
1304 W Terminal Rd
Grafton WI 53024
Information 414/ 375-0456
Call Out 414/ 425-2944

Wilderness SAR
Lois Kuntz
PO Box 9
Phillips WI 54555
Info & Call Out 715/ 682-5592

Woodruff Police Dept
Bloodhound Unit
Gerry Figge
PO Box 636
Woodruff WI 54568
Information 715/ 356-9318

WYOMING

Park County Sheriff
Linda Waggoner
1131 11th St
Cody WY 82414
Info & Call Out 307/ 587-5524

Star Valley SAR
Dep Timothy Malik
Lincoln Co SO
Afton WY 83110

There are a number of different types of hotlines available. Some of the hotlines charge for their services, so be sure to ask before you request information. All numbers that begin with 900 will be automatically billed on your next phone bill. Be very careful when using 900 numbers and do not continue with any number that requires that you call a second or third 900 number for information. This is usually a gimmick to get more money.

Animal Abusers Anonymous
212/ 505-1073

Animal Poison Hotline
800/ 548-2423

Behavior Problems
Wm Campbell, $25 per call
503/ 476-5775

Dial-A-Dog
602/ 323-3375

Dial-A-Pet
312/ 342-5738

Fight It By Reporting It
Anti-Dog Legislation
1-800-AKC-TELL

Gaines Hotline
800/ 842-4637

IAMS Canine Nutrition Hotline
800/525-4267 X44

Lost Dogs and Cats
900/ 535-1515 Lost Line
800/ 755-8111 Found Line

Nat'l Animal Cruelty Invest School
Michael Gillingham
800/825-6505

Nat'l Animal Poison Information Network
404/ 542-6751; 217/ 333-3611

National Tele-Pet
$22. for 20 minute counseling session
800/ 232-7387

New York Dog Owners Helpline
NY City Only
212/ 243-8232

Nutritional Questions
Sponsored by Hills Pet Products
8 - 8 EST
800/ 445-5777

Pet Health and Behavior
$1.00 1st minute; $.50 each additional
minute
900/ 420-6PET

Pet Line
900/ 990-7387

Pet Loss Grief Hotline
Animal Vues
717/ 784-6805; 717/ 784-5910

Pet Loss Support
M-F PST; 6:30 - 9:30 pm
916/ 752-4200

Pet Lover Hotline
3 Burroughs
Irvine CA 92718
714/ 855-8822; 714/ 855-3045

Tel-Pet
General Information
714/ 687-7387

Animal rights groups and organizations that deal with saving the wolf and/or other wildlife are listed in this chapter. Many of the organizations listed also print newsletters. Some of the listings here are services related to the preservation of wildlife, such as groups that provide information about products which when tested have not caused animal suffering. If the purpose of the organization is not clear through its name, a brief explanation is offered just below the name. The main thrust of many of the organizations listed is to educate the public; therefore they can be a good source of material that would be useful for clubs, schools, youth groups etc. They may also be a source of project ideas for youth groups.

800 For Animals
[national resource network]
PO Box 2082
Ashland VA 23005
800/ 999-4800

ASPCA
Janet Lisa Schiff
441 E 92nd St
New York NY 10128
212/ 876-7700

Action for Animals
[monthly publication of
 animal rights events]
Box 20184
Oakland CA 94620

Actors & Others for Animals
5510 Cahuenga Blvd
North Hollywood CA 91601

Alaska Wildlife Alliance
[anti-hunt/trap fur animals]
PO Box 190953
Anchorage AK 99503
907/ 277-0897

American Anti-Vivisection Society
801 Old York Rd #204
Jenkintown PA 19046-1685

American Endangered Species Foundation
Janet C Swift, president
Public Education, Wolf Propagation
PO Box 674
Black Hawk CO 30423-0674
303/ 642-3353

American Fund/Alternatives
 to Animal Research
[AFAAR]
175 W 12th St # 16-G
New York NY 10011-8275
212/ 989-8073

American Society of Mammalogists
Department of Zoology
Brigham Young University
Provo UT 84602

American Wolf Hybrid Assoc
[saving wolves/promoting hybrids]
PO Box 117
Hereford AZ 85615

Animal Care Fund Inc
Animal Care Sanctuary
PO Box A
E Smithfield PA 18817
717/ 596-2200

Animal Legal Defense Fund
[anti-exploitation & cruelty]
Box 96041
Washington DC 20077-7136

Animal Liberation Front
BCM 160
London WC1N 3XX

Animal Welfare Institute
PO Box 3650
Washington DC 20007

Animal's Lobby
1025 9th St #219
Sacramento CA 95814

Anti Cruelty Society
157 W Grand Ave
Chicago IL 60610
312/ 644-8338

Assoc of Veterinarians for Animal Rights
PO Box 6269
Vacaville CA 95696
707/ 451-1391

Associated Humane Societies
124 Evergreen Ave
Newark NJ 07114
201/ 824-7080

Beaver Defenders
Hope Sawyer-Buyukmihci
Unexpected Wildlife Refuge
PO Box 765
Newfield NJ 08344

Black Hawk Humane Society, Inc
Jeanne Burr
1166 W Airline Hwy
Waterloo IA 50703
319/ 232-6887

Bunny Huggers Gazette
[current animal rights information]
PO Box 601
Temple TX 76503

CA Political Action Committee for Animals
PAW PAC
Box 2354
San Francisco CA 94126
415/ 841-7108

California Animal Owners Assoc
Charlie Sammut
[protect exotic animal ownership]
1014 W Laurel Dr
Salinas CA 93907
408/ 424-7441

Canadian Nature Federation
[protect endangered species
 and environment]
453 Sussex Dr
Ottawa ONT   K1N 6Z4

Canine Human Rights League
545 8th Ave Suite 401-D
New York NY 10018
800/ 444-2524

Center For Marine Conservation
[fights illegal wildlife goods]
1725 DeSales St
Washington DC 20036

Christians Helping Animals & People, Inc
[free pamphlets including pet grief loss]
PO Box 272
Selden NY 11784

Citizen's Committee for Animal Rights
[animal rights update]
PO Box 483
Flushing NY 11372

Civis/Civitas
[scientific information on vivisection]
PO Box 26
Swain NY 14884-0026
607/ 545-6213

Civis/Civitas
[scientific information on vivisection]
Via Motta 51
CH-6900 Massagno Switzerland

Civis/Civitas
[scientific information on vivisection]
Per Erik Pettersson
Karhunkatu 4F-33530
Tampere Finland

Civis/Civitas
[scientific information on vivisection]
PO Box 302
London England N8 9HD

Civis/Civitas
[scientific information on vivisection]
PO Box 2130
Dublin Ireland 1

Civis/Civitas
[scientific information on vivisection]
via Flaminia Vecchia 758
1-00191 Roma Italy

Coalition to Abolish the
 LD50 & Draize Tests
Box 214 Planetarium Station
New York NY 10024

Committee to Abolish Sport Hunting
PO Box 43
White Plains NY 10605

Cousteau Society
870 Greenbrier Circle #402
Chesapeake VA 23320-2641
804/ 523-9335

Culture & Animals Foundation
3509 Eden Croft Dr
Raleigh NC 27612

DELTA Rescue
PO Box 9
Glendale CA 91201

Defenders of Animal Rights, Inc
14412 Old York Rd
Phoenix MD 21131
301/ 527-1466

Defenders of Wildlife
1244 19th St NW
Washington DC 20036

Destination/Wolf
[educational programs]
7525 Tudor Rd
Colorado Springs CO 80919

Doris Day Animal League
Ms Holly E Hazard
[anti-research]
900 2nd St NE
Washington DC 20002-3557
202/ 842-0412

Elsa Wild Animal Appeal
[wolf recovery, anti-animal cruelty]
Box 675
Elmhurst IL 60126

Environmental Magazine
Box 5098
49 Richmondville AvE
Westport CT 06881

Farm Animal Reform Movement
1010 Ashburton Lane
Bethesda MD 20817
301/ 530-1737

Farm Sanctuary
PO Box 150
Watkins Glen NY 14891
607/ 583-2225

Food Animal Concerns Trust
PO Box 14599
Chicago IL 60614

Foreningen Vare Rovdyr
[preservation predatory animals]
Postboks 17 N-2420 Trysil

Foreningen Vargruppen
[preservation of the wolf]
Box 24039
S-100 57 Stockholm Sweden

Friends of Animals, Inc
[ban steel leg-hold traps]
PO Box 1244
Norwalk CT 06856

Friends of Wolves, Ltd
5706 3 Mile Rd
Racine WI 53406

Fund for Animals, Inc, The
[anti-trapping/animal rights]
18740 Highland Vly
Ramona CA 92065

Fur-Bearers, The
[anti-trap]
2235 Commercial Dr
Vancouver BC V5N 4B6

Green Wolf of Canada
worldwide donation channel
 group supports wolf survival
429 Merten St
Toronto ONT M4S 1B3

Greenpeace
1611 Connecticut Ave NW
Washington DC 20070-2018

Groupe Loup
[protect wolves]
13 Quai Ligier Richier
54000 Nancy France

Grupo Lobo
Dept. de Zoologia e Antropologia
[conservation of the wolf]
Faculdade de Cinancias
Bloco C-2, 3o Piso Cidade University
1600 Lisboa Portugal

Help Our Wolves Live
4600 Emerson Ave S
Minneapolis MN 55409

Humane Education Committee
[teacher's committee to humane education]
PO Box 445
New York NY10028

Humane Farming Assoc
1550 California St #6
San Francisco CA 94109

Humane Society of the US
Dr Michael Fox
2100 L St NW
Washington DC 20037
202/452-1100

In Defense of Animals
816 Francisco Blvd W
San Rafael CA 94901-5360

Interfaith Council for Protection
 of Animals and Nature
2841 Colony Rd
Ann Arbor MI 48104

Interfaith Council for Protection
 of Animals and Nature
4290 Raintree Lane NW
Atlanta GA 30327

International Assoc Against Painful
Experiments on Animals
29 College Place
St Albans He England

International Fund for Animal Welfare
Animal Welfare Department
Anti-dogs-for-food: Phillipines & South
Korea
411 Main St Number 2
Yarmouth Port MA 02675
508/ 362-6487

International Primate Protection League
PO Box 766
Summerville SC 29484

International Snow Leopard Trust
4649 Sunnyside Ave N
Seattle WA 98103

International Society for Animal Rights
421 S State St
Clarks Summit PA 18411

Julian Center For Science and Education
[understanding all flora and fauna]
PO Box 1189
Julian CA 92036

LYNX
[anti-fur organization]
PO Box 509
Dunmow Essex CM6 1UH
England

Last Chance for Animals
18653 Ventura Blvd. #356
Tarzana CA 91356
213/ 271-1409

Latham Foundation
[promotes respect for all life
 through education]
1826 Clement Ave
Alameda CA 94501

Lungholm Ulvepark
Freddy W Christiansen
[wolf research & museum]
Rodbyveg 20, DK-4970 Rodby
Denmark

Marine Mammal Stranding Center
PO Box 773
3625 Atlantic-Brigantine Blvd
Brigantine NJ 08203
609/ 266-0538

Medical Research Moderization Committee
Stephen Kaufman, MD
PO Box 6036
Grand Central Station
New York NY 10163-6018
212/ 876-1368

Mexican Wolf Coalition
[intro. Mex Gray Wolf in NM]
207 San Pedro NE
Albuquerque NM 87108

Mexican Wolf Coalition of Texas
PO Box 1526
Spring TX 77383-1526

Mission: Wolf
[education center]
PO Box 211
Silver Cliff CO 81249
719/ 746-2919

Mountain Lion Preservation Foundation
PO Box 1896
Sacramento CA 95812
916/ 442-2666

National Alliance for Animals
130 Howland Circle
Brewster MA 02651

National Animal Interest Alliance
["wise use" of animals]
Patti Strand
PO Box 66579
Portland OR 97290
503/ 761-8962

National Audubon Society
950 3rd Ave
New York NY10022

National Wildlife Federation
[catalog of wildlife products]
1412 16th St NW
Washington DC 20036-2266

National Wildlife Foundation
240 N Higgins
Missoula MT 59802

National Wolf Hybrid Assoc, Inc
Colleen Schabacker
2375 Honeysuckle Lane
Hartsville TN 37074
615/ 374-3406

Natural Research Defense Council
[saving arctic wildlife refuge]
PO Box 37269
Washington DC 20013

Network for Ani-Males & Females Inc
Shirley Weber
18707 Curry Powder Lane
Germantown MD 20874

North American Wolf Foundation
98 Essex RD
Ipswich MA 01938

North American Wolf Society
PO Box 82950
Fairbanks AK 99708

North California Wolf Pack
[wolf/hybrid organization]
231 Poplar St
Vacaville CA 95688

North Michigan Wolf Sanctuary
Box 414
Negaunee MI 49866

Northwest Wildlife Preservation Society
Sherry Pettigrew
[education and science programs]
PO Box 34129 St 'D'
Vancouver BC V6J 4M3

Northwoods Audubon Center
[all wildlife]
RT 1
Sandstone MN 55072

People for the Ethical Treatment
 of Animals [PETA]
Box 42516
Washington DC 20015
301/ 770-7444

Performing Animal Welfare Society
PAWS
PO Box 849
Galt CA 95632
209/ 745-2606

Pet and People Foundation
Dr Jan Dunlap
PO Box 14603
Raleigh NC 27620-4603
919/ 231-1710

Physicians Committee for Responsible
Medicine
[against using animals for research]
PO Box 6322
Washington DC 20015

Preserve Arizona's Wolves [PAW]
[reintroduce Mex Gray Wolf in the SW]
1413 E Dobbins Rd
Phoenix AZ 85040

Primarily Primates
Box 15306
San Antonio TX 78212

Project Wolf
[monitors wolf kills]
PO Box 48446
Vancouver BC V7X 1A2

Protective Assoc for World Species
PAWS
PO Box 121
New Berlin WI 53151

Psychologists For Ethical Treatment
 of Animals
Kenneth J Shapiro, PhD
PO Box 1297
Washington Grove MD 20880-1297
301/ 963-4751

Red Wolf Coordinator
US Fish and Wildlife Service
330 Ridgefield Ct
Asheville NC 28806

Red Wolf Sanctuary
Paul Strasser
Dillsboro IN 47018

Scientists Center for Animal Welfare
Lee Krulisch
4805 St Elmo Ave
Bethesda MD 20814
301/ 654-6390

Sea Shepherd
[marine life conservation]
PO Box 7000-S
Redondo Beach CA 90277

Sierra Club
730 Polk St
San Francisco CA 94109
415/ 776-2211

Sinapu
PO Box 3243
Boulder CO 80307

Sonoma People for Animal Rights
701A Fourth St
Santa Rosa CA 95404
707/ 576-1415

Teton Science School
PO Box 68
Kelly WY 83011

Timber Wolf Alliance
Sigurd Olson Environmental Institute
[resource directory for teachers
 about wolves]
Northland College
Ashland WI 54806
715/ 682-1223

Timber Wolf Information Network
[TWIN]
Waupaca Field St N
E110 Emmons Crk Rd
Waupaca WI 54981

Timber Wolf Project [WDNR]
Bureau of Endangered Resources [DNR]
PO Box 7921
Madison WI 53707

Timberwolf Preservation Society
6669 S 76th St
Greendale WI 53129

United Action for Animals
205 E 42nd St
New York NY10017

Voice of Nature Network
environmental protection,
 print/TV campaigns
PO Box 68
Westport CT 06881

W-holf
Wolf Hybrid Owners League of Friends
2610 E Danbury Rd
Phoenix AZ 85032

Washington Wolf Project
Committee of Wolf Haven
[re-establish Grey Wolf in WA]
4th & Blanchard Bldg
2121 4th Ave #2300
Seattle WA 98121

West Coast Wolf Hybrid Assoc Inc
5785 Little Uvas Rd
Morgan Hill CA 95037

Wild Canid Survival and Rescue Center
Wolf Sanctuary
PO Box 760
Eureka MO 63025

Wild Horse Sanctuary
PO Box 30
Shingletown CA96088-0030

Wildlife Education Program/Living Future
1595 Bittners Rt. Rd
Bovey MN55709

Wildlife Society, The
5410 Grosvenor Lane
Bethesda MD 20814

Wildlife Waystation
14831 Tujunga Canyon Road
Angeles National Forest, SF. CA91342

Windstar Foundation, The
John Denver
[environmental ethics]
2317 Snowmass Creek Rd
Snowmass CO 81654

Wolf Action Group
2118 Central SE Ste 46
Albuquerque NM87108

Wolf Action Network
PO Box 6733
Bozeman MT59771

Wolf Awareness, Inc
G.2 Farms
RR3
ONT N0M 1A0

Wolf Fund, The
PO Box 471
Moose WY 83012

Wolf Haven
3111 Offut Lake Rd
Tenino WA 98589

Wolf/Moose Study
[I.R.] Alumni House
MI Tech University
Houghton MI 49931

Wolf Mountain Sanctuary
Tonya Carloni
PO Box 385
Lucerne Valley CA 92356

Wolf Park
Dr Erich Klinghammer
[captive wolf research]
North American Wildlife Park Foundation
Battleground IN 47920
317/ 567-2265

Wolf Project, Riding Mtn Nat'l Park
World Wildlife Fund- Canada
60 St Clair SE E, #201
Toronto ONT M4T 1N5

Wolf Recovery Foundation
PO Box 793
Boise ID 83701

Wolf Ridge Environmental Learning Center
230 Cranberry Rd
Finland MN 55603

Wolf Sanctuary
PO Box 760
Eureka MO 63025

Wolf Society of Great Britain
Cottage Kings Woodland
Hindhead Surrey GU26 6DQ
England

Wolf Song of Alaska
6430 Ridge Tree Circle
Anchorage AK 99516

World Pet Society
Box 343
Tarzana CA 91356

World Society for the Protection of Animals
[protection of use of animals in film]
215 Lakeshire Blvd. E #113
Toronto ONT M5A #W9

World Society for the Protection of Animals
Box 190
29 Perkins St
Boston MA 02130

World Wildlife Fund
PO Box 37002
Washington DC 20013-9976

World Wildlife Fund SW/
World Conservation Center
1196 Gland
Switzerland

Write Cause, The
Carol RS Treacy
[letter campaign service]
PO Box 2524
Petaluma CA 94953-2524
707/ 769-0116

Yukon Conservation Society
PO Box 4163
Whitehorse Yukon Y1A 3I3

This chapter lists organizations that offer specially trained dogs to help handicapped persons. Many of the organizations listed use dogs that are donated or rescued from shelters. Some of the organizations listed offer training courses for people who are interested in working in this field of dog training.

Access K-9 Co-workers
[handicapped raise & train their own K-9s]
PO Box 30142
Indianapolis IN 46230

Aid Dogs for the Handicapped
Mrs Everett Hayes
1312 Bergan Rd
Oreland PA 19075
215/ 233-2722

Animals for Independence & Mobility
Carilee Cole
11071 E Sanley Rd
Davison MI 48423
313/ 653-3842 voice
313/ 655-4129 [TTY]

Arlington Humane Society
7817 S Cooper St
Arlington TX 76017

Assistance Dogs Internat'l
Shiela O'Brien
[sets standards for assistance dog groups]
NEADS
PO Box 213
W Boylston MA 01583
508/ 835-3304

Assistance Dogs of America, Inc
5236 Bethel Center Mall
Columbus OH 43220
614/ 451-2969

Canadian Guide Dogs for the Blind
PO Box 280
Rideau Valley Dr N
Manotuck ONT K0A 2N0
613/ 692-7777

Canine Companions For Independence
Southeast Regional Center
[service, signal, social & therapy dogs]
PO Box 547511
Orlando FL 32854
407/ 682-2535 voice

Canine Companions for Independence
Northeast Center
PO Box 205
Farmingdale NY 11735-0205
516/ 694-6938

Canine Companions For Independence
Support Dog Center
[assistance, therapy, hearing-ear dogs]
4989 State Rt 37 E
Delaware OH 43015
614/ 548-4447

Canine Companions for Independence
Northwest Regional Training Center
1215 Sebastopol Rd
PO Box 446
Santa Rosa CA 95402-0446
707/ 528-0830

Canine Companions for Independence
Southwest Regional Training Center
San Dieguito Rd & Calle del Nido
PO Box 8247
Rancho Santa Fe CA 92067

Canine Hearing Companions, Inc
Debby Gatier
247 E Forest Grove Rd
Veneland NJ 08360
609/696-0969

Canine Helpers for the Handicapped Inc
Beverly Underwood
[hearing ear & service dogs]
5705 Ridge Rd
Lockport NY 14094
716/ 433-4035 voice

Canine Partners For Life
Darlene Sullivan
[assistance dogs]
130D RD 2
Cochranville PA 19330
610/ 869-4902

Canine Vison Canada
PO Box 907
Oakville ONT L6J 5E8
416/ 842-2891

Canine Working Companions, Inc
Pat McNamara, Director
[hearing dogs, service dogs
 & therapy dogs]
RD 2 Box 170
Gorton Lake Rd
Waterville NY 13480
315/ 861-7770 voice

Connecticut K-9 Hearing Dog Training
Robert Schatz
239 Maple Hill Ave
Newington CT 06111
203/ 666-4646 voice; 203/ 666-4684 [TTY]

Dogs For Independent Living
PO Box 2055
Montrose CO 81402

Dogs for Independence
Joyce Munguia
PO Box 965
Ellenburg WA 98926
509/ 925-4535

Dogs for the Deaf
Robin Dickson
10175 Wheeler Rd
Central Point OR 97502
503/ 826-9220 voice

Feeling Heart Foundation
RFD 2 Box 354
Cambridge MD 21613
301/ 228-3689

Florida Dog Guide for the Deaf, Inc
PO Box 20662
Brandenton FL 34202-0662
813/ 748-8245 voice

Freedom Bonds
Lillian E Klien
[service dogs for the handicapped]
64 Regency Dr Apt 402
Mt Holly NJ 08060

Freedom Service Dogs
[dogs for the handicapped]
PO Box 150217
Lakewood CO 80215
303/ 234-9512

Friends for Folks
Lexington Correctional Center
[adopts dogs to special needs people]
Lexington A & R Center
Box 260
Lexington OK 73051
405/ 527-5676

Guide Dog Assoc of New South Wales
77 Deepfield Rd
Catherine Field, NSW 2171
Sydney Australia
02-606-6616

Guide Dog Foundation for the Blind Inc
Peggy Teufel
371 E Jericho Tpk
Smithtown NY 11787-9897
516/ 265-2121; 516/361-5192

Guide Dogs for the Blind, Inc
PO Box 151200
San Rafael CA 94915
415/ 499-4000

Guide Dogs of the Desert
PO Box 1692
Palm Springs CA 92263
619/ 329-6257

Guiding Eyes for the Blind
611 Granite Springs Rd
Yorktown Heights NY 10598
914/ 245-4024

Handi-Dogs Inc
Alamo Reavers
[support dogs]
PO Box 12563
Tucson AZ 85732
602/ 326-3412; 602/ 325-6466

Happy Canine Helpers Inc
16277 Montgomery Rd
Johnstown OH 43031
614/ 965-2204

Hearing Dog For The Deaf
6940 48th St
Coloma MI 49038
616/ 468-6154

Hearing Dog Inc
Martha Foss
5901 E 89th Ave
Henderson CO 80640
303/ 287-3277

Hearing Dog Program of Minnesota
2223 East 35th St
Minneapolis MN 55407
612/ 729-5986 voice; 612/ 729-5914 TDD

Hearing Dog Resource Center
Michelle Cobey
PO Box 1080
Renton WA 98057-1080
800/ 869-6898

Hearing Dogs For The Deaf
London Rd [A-40]
Lewknor, Oxford 0X9 5RY
London England

Hearing Dogs Inc
Cathy Nagaich
4623 Pleasant Chapel
Newark OH 43055
614/ 763-4282 V/TTY
614/ 471-7397 TTY/V

Hearing Dogs of the South
Barbara Hennessy
998 Sousa Dr
Largo FL 34641
813/ 530-4929 voice

Hearing Dogs, Inc
290 North Hamilton
Gahanna OH 43230
614/ 471-7397 voice
614/ 763-4282 voice

Hearing Ear Dogs of Canada
Jacqueline Harbour
1154 Hwy 2 W
Ancaster ONT L9G 3K9
416/ 648-1522 voice
416/ 648-2262 TDD

Hearing Ear Dogs of New England, Ltd
420 Groton Long Point Rd
Groton CT 06340
203/ 536-4849

Helping Paws
Geraldine Gage
c/o Censhare
290 McNeal Hall
1985 Buford AvE
St Paul MN 55108
612/ 625-5741

Independence Dogs for
 Mobility Handicapped
146 State Line Rd
Chadds Ford PA 19317
610/ 358-2723

Internat'l Guiding Eyes
Jane Brackman
13445 Glenoaks Blvd
Sylmar CA 91342
818/ 362-5834

Iowa Hearing Dog Program Inc
Scott Franke
2258 Logan Ave
Waterloo IA 50703
319/ 236-2987 voice

La Foundation MIRA
1820 Rang Nord-ovest
Ste Madeleine QUE J0H 1S0
514/ 467-7524

Leader Dogs for the Blind
PO Box 5000
Rochester MI 48307-3115
313/ 651-9011; 313/ 651-5812

Mary Ann Salem Companion
Animal Program for Deaf
Riverside Humane Society PCA
Karen Detterich
5791 Fremont St
Riverside CA 92504
714/ 688-4382 voice
714/ 688-8612 TDD

Mile High Hearing & Handi Dog, Inc
12395 N Piney Lake Rd
Parker CO 80134-8434
303/ 288-7297 voice

Nanhall Training Center
2206 Martin Luther King Blvd
Greensboro NC 27406
919/ 272-6584

National Hearing Dog Center
1116 S Main St
Athol MA 01331
508/ 249-9264

New England Assistance
 Dog Service Inc
Sheila O'Brien
PO Box 213
West Boylston MA 01583
508/ 835-3304 voice

Okada Ltd.
Patti Putnam
[assistance dogs]
RR 1 Box 640F
Fontana WI 53125
414/ 275-5226 voice

Pacific Assistance Dogs Society
10060 #5 Rd
Richmond BC V7A 4E5
604/ 597-9268

Paws To Listen, Inc
PO Box 2941
South Bend IN 46680
219/ 287-4273

Paws With A Cause
1235 100th St SE
Byron Center MI 49315
616/ 698-0688

PawsAbilities
2827 Ft Missoula Rd
Missoula MT 59801
406/ 728-4100

Phydeauxs For Freedom Inc
[support dogs for handicapped]
1 Main St
Laurel MD 20707
301/ 498-6779

Prison Pet Partnership Program
PO Box 17
Gig Harbor WA 98335
206/ 858-9101 X 240

Pro-Dogs, The Dog House
Rocky Bank, 4, New Rd, Ditton
Maidstone Kent MEZ0 7AD
England

Red Acre Farm Hearing Dog Center
Carolyn Bird
Box 278
Stow MA 01775
508/ 897-8343 voice

San Francisco SPCA
Hearing Dog Program
Ralph Dennard
2500 16th St
San Francisco CA 94103
415/ 544-3020 voice; 415/ 554-3022 TDD

Seeing Eye Guide Dogs for the Blind
PO Box 375
Morristown NJ 07963-0375
201/ 539-4425

Service Dogs of Canada
Box 128
Stirling ONT K0K 3E0

Southeast Hearing EAR Dog Program
Sonya Walley Tate
The Ear Foundation, Baptist Hospital
Box 111
2000 Church St
Nashville TN 37236
615/ 329-7807 voice; 615/ 329-7809 TTY

Southeastern Assistance Dogs
Cindy M Teal
811 Pendleton St
9-11 Medical Ct
Greenville SC 29601
803/ 235-9689 voice; 704/ 843-3459 voice

Support Dogs for the Handicapped Inc
301 Sovereign Ct #113
St Louis MO 63011
314/ 394-6163

Texas Hearing Dogs, Inc
[service dogs, hearing ear dogs]
1147 Tulane St
Houston TX 77008-6846
713/ 869-0030 voice

W Canada Handicapped
/Hearing Ear Dog Soc
10060 #5 Rd
Richmond BC V7A 4E5

Working PAWS Inc
PO Box 81
Wyatt IN 46595
219/ 277-6525

This chapter lists various dog-related videos. Videos are very important for certain aspects of study concerning dogs since the viewer is able to see the message the author wants to get across. This would be especially helpful for areas such as grooming, training or movement in dogs.

If the video is available through a well-known organizaiton such as the American Kennel Club (AKC), then the AKC is listed next to the name of the video. If it is offered through another organization, then the name and address is given under the name of the video.

Some of the videos listed are available for rent and do not have to be purchased. Be sure to contact the organization listed and ask.

Please note that the AKC library is not a lending library, but the librarians are willing to help you in any way they can to obtain the videos listed with AKC after their title. Many of the AKC videos are for sale. For more information, write to the AKC, ATTN: Videos. European format (PAL) is also available. Many of the AKC videos are offered through supply catalogs such as those listed in the *Supply Catalogs* chapter of this book.

Also listed in this chapter are those organizations that only supply videos for sale.

When ordering videos be sure to specify VHS or BETA.

Some organizations offer computer bulletin boards or other computer-related services, such as software designed for kennel management. These have been listed as well.

AFFENPINSCHER
AKC

AFGHAN HOUND
AKC

AIREDALE, HOW TO GROOM AN
Jane Harvey, AKC
2 cassettes, 95 & 87 minutes

AIREDALE TERRIER
AKC

AIREDALES FOR AGILITY, TRAINING
AKC

AIRSCENTING SAR DOG, AN INTRO TO
THE
NASAR
PO Box 3709
Fairfax VA 22038
703/ 352-1349

AKC AND THE SPORT OF DOGS
30 minutes

AKITA
AKC

ALASKAN MALAMUTE
AKC

AMERICAN DOG MAGAZINE ON VIDEO
$49.95—6 mo; $79.95—yr.
PO Box 127
Montpelier IN 47359
317/ 728-2144

American Pet Industires, Inc
Shari Brooks
PO Box 340
Old Bethpage NY 11804
516/ 938-2410

AMERICAN STAFFORDSHIRE TERRIER
AKC

ANATOMY OF A DOG [GAINES]
In-Sight Into Communications
23 minutes; $35.00]
288 Fillow St
Norwalk CT 06850

ANTARCTICA, BOUND FOR
Hills Pet Products
17 minutes
PO Box 148
Topeka KS 66601
913/ 231-5619

ARCTIC WOLF: LIVING WITH THE PACK,
THE
Wolves and Related Canids
PO Box 1026
Agoura CA 91301

AUSTRALIAN CATTLE DOG
AKC

AUSTRALIAN TERRIER
AKC

BASENJI
AKC

BASICS AND BEYOND, THE
Carter Whitney Border Collies
PO Box 877
Center Point TX 78010
512/ 792-5645

BASSET HOUND
AKC

BEAGLE
AKC

BEAGLE FIELD TRIALS, CARRYING THE
LINE -
AKC, 30 minutes

BEARDED COLLIE
AKC

BELGIAN SHEEPDOG
AKC

BELGIAN TERVUREN
AKC

Bennu Productions Inc
Wayne Keelye
165 Madison Ave 6th Floor
New York NY 10016
212/ 213-8511

BERNESE MOUNTAIN DOG
AKC

BICHON FRISE, THE
AKC

BILL MASON'S CRY OF THE WILD
The Boundary Waters
$29.95
800/ 223-6565

BILL TRAINOR: A PROFILE
AKC

BJ's Software & Computer Service
DOGPED [Version 3.1B]
Pedigree Records System DB
PO Box 500140
Palmdale CA 93550-0140
805/ 264-4628

BLACK AND TAN COONHOUND
AKC

BLOODHOUND
AKC

BORDER COLLIE, TRAINING A WORKING
Carter Whitney Border Collies
PO Box 877
Center Point TX 78010
512/ 792-5645

BORDER TERRIER
AKC

BORZOI
AKC

BOSTON TERRIER
AKC

BOUVIER DES FLANDRES
AKC

BOXER
AKC

BRIARD
AKC

BRITISH DOG SHOWS [GAINES]
In-Sight Into Communications
26 minutes, $35
288 Fillow St
Norwalk CT 06850

BRITTANY
AKC

BULL TERRIER
AKC

BULLDOG
AKC

CAIRN TERRIER, THE
AKC

CANINE CHRONICLE VIDEO MAGAZINE
Routledge Publishing
58 minutes for each edition
AKC

Canine Film Corporation
PO Box 262
Summerfield FL 32691
800/ 835-2246

Canine Video Library
PO Box 816312
Dallas TX 75381

CARDIGAN WELSH CORGI
AKC

Centra Productions
John Cravotta
8236 E 71st St #188
Tulsa OK 74133
918/ 481-5388

Championship Software
[Total Ownership & Pedigree Systems]
PO Box 9806
Coral Springs FL 33075
305/ 344-1626

CHESAPEAKE BAY RETRIEVER
AKC

CHIHUAHUA
AKC

CHOW CHOW
AKC

Cincecraft Inc
Gary Brown
215B Central Ave
Farmingdale NY 11735
516/ 752-0700

CLUMBER SPANIEL
AKC

Coastal Pet Products
Jim Stout
46 N Rockhill Ave
Alliance OH 44601
800/ 321-0248

COCKER SPANIEL
AKC

COLLIE
AKC

COME BYE! AND AWAY!
Early Stages Sheepdog Training
Diamond Farm Book Publishers
Box 537
Alexandria Bay NY 13607
613/ 475-1771; 613/ 475-3748

COMPUTER BULLETIN BOARD
CompuServe
5000 Arlington Ctr Blvd
PO Box 20212
Columbus OH 43220
800/ 848-8199

DACHSHUND
AKC

DALMATIAN
AKC

DALMATION, A REVIEW OF COLOR IN
THE
AKC, 16 minutes

DANDIE DINMONT TERRIER
AKC

DELTA SOCIETY
Professional Programs Inc
Various Video's on
the Human Animal Bond
12035 Sticoy St #B
North Hollywood CA 91605
818/ 764-7087

DEREK RAYNE: A PROFILE
AKC

Direct Book Service
Charlene Woodward
PO Box 3073
Wenatchee WA 98807-3073
800/ 776-2665

DOBERMAN PINSCHER
AKC

DOG, STARTING THE YOUNG
AKC

DOG SHOW, THE QUEST FOR
A QUALITY
AKC

DOG SHOW, WAY OF A [GAINES]
In-Sight Into Communications
288 Fillow St
Norwalk CT 06850

DOG TRAINING, THE NO-FORCE
METHOD OF
Goldrush Pet Care Center
1991 E Allovez Ave
Green Bay WI 54311

DOG TRICKS I & II
Canine Training Systems Ltd.
$34.95 ea
7550 W Radcliff Ave
Littleton CO 80123

DOGSTEPS: STUDY OF CANINE
 STRUCTURE/MOVEMENT
Ruth Page Elliott, AKC
69 minutes $49.95

Doral Publishing
2619 Industrial St NW
Portland OR 97210
503/228-6625; 503/228-6632 [FAX]
Pack A: First Things First
Getting Started in Purebred Dogs
Sportsmanship
Fundamentals of Gait
Pack B: Before You Breed
The Basics of Heredity
Puppies, Puppies, Here They Come:
Ready or Not!
Raising the Litter
Pack C: Now You Have a Star
Choosing a Professional Handler
Campaigning a Specials Dog
Come Blow Your Horn
Single video: $24.95
The 3-pack (A, B or C):$49.95
The 6-pack (any two 3-packs): $89.95
The entire program (all 9 videos): $139.95
Rental (3-packs only): $29.95
Postage: Add $3.50 for single or any 3-pack;
add $5 for any 6-pack or all nine

ENGLISH COCKER SPANIEL
AKC

ENGLISH SETTER
AKC

ENGLISH SPRINGER SPANIEL
AKC

EXERCISE FINISHED-OBEDIENCE
 FROM JUDGES' VIEW
AKC,   20 minutes

FIELD SPANIEL
AKC

FLAT-COATED RETRIEVER
AKC

FLUSHING SPANIEL TEST, HIGH ON
HUNTING:
AKC

GAIT: OBSERVING THE DOG IN MOTION
AKC,   37 minutes

Galerie
Pat Fresener
12629 N Tatum Blvd #605
Phoenix AZ 85032
602/ 483-6553

GERMAN SHEPHERD DOG
AKC

GERMAN SHORTHAIRED POINTER
AKC

GIANT SCHNAUZER
AKC

Glendhenmere Kennels/Canine Videos
Mary Adelman
RD 2 Box 54B
Hazel KY 42049
502/ 436-2858

GOLDEN RETRIEVER
AKC

GORDON SETTER
AKC

GREAT DANE
AKC

GREAT PYRENEES
AKC

GREYHOUND
AKC

HUNTING TEST FOR POINTING
 BREEDS, THE POINT IS
AKC

IBIZAN HOUND
AKC

IN THE RING WITH MR WRONG
AKC, 20 minutes

Infomedia, Inc
Terry Pochert
PO Box 304
Novi MI 48050
313/ 348-2444

IRISH SETTER, THE
AKC

IRISH TERRIER
AKC

IS YOUR DOG DRIVING YOU CRAZY
BKCA Inc
45 minutes
PO Box 65656
Lubbock TX 79464
800/ 441-3294

ITALIAN GREYHOUND
AKC

Jiffy Jumps Obedience Videos
Marcis Koenig
PO Box 625
Redmond WA 98073
206/ 823-6030

K-9 BBS
DOG SPORTS MAGAZINE
set software 8-1-N, 300,
 1200, 2400 Baud
707/ 745-6225

KEESHOND
AKC

KERRY BLUE TERRIER
AKC

KOMONDOR
AKC

Konari Outfitters, Ltd
Ed Blechner
PO Box 752
Middlebury VT 05253
802/ 388-7447

Kramer Computer Aids, Inc
PO Box 57
Red Bank NJ 07701
201/ 747-3257

KUVASZ
AKC

KUVASZ ENTRY-CKC CENTIENNIAL
 SHOW 1988
AKC, 43 minutes

LABRADOR RETRIEVER
AKC

LAKELAND TERRIER
AKC

Leader Dogs For The Blind
Computer Bulletin Board
313/ 651-4009

Leerburg Video Production
50 videos on all aspects of dog training
PO Box 218C
Menomonie WI 54751
715/ 235-6502

LHASA APSO
AKC

LIVESTOCK GUARDING DOGS
Roger Woodruff
available through any state
 extension agency
APHIS/ADC
61396 S Hwy. 97
Bend OR 97702

Made-For-Dog Videos, Inc
Harley Toberman
PO Box 300122
Minneapolis MN 55403
800/ 359-8750

MALTESE
AKC

Mark Recording Co
Floye K Dreyer
101 NE 165th St
N Miami Beach FL 33162
305/ 945-7922

MASTIFF
AKC

Media West Home Video
Tim Barker
PO Box 1563
Lake Oswego OR 97035
800/ 888-TAPE

MEXICAN DOG SHOWS, HIGHLIGHTS
 OF THE   [GAINES]
In-Sight Into Communications
31 minutes, $35
288 Fillow St
Norwalk CT 06850

MINIATURE PINSHCER
AKC

MINIATURE SCHNAUZER
AKC

MURIEL FREEMAN: A PROFILE
AKC

NEWFOUNDLAND, THE
AKC

NORFOLK TERRIER
AKC

NORWEGIAN ELKHOUND
AKC

NORWICH TERRIER
AKC

OLD ENGLISH SHEEPDOG
AKC

OTTERHOUND
AKC

PAPILLON
AKC

PAW
Advantages of Seniors Owning Pets
PO Box 66122
Washington DC 20035-6122
202/ 857-1120; 202/ 223-4579

PEKINGESE
AKC

PEMBROKE WELSH CORGI
AKC

Petvision, Div ASPC, Inc
Colette Fairchild
PO Box 134
Lady Lake FL 32159-0134

PHARAOH HOUND
AKC

POINTER
AKC

Pollack Software
Dog Breeders Asst Kennel
 Mgt Software
PO Box 360892
Melbourne Beach FL 32936-0892
407/ 727-0740

POMERANIAN
AKC

POODLE
AKC

PORTUGUESE WATER DOG
AKC

PUG
AKC

PULI
AKC

PUPPIES, HOW TO RAISE A LITTER OF
Jane Harvey, AKC
170 minutes

R C Steele
Brenda Bauch
1989 Transit Way
Brockport NY 14420
800/ 872-3773

Radius Press Home Video
Jan Brighton
PO Box 1271
FDR Station NY 10150
212/ 988-4715

Ray Allen Mfg. Co
Patrick O'Connor
975 Ford St
Colorado Springs CO 80901

RETRIEVER, WITH COURAGE AND
 STYLE: FIELD TRIAL
AKC

RETRIEVER HUNTING TEST,
 LOVE EM/HUNT EM/TEST EM
AKC

RHODESIAN RIDGEBACK
AKC

RING SPORT VIDEOS
Bob Dixon
PO Box 157
Wells ME 04090-0157
207/ 646-5911

ROTTWEILER
AKC

ROTTWEILER PUPPY/DEVELOP
 A CHAMPION, SELECT A
AKC

Routledge Publications, Inc
132 W High St
Montpelier IN 47359
317/ 728-2464

SAINT BERNARD
AKC

SALUKI
AKC

SAMOYED
AKC

SCENT: THE FORGOTTEN EVIDENCE
Media Productions
217 S Transit Rd
Lockport NY 14094

SCHIPPERKE
AKC

SCOTTISH DEERHOUND
AKC

SCOTTISH TERRIER
AKC

SEALYHAM TERRIER
AKC

Sentinel Consultants Inc
Pedmaker, Entry-Matic, Show-Tracker
Canine Management Computer System
29 Miller Rd
Wayne NJ 07470
201/ 694-0424

Sheepherding Videos
Rural Route Videos
Box 113 River John
Pictou Co NS B0K 1N0
902/ 351-2788

SHETLAND SHEEPDOG
AKC

SHIH TZU
AKC

SHIH TZU CLUB VOL. I,
  TWIN CITIES AREA
AKC

Show Quality Pet Products
Joanna Yund
601 Excelsior Ave E
Hopkins MN 55343
612/ 933-7758

SIBERIAN HUSKY
AKC

SILKY TERRIER
AKC

SIRIUS PUPPY TRAINING,
  IAN DUNBAR
AKC

SKYE TERRIER
AKC

SMOOTH FOX TERRIER
AKC

SOFT-COATED WHEATEN TERRIER
AKC

STAFFORDSHIRE BULL TERRIER
AKC

STANDARD SCHNAUZER
AKC

Starline
Pet Record System
7131 Kermore Ln
Stanton CA 90680
714/ 826-5218

STOCK DOG, TRAINING THE WORKING
Extension Services, Jim Freeman
Olds College
Olds Alberta T0M 1P0
403/ 556-8344

TPS
Scott Criswell
3448 Ridge Road
Lansing IL 60438
708/ 474-4917

Tattoo-A-Pet
Julie Moscove
1625 Emmons Ave
Brooklyn NY 11235
800/ 828-8667

TGM Software
"Dog Trax" Canine
  Management Software
6105 Via Fortuna
El Paso TX 79912
915/ 585-8045

TIBETAN SPANIEL
AKC

TIBETAN TERRIER
AKC

TOP DOG
AKC

TRAINING YOU TO TRAIN YOUR
 DOG—BASIC [GAINES]
In-Sight Into Communications
288 Fillow St
Norwalk CT 06850

VideoHouse, Inc
Robert A Moss
PO Box 10630
Arlington VA 22210
703/ 524-8190

VIZSLA
AKC

WATER SEARCHING WITH DOGS
Jiffy Jumps
PO Box 625
Redmond WA 98073
206/ 823-6030

WEIMARANER
AKC

WELSH SPRINGER SPANIEL
AKC

WELSH TERRIER
AKC

WEST HIGHLAND WHITE TERRIER
AKC

WESTMINISTER DOG SHOW,
 THE 100th [GAINES]
In-Sight Into Communications
288 Fillow St
Norwalk CT 06850

WHIPPET
AKC

Williams, Edward
1992 BBC "One Man and
 His Dog" Competition
59 Pleasant Way
Penfield NY 14526

WIRE FOX TERRIER
AKC

This chapter contains information that might be of interest to the reader. It is not necessarily dog related, but is the kind of information that is not well known or readily availabe.

Adopt-A-Cow
[Farm Animal Protection]
RD 1 Box 839
Port Royal PA 17082

Adopt-An-Acre Program,
 Latin Rain Forest Pres.
The Nature Conservancy
1815 North Lynn St
Arlington VA 22209
 800/ 628-6860

American Bantam Assoc
Eleanor Vinhage
Box 127
Augusta NJ 07822
201/ 383-6944

American Bison Assoc, Inc
PO Box 16660
Denver CO 80216
303/ 292-2833; 303/ 292-2564

American Cichlid Assoc
706 Balfour
San Antonio TX 78239
512/ 656-4844

American Council of Spotted Asses
John Conter
2126 Fairview Plaza
Billings MT 59102
406/ 259-4926

American Donkey & Mule Society
The Brayer
Betsy Hutchins
2901 N Elm St
Denton TX 76201
817/ 382-6845

American Dove Assoc
Rita M Courtney
PO Box 21
Milton KY 40045

American Minor Breeds Conservancy
Box 477
Pittsboro NC 27312
919/ 542-5704

American Pheasant & Waterfowl Society
Lloyd Ure
RT 1 Box 164-A
Granton WI 54436
715/ 238-7291

American Pigeon Journal
PO Box 278
Warrenton MO 63383

American Poultry Assoc
Nona Shearer
26363 S Tucker Rd
Estacada OR 97023
503/ 630-6759

American Rabbit Breeders Assoc
Box 426
Bloomington IL 61702
309/ 827-6623

American Wooden Leg Goat/ Club
Butch & Linda Rehfeld
RT 4 Box 304
Seguin TX 78155
512/ 379-7750

Angora & Cashmere Quarterly
PO Box 322
Interlochen MI 49643

Araucana Magazine
Max Huff
PO Box 416
Lindale GA 30147

Black Sheep Newsletter
25455 NW Dixie Mtn Rd
Scappoose OR 97056

Bureau of Land Mgt Eastern States Office
Adopt-A-Horse & Burro Program
7450 Boston Blvd
Springfield VA 22153-3121
703/ 461-1300

Cat Industry Newsletter
511 Harbor View Circle
Charleston SC 29412
803/ 795-9555; 803/ 795-2930

Dairy Goat Journal
W2997 Market Rd
Helenville WI 53137
800/ 272-4628

Delaware Valley Pot
 Bellied Pig Assoc
Susan Armstrong
2370 Old York Rd
Suite D-5
Jamison PA 18956
215/ 322-1539

Florida Fish Cooperative
PO Box 25394
Tampa FL 33622
 813/ 677-7136

Florida Marine Life Assoc
801 NW 67 Ave
Plantation FL 33317
305/ 581-3238

Florida Tropical Fish Farms Assoc
PO Box 1519
Winter Haven FL 33880
813/ 293-5710

Footnotes, Nigerian Dwarf Goats
Shaula Parker
209 Crown Rd
Willow Park TX 76087

Game Bird Gasette Magazine
1155 E 4780 S
Salt Lake City UT 84117

Gamefowl Magazine
Drawer 280
Gaffney SC 29342

International Dove Society
Debbie Pire
3013 Tarpey Ave
Texas City TX77590
409/ 945-8381

International Ferret Assoc
PO Box 522
Roanoke VA 24003
703/ 343-5889

International Llama Assoc
PO Box 37505
Denver CO 80237
303/ 756-9004

International Potbelly Pig/
 Registry Service
PO Box 277
Pescadero CA 94060
415/ 879-0061

International Waterfowl Breeders Assoc
Elaine Nelisse
1167 Madison Rd
Montville OH 44064
216/ 968-3381

Jumpin Pouch Newsletter:
 On Kangaroo and Kin
RR 9 Box 47
Bloomfield IA 52537
515/ 722-3374

Llama Life
2259-B County Rd 220
Durango CO 81301

Miniature Donkey Talk
1338 Hughes Shop Rd
Westminister MD 21157
301/ 875-0118

National Call Duck/ Breeders Assoc
Terry Campbell
853 County Farm Rd
Murfreesboro TN 37130
615/ 980-4420

National Cockatiel Society
PO Box 26
Dalzell SC 29040
803/ 469-8730

National Herford Hog Record Assoc
Mrs Ruby Schrecengost
RD 1 Box 37
Flandreau SD 57028
605/ 997-2116

National Poultry News
PO Box 1647
Easley SC 29641
803/ 855-0140

North American Dir/Exotic
 Animal & Bird Owners
Pat & Connie Corbett
Skaar Rte Box 4028
Sidney MT 59270
406/ 482-7196

Old English Game Bantam Club of America
Fred P Jeffrey
PO Box 494
North Amherst MA 01059

Ornamental Fish International
Empire Fisheries
102 Charlton St
New York NY 10014
212/ 741-1023

PA Council Horseback Riding
 for Handicapped
1 Armsby Hall
PA State University
University Park PA 16802
814/ 865-6551

Peafowl Newsletter
Dennis Fett
RR 1
Minden IA 51553

Pig Tale Times
Kiyoko & Co
[potbelly pigs]
PO Box 277
Pescadero CA 94060
415/ 879-0061

Potbellied Pig Rescue
PIGS
RR1 Box 317-X
Charlestown WV 25414
304/ 725-7447

Poultry Press
William F Wulff
Box 542
Connersville IN 47331
317/ 827-0932

Pygmy Goat Digest
1320 Mountain Ave
Norco CA 91760
714/ 371-4307

Rare Breeds Journal
[All rare breeds of animals]
HC 77 Box 66
Crawford NE 69339

Rare Breeds Survival Trust
NAC, Kenilworth
Warwickshire DV8 2LG

Rocky Mountain Feed and Livestock Journal
425 West Griggs
Las Cruces NM 88005
800/ 524-0070

Scottish Blackface Sheep Breeders Assoc
R J Harward
39282 River Dr
Lebanon OR 97355
503/ 258-2373

The American Cavy Breeders Assoc, Inc
Linda Mowers
Box 386
East Derby NH 03041

The Angora & Cashmere Quarterly Journal
PO Box 112
Hastings MI 49058-0112

The Guinea Hog Assoc
Gabriella Nanci
14335 Pauma Vista Dr
Valley Center CA 92082
619/ 749-2126

The Ostrich News
502 "C" Street
PO Box 860
Cache OK 73527
405/ 429-3765

The Piggy Bank
John E Bickel
2005 Johns Ave
Alva FL 33920-1417

The Sheep Producer, Farm,
Flock & Ranch Journal
RT 2 Box 131A
Arlington KY 42021
502/ 655-6871

USDA Murry Walton
Predator Mgt Certification/Training Spec
PO Box 12847
Austin TX 463-0013

Welsh Cob Horses
Victoria Headley
Box 2977
Winchester VA 22601
703/ 667-6195

Wings & Hooves
RT 3 Box 65
Chandler OK 74834

Zoological Publications
Rte 5 Box 435
Lexington VA 24450
703/ 463-2592

This is not a comprehensive index. It highlights those topics that may not be easily found in the text. Listings that are clearly identified by the chapter title will not be listed. An example would be the different breeds of dogs.

The index is arranged in alphabetical order by subject. The topic is printed in upper and lower case letters and the chapter title is printed in upper case letters.

Example:

Search and Rescue	GENERAL PUBLICATIONS
Carting supplies	SUPPLY CATALOGS

Dog training .... GENERAL PUBS, SUPPLY CATALOGS, ASSOCIATIONS

Dog writers .... ASSOCIATIONS

Electric fences .... SUPPLY CATALOGS

Electronic flea collars....................... SUPPLY CATALOGS

Emergency pet care .... GENERAL PUBS, HOTLINES

Federation of dog clubs/breeders.... ASSOCIATIONS

Field dogs.. ACTIVITY CLUBS

Food .... ASSOCIATIONS

Frisbee .... GENERAL PUBS

Grooming supplies........................... SUPPLY CATALOGS

Health insurance .... HEALTH & SAFETY

Home pet care .... ASSOCIATIONS

Human/animal bond .... ASSOCIATIONS

Hunting .... ACTIVITY CLUBS, GENERAL PUBS, REGISTRY
ORGS., SUPPLY CATALOGS, AWARDS & CONTESTS

Hunting retrievers .... GENERAL PUBS

Showing altered dogs .... ASSOCIATIONS

Showing rare breeds .... ASSOCIATIONS

Sled racing .... SUPPLY CATALOGS, GENERAL PUBS

Solar dog houses .... SUPPLY CATALOGS

Stationery .... SUPPLY CATALOGS

Temperament testing .... HEALTH & SAFETY

Therapy dogs .... HEALTH & SAFETY

Vegetarian diets.............................. SUPPLY CATALOGS

Veterinary nutritionists .... ASSOCIATIONS

Waste disposal .... SUPPLY CATALOGS

Weight pulling................................. GENERAL PUBS, WOLF/WILDLIFE

Wolf publications .... GENERAL PUBS, WOLF/WILDLIFE

Working dogs .... ACTIVITY CLUBS, MISCELLANEOUS CLUBS

Working Terrier .... ACTIVITY CLUBS

THE CANINE SOURCE BOOK

is available on self-sticking labels

For more information contact:

Bulanda Enterprises
106 Halteman Road
Pottstown PA 19464
215/323-6725